T0303144

Wikipedia and Academic Libraries

Wikipedia and Academic Libraries

A Global Project

Edited by

Laurie M. Bridges, Raymond Pun,
and Roberto A. Arteaga

Maize Books
2021

Copyright © 2021 by Laurie M. Bridges, Raymond Pun, and Roberto A. Arteaga
Some rights reserved

This work is licensed under the Creative Commons Attribution 4.0 International Public License. To view a copy of this license, visit https://creativecommons.org/licenses/by/4.0/ or send a letter to Creative Commons, PO Box 1866, Mountain View, California, 94042, USA.

Published in the United States of America by
Michigan Publishing
Manufactured in the United States of America

DOI: http://doi.org/10.3998/mpub.11778416

ISBN 978-1-60785-670-2 (paper)
ISBN 978-1-60785-671-9 (ebook)
ISBN 978-1-60785-672-6 (open access)

An imprint of Michigan Publishing, Maize Books serves the publishing needs of the University of Michigan community by making high-quality scholarship widely available in print and online. It represents a new model for authors seeking to share their work within and beyond the academy, offering streamlined selection, production, and distribution processes. Maize Books is intended as a complement to more formal modes of publication in a wide range of disciplinary areas.

www.maizebooks.org

"Beyond underscoring the core values that Wikipedia and librarians share in relation to the democratization of ideas and the free flow of information through the open movement, this book offers valuable insights into how productive engagement with Wikipedia can act as the catalyst for professional development and workplace learning. The case studies illustrate how academic librarians can proactively build their skills to enhance the discoverability of the library collection, to work in creative ways with digital media, to use information and digital literacy as powerful pedagogical tools and to establish meaningful partnerships with groups within and beyond the university."

Gill Hallam, PhD
Freelance Information Consultant, Brisbane, Australia
Co-Chair, IFLA Section for Continuing Professional
Development and Workplace Learning (CPDWL)

"From a forbidden space for students, academics, and librarians, to an open enabler for community collaboration, Wikipedia has ignited a worldwide movement.

"*Wikipedia and Academic Libraries* is an insightful contribution of libraries' diverse intersections with Wikimedia-related projects and activities. It outlines some of the most important features that shape our digital lives: collaboration and the need to make visible the infodiversity we produce.

"Stunning, critical, and diverse, *Wikipedia and Academic Libraries* will empower libraries to lead the open movement. It is a must-read for every information professional."

Jonathan Hernández, PhD
Associated Researcher, Library and Information Institute
at the National Autonomous University of Mexico

Contents

SECTION 2: PRACTICAL APPLICATIONS
OUTSIDE THE CLASSROOM

Acknowledgments

This Open Access book was made possible thanks to funding from the following sources:

- Creative Commons Global Network Community Activities Fund
- Wikimedia Foundation Rapid Grant
- Oregon State University Robert Lundeen Faculty Development Award

We thank the following individuals for serving as peer reviewers of chapters submitted for this book. Each chapter was reviewed by two individuals in a single-blind process.

Alex Stinson, Andrew Carlos, Bronwen Maxson, Camille François, Cliff Landis, Denise Kane, Diana Park, Joseph Yap, Kellee Warren, Kelly McElroy, Liam Wyatt, Meghan Dowell, Michael Gutierrez, Moon Kim, Nicollette Davis, Rachel Wexelbaum, Reysa Alenzuela, Robin Kear, Ryan Randall, Stacy R Williams, Stefani L Baldivia, and Tiah Edmunson-Morton

Last, we would like to thank our University of Michigan sponsors who supported this project and made it possible for us to partner with Maize Books and Michigan Publishing:

Alexandra Rivera, Amanda Peters, Anne Cong-Huyen, Karen E. Downing

INTRODUCTION

The publication of this book—in 2021—will coincide with Wikipedia's twentieth birthday. Much has been written about Wikipedia's beginning and evolution over the past twenty years, and we won't go into detail here, but you can read about the history in other publications such as *The Wikipedia Revolution: How a Bunch of Nobodies Created the World's Greatest Encyclopedia* by Andrew Lih (2009) or *Wikipedia @ 20: Stories of an Incomplete Revolution* edited by Joseph Reagle and Jackie Koerner (2020). What has remained constant since its inception in 2001 is Wikipedia's radically open model. As a result, Wikipedia was initially derided in higher education because this model allowed anyone to edit its content. However, what was initially seen as a flaw in many education circles has now become Wikipedia's strength, when compared with other social media platforms (Cooke, 2020). Although opinion has slowly started to shift over the past decade, Wikipedia is still often considered a "forbidden space" for educators and students in the classroom (Lockett, 2020, p. 208).

In 2019, when we began this project, we set out to create a book that would represent different perspectives from around the globe. *Wikipedia and Academic Libraries: A Global Project* contains nineteen chapters by fifty-two authors from Brazil, Canada, Hong Kong, Ireland, Kyrgyzstan, Mexico, the Netherlands, Nigeria, Scotland, Spain, and the United States. In keeping with the Wikipedia commitment and spirit to open access, each chapter has a CC BY 4.0 license, which means that

DOI: https://doi.org/10.3998/mpub.11778416.intro.en

anyone is free to copy and redistribute the chapters in any material or format, making sure to give the authors credit for their work.

The chapters in this book are authored by both new and longtime members of the Wikimedia community, representing a range of experiences. Obuezie and Horsfall (chapter 8), for example, joined the Wikimedia movement when they participated in the #1Lib1Ref campaign organized by the African Library and Information Associations and Institutions; while Dengra i Grau (chapter 11) first edited Catalan Wikipedia at age fourteen, in 2009, when he created an article about mashed potatoes: Puré de patates; Miller (chapter 7) first engaged with Francophone Wikipedia in 2017 to create an article about Mado Lamotte, a celebrated drag queen in Canada; and Peschanski (chapter 17) first edited Wikipedia in 2011, as part of a call to action by his graduate advisor, renowned sociologist Erik Olin Wright, at the University of Wisconsin.

We want to thank all of our contributors who proposed, wrote, and completed their chapters during the COVID-19 crisis. The crisis reminded us, once again, of the importance of open-access information—not just as a source of educational content but also health information. Our contributors are librarians, library staff, disciplinary faculty, and Wikimedia volunteers—acting as intermediaries between Wikimedia projects, faculty, and students. As more librarians engage with Wikipedia in the coming years, we hope this publication will act as a launching pad for future international collaborations, projects, and publications.

References

Cooke, R. (2020, February 17). Wikipedia is the last best place on the internet. *Wired*. Retrieved January 24, 2021, from www.wired.com/story/wikipedia-online-encyclopedia-best-place-internet/.

Lih, A. (2009). *The Wikipedia revolution: How a bunch of nobodies created the world's greatest encyclopedia*. Aurum.

Lockett, A. (2020). Why do I have authority to edit the page? The politics of user agency and participation on Wikipedia. In J. M. Reagle & J. Koerner. J. (Eds.), *Wikipedia @ 20: Stories of an incomplete revolution*. MIT Press.

Reagle, J. M., & Koerner, J. L. (Eds.). (2020). *Wikipedia @ 20: Stories of an incomplete revolution*. The MIT Press.

SECTION 1
PRACTICAL APPLICATIONS IN THE CLASSROOM

CHAPTER 1

LIBRARY-FACULTY COLLABORATION USING WIKIPEDIA FOR LEARNING AND CIVIC ENGAGEMENT

Jyldyz Bekbalaeva[1], Aisuluu Namasbek kyzy[1], Shirin Tumenbaeva[1], and Zhuzumkan Askhatbekova[1]

[1] American University of Central Asia

Abstract

Wikipedia uses collaborative models of content creation and fosters a culture of collaboration. Understanding how it works and mastering editing skills often calls for partnerships between different members of the university community. Library-faculty Wikipedia-centered collaboration can open new opportunities to develop information and media literacy, student agency, and civic participation. This chapter shares faculty and librarians' experience with using Wikipedia as a teaching tool as part of an initial pilot project aimed at using open educational resources. The library-faculty team from the American University of Central Asia worked together to use Wikipedia as a tool for collaborative learning and civic participation among students in sociology classes.

Keywords

Wikipedia in education, Wikipedia as a teaching resource, Wikipedia and academic libraries.

DOI: https://doi.org/10.3998/mpub.11778416.ch1.en

Introduction

Wikipedia is a global, open-source encyclopedia of information that engages users around the world in the creation, storage, and dissemination of knowledge. It has become an established starting point for preliminary research on the web. Over the last nineteen years, the encyclopedia has grown to 54 million articles in over 312 languages (Wikipedia, 2020). Consistently ranking as one of the most popular sites on the web, Wikipedia has over 200,000 volunteer contributors around the world who help to improve free access to knowledge in their languages (Wikimedia Foundation, 2020).

The use of Wikipedia as a teaching and learning tool has been increasingly implemented in a significant number of educational contexts and has become a common practice in many countries (Wikimedia Education, 2020). The platform has drawn the attention of faculty, librarians, instructional technologists, students, and other stakeholders in the academic community, and many have come to see it as a useful tool in fulfilling their mission. Librarians welcome Wikipedia as an open resource that aims to expand access to information, while faculty have become interested in how they can use Wikipedia in teaching and in the achievement of their pedagogical goals. Wikipedia is among the most popular open sources that students consult to gain an initial grounding in a topic before delving further for study or research purposes. Despite variation in the perception and acceptability of usage of Wikipedia, people in academia consult, edit, and contribute to the online encyclopedia.

The pedagogical use of Wikipedia is often limited to certain activities such as the critical analysis of existing articles, the editing of these, and/or the creation of new ones. However, even these limited practices are believed to improve students' basic skills in reading comprehension, writing, research, and motivation (Lerga & Aibar, 2015). Faculty members who use Wikipedia have a positive perception of the online resource when it comes to using it as a teaching tool. Nevertheless, conflicts can arise with regards to standard knowledge-building procedures habitual in the academic setting and the open collaborative model common to Wikipedia (Aibar et al., 2015)

This platform uses collaborative models of content creation and fosters a culture of collaboration. Understanding how it works and mastering the editor's skills often call for partnerships between different members of the university community. Wikipedia projects can bring extra value to academic libraries and be used for information literacy instruction and digital and media literacy programs (Lubbock, 2018). Library-faculty collaboration can open new opportunities for information and media literacy and increase student agency and civic participation. This chapter shares faculty and librarians' experience using Wikipedia in the context of an initial pilot project aimed at adopting open educational resources (OER). The library-faculty team from the American University of Central Asia worked together to use Wikipedia as a tool to increase collaborative learning and civic participation of students in sociology courses.

Context

The American University in Central Asia (AUCA) is an international liberal arts university located in Kyrgyzstan, a former Soviet republic. The university offers a multidisciplinary learning environment and aspires to develop leaders for the democratic transformation of the Central Asian region. Students come from twenty-five countries around the world, including all the Central Asian countries, as well as Afghanistan, China, Pakistan, Russia, and South Korea, among others. AUCA faculty and librarians implement various instructional approaches to support learning and to promote critical inquiry and free expression. Wikipedia has become one of such tools helping to complement classroom learning and library instruction at the university.

In Kyrgyzstan, Wikipedia is listed among the most visited websites (SimilarWeb, 2020). The development of Wikipedia in the local context was implemented by nonprofit organizations that aimed to launch a Kyrgyz version of the platform. In the early 2010s, the local organization "Bizdin Muras," with the support of the Open Society Foundation, attracted more than 10 universities, 30 academics, and about 300 students from across the country to start creating content for Kyrgyz Wikipedia (Saadanbekov, 2013). In March 2011, the first "Week of Wikipedia" was held at five universities by the Movement of Kyrgyz Wikipedians. Each university committed to producing 500 articles in the first half of the year in exchange for Wi-Fi installation on their campuses. Kyrgyz Wikipedia has grown rapidly from 1,300 entries at the beginning of the project to 23,000 entries by the end of the project. Currently, the Kyrgyz version of Wikipedia has 80,271 entries (Kyrgyz Wikipedia, 2020).

The development of Kyrgyz Wikipedia coincided with the rise of a countrywide movement to promote OER. A series of events and activities was launched by education practitioners and institutions, with the development of Kyrgyz Wikipedia as an integral part of these (Roza Otunbayeva Initiative, 2015).

OER as a Starting Point

At AUCA, the faculty-library partnership around Wikipedia evolved from a pilot project aimed at implementing the use of OER. It has become common for academic libraries to pioneer OER at the institutional level through the raising of faculty awareness and providing needed support in adopting open-license materials (Crozier, 2018; Walz, 2015). OER and open educational practices can receive a great deal of support at different levels within an institution, but past experiences have shown that small-scale projects and tailored support for educators lead to more effective results (Jong et al., 2019). AUCA faculty and staff members chose to follow the above mentioned model, taking small steps in small teams to explore the potential of OER.

There were several reasons AUCA librarians chose to invest time in learning about OER. These included financial considerations with regards to the acquisition of multiple copies of textbooks, which is required by the government. Beyond the financial benefits, OER could be edited and customized by faculty to suit course needs and to reflect the local context. Furthermore, OER could have multiple applications across the university as different campus members were encouraged to adopt, edit, create, and share them.

In spring 2017, AUCA librarians launched a series of events to raise awareness of OER in the university. They reached out to interested faculty members in order to develop the first OER project at the university level, and the library-faculty collaboration team began to pilot the use of openly licensed textbooks for the introductory class in sociology in the 2017 fall semester. The experience of using an open textbook was rated as quite positive by students and faculty members in the end of semester survey. In the 2018 spring semester, the project went beyond the simple adoption of OER and expanded into the creation of open educational content by students.

Although the adopted textbook covered major topics in the discipline and helped students to grasp the main concepts, the cases and examples used in the text were predominantly Western focused and did not always allow students to relate the concepts to their experience. Adapting the textbook to the local context was needed, and the nature of open licenses made this possible. Engaging students in the creation of content that could complement the textbook seemed a reasoned step to follow. Students in the *General Sociology for Non-Sociologists* class were given the assignment to write about a pressing societal issue in their immediate surroundings as reflected through the lens of common sociological theories. The student papers submitted were then assembled for further use as supplementary course reading material.

At that stage of the project, librarians conducted a session for students to introduce them to the notion of Creative Commons and the ways authors may share and modify creative content through open licenses. The AUCA librarians also helped to compile student work into a handbook that could be further used as open educational content.

The move from OER adopters to contributors expanded the scope of activities the team could embrace as participants of the contemporary knowledge community. Following the themes of openness and contribution, faculty and librarians wanted to explore other ways of engaging students in participatory and collaborative learning experiences. This became one of the goals of the next stage in the faculty-library partnership.

Wikipedia as a Work in Progress and Its Potential in the Classroom

Why Wikipedia?

Wikipedia is based on the idea of openness and collaboration. Its Five Pillars align perfectly with what the team was looking for: an "online encyclopedia" with a "neutral point of view" providing "free content that anyone can use, edit and distribute," encouraging contributors to "treat each other with respect and civility" without imposing "firm rules" (Wikipedia: Five pillars, n.d.). The Five Pillars inspired the team to continue their work with open resources in other courses taught by the same instructors. In the 2019 fall semester, two courses, *Introduction to Gender Studies* and *State and Society*, provided students with the opportunity to become Wikipedia editors and to contribute to raising awareness on gender issues in the country. While one of the courses focused on gender issues, the second course included topics of gender roles in society. Gender-related topics became an intersection of team members' personal interests. Wikipedia, as an online open platform promoting a "neutral point of view," seemed the right tool for classes aiming to explore gender justice, still a sensitive topic in Kyrgyzstan (Rysbekova, 2020).

Working with Wikipedia, the team also learned about some gaps that could be addressed on the platform, such as the lack of global coverage and geographic and language underrepresentation. Gender imbalance in Wikipedia has been continuously studied in recent years. Graells-Garrido et al. (2015) argued that multiple groups are underrepresented in Wikipedia and one of these groups is women. Women only constitute 16 percent of the Wikipedia editors, which affects the generated content. Research indicated that, out of 1,445,021 biographies, only 15 percent were about women. The researchers also found that the significant gender disparity in the number of editors had influenced not only the content but also the narratives and attitudes expressed in those pages.

The literature has suggested that gender bias goes beyond a lack of representation. Lam et al. (2011) found that coverage of topics of potential interest for women was significantly less, and that male and female editors focused on different content areas when writing for Wikipedia. Wagner et al. (2016) found that there is topical gender bias on Wikipedia, as the most searched terms in relation to women (pre- and post-1900) were *her husband, women's, actress,* and *female,* whereas for men words included *served, elected, politician, played, league,* and *football.* Research on gender imbalance on Wikipedia demonstrates that the content of the platform cannot always be "neutral" due to the gender bias among the contributors.

The lack of representation of women on Wikipedia motivated the team to address the issue by contributing to Wikipedia content about women activists in the region and the impact these women have had on their communities. The idea was also influenced by a public event that touched upon gender issues in the country. In the fall of 2019, Kyrgyzstan experienced an incident that caused heated discussions in the country about gender justice. The feminist art exhibition, Feminnale, brought whip-wielding nationalists out to protest. "Controversial" performances and installations, designed to call attention to women's problems, appeared in the press and became the fulcrum of public debates (Suyarkulova, 2020a). Public opinion was divided and both sides were presented in the media. However, the prevailing coverage appealed to traditions pertaining to patriarchal cultural norms, leaving aside such issues as women's economic empowerment and gender violence, both of which had been central themes of the exhibition (Tuitunova, 2019).

Students in both courses were given the space to discuss the event from different perspectives. These discussions resulted in the creation of Wikipedia content aimed at filling the gaps in coverage of women issues in the region. For both courses, the faculty-library team designed Wikipedia assignments aimed at developing students' research skills, while also increasing their motivation, enthusiasm, and overall learning experience. In one of the courses, students were offered the chance to create Wikipedia pages about female political leaders in Central Asia, including members of parliaments. In the other course, the assignment included writing pages about feminist activism in the region, including about women-led initiatives, biographies of activists, and women leaders.

Librarians worked closely with the instructors to help ensure the assignments met the learning objectives and to facilitate students' needs in searching of information, source evaluation, and citation. Librarians delivered training sessions on Wikipedia editing for both courses. Even though all students had previously used Wikipedia for personal or academic purposes, none of them knew about the Wikipedia policies and guidelines. The training session covered information about the history, purpose, and mission of the platform, with a focus on the rules and regulations for editing and creating articles. It was important to help students understand the collaborative culture and philosophy of the platform, so they could feel connected to the Wikipedia community while bringing their perspectives into the construction of knowledge.

Students were given freedom in selecting topics, individuals, or events to cover in their assignments. Several students wrote Wikipedia pages about outstanding women they had known in their communities. One student wrote about one of the first female members of parliament in her country and the contribution of that woman to fighting gender inequality. This was especially important since gender inequality in the higher echelons of power is high in the region (IWPR Central Asia, 2020). Another student created a page about one of the feminist activists in Kyrgyzstan whose popularity increased after she had organized the earlier-mentioned "controversial" Feminnale art exhibition. The page included her achievements as a feminist, a writer of children's books, and a researcher.

Several pages were created to acknowledge women's accomplishments that were quite remarkable and important in their communities. For example, a well-known *Village Girl* project aiming to empower young girls in rural areas evolved from a small community project into a big countrywide initiative ("Village Girl Project," 2019). A Wikipedia page gathered information about that project and its activities and included information about the young woman activist who initiated the initiative.

Women in STEM became another topic of interest for students. One of the pages was dedicated to the *First Satellite Launch in Kyrgyzstan* project, the very first girls-only space program (BBC News, 2018). The page included information about the project goals, the training of the team, and the engineering process.

Students in the courses used various methods to collect information for their projects. Supporting students in the search for and ethical use of information was important in this project. Students collected information from openly available resources, such as public websites, news sites, social media, personal blogs, or official web pages. Some students even conducted interviews with the founders of women initiatives. After completing preliminary research, students received guidance from librarians on how to write, edit, and format pages on Wikipedia.

Students were given freedom in selecting the language of their pages, and the majority preferred their native languages, which included Kazakh, Turkish, Dari, and Russian. This helped contribute to the development of Wikipedia content in languages other than English. It is recognized that English is the dominant language of today's online knowledge ("Top Ten Languages Used in the Web," 2020). The development of Wikipedia pages in local languages helps to deliver information to non-English-speaking communities. This also aligns with the idea of making knowledge more accessible, which supports the concept of openness, and which had at first inspired the team to start the OER collaboration.

What Did We Learn?
THE ONLINE ENVIRONMENT NECESSITATES RESPONSIBILITY

While working on Wikipedia assignments, several issues came to light including online privacy and safety. Concerns remain about online violence toward different groups of people. Women and people with nonheterosexual gender identities are more at risk of online harassment and bullying (UN Women, 2015). Cases of discrimination based on gender, sexual orientation, or ethnicity are known in Central al Asia, as conservative norms prevail in the region (Suyarkulova, 2020b). The safety of the individuals and organizations selected by students for the Wikipedia assignment raised some concerns because of patriarchal attitudes. The questions of online security were discussed with students during the course to ensure the information used was taken from public and open sources.

Inclusiveness May Require Additional Work

By giving students freedom in choosing the language of the assignment, the team hoped to increase the inclusivity and accessibility of knowledge. At the same time, it created more work for instructors when evaluating the assignments. Some pages were written in languages in which faculty members did not speak. However, the instructors did not want to put extra work on the students with translating the content. For the pages created in languages other than Russian, Kyrgyz, Kazakh, and English, which were familiar to the instructors, students were asked to submit their original texts as Word documents, which were then translated with the help of an online translation tool.

Censorship of Wikipedia

The issue of censorship of Wikipedia also came up during the project. A Wikipedia ban has been implemented in several countries, either as a part of more general internet censorship or as a targeted block of the online encyclopedia (Ant, 2017; Vinton, 2015). This had an impact on the work of one of the students who was not able to create a Wikipedia page in Turkish. Wikipedia has been banned in Turkey for over two years, with access being restored in early 2020 (BBC News, 2020). Therefore, the student working on the assignment in the 2019 fall semester had to write a page about a Turkish female activist in English.

Wikipedia for Civic Activism

Like many other online platforms, Wikipedia can be used as a tool to engage students in a discussion of important societal problems. As students progressed in their assignments, they became more aware of issues around gender justice in the region, studying them from various perspectives. Creating Wikipedia pages on feminist activists and female political leaders of the Central Asia region not only allowed students to address the lack of content in the local languages but also became a small, yet important, step in minimizing the impact of patriarchal history on the representation of women in the region. This also is an avenue to help raise awareness of women's issues in communities where such online content could be limited.

Conclusion

As the landscape of knowledge and information has changed, the perception of Wikipedia has also changed from a quick online reference platform to a potential teaching resource. University members can find many benefits in using Wikipedia to fulfill their academic missions. At AUCA, the library-faculty collaboration provided new opportunities for instruction, learning, and participation. The partnership worked well and enriched team members' and students' experiences. Faculty members experimented with using open resources and new ways of engaging students in discussion. Students had an opportunity to participate in collaborative knowledge production and sharing and to contribute to the advancement of important topics in the public discourse. Librarians went beyond the traditional information literacy instruction by supporting both students and faculty throughout several semesters. Wikipedia editing workshops have become a part of the library instruction agenda and are currently delivered upon invitation from faculty as in class training sessions.

The role of Wikipedia in higher education is an ongoing discussion, and further studies can be very useful in deepening the understanding of this. One of the key features worthy of further exploration is the use of Wikipedia as a collaborative and open model that fosters, promotes, and provides the grounds for both engagement with the knowledge it provides and the further development of the platform itself. Given the increasing role of online learning today, Wikipedia has the potential to become a useful tool for diversifying learning experiences and motivating students.

References

Aibar, E., Lladós-Masllorens, J., Meseguer-Artola, A., Minguillón, J., & Lerga, M. (2015). Wikipedia at university: What faculty think and do about it. *Electronic Library, 4,* 668.

Ant, O. (2017). Turkey shuts Wikipedia as opposition party cries censorship. Bloomberg.Com.

BBC News. (2018). The women launching Kyrgyzstan's first satellite. Retrieved from www.bbc.com/news/av/world-europe-46347757.

BBC News. (2020). Turkey's Wikipedia ban ends after almost three years. Retrieved from www.bbc.com/news/technology-51133804.

Crozier, Heather. (2018). Promoting open access and open educational resources to faculty. *The Serials Librarian*, *74*,1–4, 145–50. doi: 10.1080/0361526X.2018.1428470

Graells-Garrido, E., Lalmas, M., & Menczer, F. (2015). First women, second sex: Gender bias in Wikipedia. *Proceedings of the 26th ACM Conference on Hypertext & Social Media*, 165–74.

Internet World Stats (2020). Top ten languages used in the web. Retrieved from www.internetworldstats.com/stats7.htm.

IWPR Central Asia. (2020). Kyrgyzstan: Bringing women into politics. Retrieved from https://iwpr.net/global-voices/kyrgyzstan-bringing-women-politics.

Jong, M. D., Munnik, M., & Will, N. (2019). Innovation opportunities for academic libraries to support teaching through open education: A case study at TU Delft, the Netherlands. *New Review of Academic Librarianship*, *25*, 392–407.

Kyrgyz Wikipedia. (2020). About. Retrieved from https://ky.wikipedia.org/wiki/Башбарак

Lam, S. K., Uduwage, A., Dong, Z., Sen, S., Musicant, D. R., Terveen, L., & Riedl, J. (2011). WP: Clubhouse? An exploration of Wikipedia's gender imbalance. *Proceedings of the 7th International Symposium on Wikis and Open Collaboration*.

Lerga, M., & Aibar, E. (2015). Best practices guide to use Wikipedia in university education. Retrieved from http://openaccess.uoc.edu/webapps/o2/handle/10609/41662.

Lubbock, J. (2018). Wikipedia and libraries. *Alexandria*, *28*(1), 55–68. https://doi-org.ldb.auca.kg:6443/10.1177/0955749018794968.

Roza Otunbayeva Initiative. (2015). Results of the gathering for The Coalition for "Open Education". Retrieved from https://roza.kg/en/press-center/photos/291.

Rysbekova, G. (2020). Why care about feminism in Kyrgyzstan? Retrieved from https://cabar.asia/en/why-care-about-feminism-in-kyrgyzstan.

Saadanbekov, C. (2013). A Kyrgyz Wikipedia. Retrieved from www.opensocietyfoundations.org/voices/und-44.

SimilarWeb. (2020). Top website ranking. Retrieved from www.similarweb.com/top-websites/kyrgyzstan/.

Suyarkulova, M. (2020a). Fateful Feminnale: An insider's view of a "controversial" feminist art exhibition in Kyrgyzstan. Retrieved from www.opendemocracy.net/en/odr/fateful-feminnale-an-insiders-view-of-a-controversial-feminist-art-exhibition-in-kyrgyzstan/.

Suyarkulova, M. (2020b). The struggle against patriarchal violence in Kyrgyzstan. Retrieved from www.opendemocracy.net/en/odr/your-traditions-our-blood-the-struggle-against-patriarchal-violence-in-kyrgyzstan/.

Tuitunova, S. (2019). Minister poshel na ustupki "choro" [The minister made concessions to "choro"]. Retrieved from https://rus.azattyk.org/a/zakri tiye_vistavki_femminale_v_bishkeke/30304553.html.

United Nations Women. (2015). Cyber violence against women and girls: A world-wide wake-up call. Retrieved from www.unwomen.org/~/media/headquarters/attachments/sections/library/publications/2015/cyber_vio lence_gender%20report.pdf.

Village Girl Project. (2019). Retrieved from https://sidp.auca.kg/wp-content/uploads/2019/10/Village-Girl-One-Pager.pdf.

Vinton, K. (2015). Wikipedia is now using HTTPS by default to prevent snooping and censorship. Retrieved from https://www.forbes.com/sites/katevinton/2015/06/12/wikipedia-is-now-using-https-by-default-to-pre vent-snooping-and-censorship/?sh=5d3601a17856, 22.

Wagner, C., Graells-Garrido, E., Garcia, D., & Menczer, F. (2016). Women through the glass ceiling: Gender asymmetries in Wikipedia. *EPJ Data Science*, *5*, 1–24.

Walz, A. R. (2015). Open and editable: Exploring library engagement in open educational resource adoption, adaption and authoring. *Virginia Libraries*, *61*, 23–31. doi:10.21061/valib.v61i1.1326.

Wikipedia: About. (2020). In Wikipedia. Retrieved from https://en.wikipedia.org/wiki/Wikipedia:About.

Wikipedia: Five pillars. (n.d.). In Wikipedia. Retrieved from https://en.wiki pedia.org/wiki/Wikipedia:Five_pillars.

Wikimedia Education. (2020). About. Retrieved from https://outreach.wiki media.org/wiki/Education/About

Wikimedia Foundation. (2020). About. Retrieved from https://wikimedia foundation.org/about

CHAPTER 2

"YEAH, I WROTE THAT!": INCORPORATING CRITICAL INFORMATION LITERACY TO BUILD COMMUNITY INSIDE AND OUTSIDE OF WIKIPEDIA

Kristina M. De Voe[1] and Adrienne Shaw[1]

[1]Temple University

Abstract

In this chapter, we examine the relationship between open pedagogical practices and critical information literacy and how they intersect when Wikipedia is introduced in the classroom. Specifically, we discuss the collaboration between a librarian and a course instructor on iterations of Wikipedia assignments across three years and two classes. We unpack the importance of existing infrastructures, such as edit-a-thons and the WikiEdu dashboard, to support bringing Wikipedia assignments into the classroom. We also explore how we worked to connect course content to the renewable assignments and brought larger discussions of representation and community on Wikipedia into the classroom and assignments. Finally, we outline the lessons we learned through this collaboration. In sum, scaffolded projects allowed students to practice their contributions to Wikipedia in a supportive space and fostered critical engagement with course content. In their end-of-semester reflections, students stated that

DOI: https://doi.org/10.3998/mpub.11778416.ch2.en

contributing to Wikipedia felt more meaningful and elicited feelings of pride that traditional, disposable assessments did not. They saw themselves as knowledge creators and scholarship creation as part of an ongoing conversation rather than an "end product." By engaging in peer-review assignments, participating in edit-a-thons, and discussing the assignments with librarians who were not their professors, students also saw their work as part of a broader academic conversation. Through Wikipedia assignments, students can appreciate their own information privilege in terms of access to costly resources and become proactive in sharing that knowledge and their own growing expertise with a wider public.

Keywords

Open education, information literacy, open educational practices, open pedagogy.

Introduction

Critical approaches to information literacy invite us to "co-investigate the political, social, and economic dimensions of information, including its creation, access, and use" (Tewell, 2016, para. 1). Drawing from critical pedagogy and extending beyond merely learning to use library resources, critical information literacy develops a critical consciousness in students around information so that they might take control of their own lives and learning (Freire, 2003; Giroux, 1988; hooks, 1994). As active agents in their own learning, students need a community with which to explore their information privilege, test and contest ideas, and create meaning. When students see themselves as authentic contributors to an ongoing conversation, instead of as mere consumers of information, their level of motivation increases (Elmborg, 2006; Jacobson & Xu, 2002).

Open pedagogical practices complement critical information literacy. These practices have clear connections to the open education movement and offer students opportunities to do inquiry-based work that is both available and accountable to a public beyond the classroom. With open pedagogy, assignments transition from being disposable to renewable. Laid to rest are assignments that both students and faculty know will likely be tossed in the recycle bin once the semester is over, such as the quintessential research paper, in favor of assignments where students actively engage in the creation or adaption of open educational resources (OER) (Wiley & Hilton, 2018). While supporting individual student learning, these OER add value as they can be seen, used, and improved upon by a broader community once completed (Wiley, 2015). Renewable assignments allow students to "contribute to the knowledge commons, not just consume it, in meaningful and lasting ways . . . shap[ing] the world as they encounter it" (DeRosa & Jhangiani, 2017, p. 9). Open pedagogy focuses on open teaching, open content, and having student work and interactions brought into the public sphere. As Bali (2017) suggested, it has an ethos of sharing and a social justice orientation. This emphasis on equitable participation in knowledge creation, centered around affordability, exemplifies the ways in which critical information literacy seeks to intervene upon information systems of oppression. Wikipedia offers an ideal site of praxis for critical information literacy and open pedagogy to intersect, demonstrating to students how knowledge is constructed and made accessible in open systems (Fields & Harper, 2020).

Wikipedia offers an outlet for publishing information on topics that are underrepresented in traditional publishing and mainstream media. Wikipedia provides a platform for diverse stories and histories while promoting collaboration among content creators with varying levels of expertise. In the classroom, learning how to improve Wikipedia gives students the opportunity to intervene upon the inner workings of a resource they all use while translating and publishing concepts from the course to a wider, public audience (Davis, 2018). Editing Wikipedia in class is also an example of what Hartley (2011) has termed "out-learning," a distributed way to venture into "that intermediate space between expert elites and the citizen-consumer" (p. 163). Although one of our goals of incorporating Wikipedia into the classroom is teaching and practicing critical information literacy, it also produces a secondary effect of showing students that research is a community-building process.

This chapter discusses the importance of existing infrastructures, such as edit-a-thons and WikiEdu, to support bringing Wikipedia assignments into the classroom and the iterative nature of collaboration between a librarian and professor working on Wikipedia assignments across three years and two different classes. We also talk about how we worked to connect course content to the assignment and brought broader discussions of representation on Wikipedia into the classroom and assignment. Finally, we talk about some of the lessons we have learned through this collaboration. In sum, scaffolded projects allowed students to practice their contributions to Wikipedia in a supportive space and made them engage critically with course content. In their reflections, students stated that contributing felt more meaningful and elicited feelings of pride that traditional, disposable assessments did not. They saw scholarship creation as part of an ongoing conversation rather than an "end product." By engaging in peer-review assignments, participating in edit-a-thons, and discussing the assignment with librarians who were not their professors, students also saw their work as part of a broader academic conversation. Through Wikipedia assignments, students can appreciate their own privilege in terms of access to costly resources and become proactive in sharing that knowledge and their own growing expertise with a broader public.

Tapping into Existing Infrastructures

Incorporating Wikipedia assignments in the classroom is made substantially easier when there are existing support structures for this work (Bridges & Dowell, 2020; Cassell, 2018; Davis, 2018). For instance, although we had previously worked together to incorporate scaffolded information literacy learning opportunities into courses, the Library's Art+Feminism edit-a-thon served as the jumping off point for our Wikipedia collaboration. This was then further supported by Wiki Education's training modules and course dashboard system.

Wikipedia edit-a-thons are planned, public programming events organized by galleries, libraries, archives, and museums (GLAMs) where attendees contribute edits to articles around a special theme, collection, or exhibition (Snyder, 2018). GLAMs view these communal events as "being a great outreach and engagement initiative" as they bring community members into their spaces, making them aware of services, holdings, and expertise (Robichaud, 2017, p. 2). Edit-a-thons gained momentum and mainstream consciousness beginning in 2014 with the Art+Feminism organization coordinating its edit-a-thon series, an annual event taking place at GLAMs worldwide with the aim to address gender disparities found within Wikipedia—including biased and/or underrepresented content as well as a lack of diverse, contributing editors (Art+Feminism, 2020; Evans et al., 2015).

At Temple University, Art+Feminism edit-a-thons have been hosted or cohosted by the library since 2016. Efforts to extend reach have included partnering with the university's art school and nearby academic libraries, bringing in panel speakers, as well as having librarians identify relevant courses whose faculty may wish students to participate or who may design assignments around the event. Art+Feminism's ambassador network and online event kits—complete with organizing how-to guides, CC-licensed promotional materials, safe/brave space policies, lesson plans, video tutorials, training slide decks—have ensured that GLAM staff are supported and prepared to host edit-a-thons that foster communities of possibility.

Our collaboration on Wikipedia assignments began in December 2017, after an announcement about Wiki Education's resources and training modules (WikiEdu) was sent through a feminist academic listserv. Paired with the announcement of the spring 2018's Art+Feminism edit-a-thon, this seemed like a good moment to find a way to incorporate a Wikipedia editing assignment into a course called LGBTQ Media Representation. The goals of the edit-a-thon directly intersected with the course content, and there would be staff on hand to help students navigate the editing process. WikiEdu's dashboard allowed us to structure training modules, exercises, discussion questions, and assignments within a timeline so that students could work their way through learning Wikipedia policies, how the site works, and how to use the editor functions. The dashboard also permitted students to create sandboxes where they could draft edits and get peer and faculty feedback on them before migrating them to "Live" Wikipedia articles during the edit-a-thon. This also made it easier to assess their edits, even if changes they make end up getting overwritten or rejected by later editors.

We worked together to find a way to experiment with an assignment that would feel meaningful to as well as manageable for students. We decided creating new Wikipedia articles from scratch would be unnecessary if the goal was to have students learn enough about editing to contribute to the edit-a-thon. Thus, we focused on creating a list of Wikipedia articles related to the course that needed improvement. We considered what contributions students could make to those articles, ranging from adding citations or external references, revising narrative text, or uploading public domain and/or CC-licensed content. We also discussed the logistics for preparing students for the edit-a-thon (e.g., including when specific WikiEdu training modules should be completed in relation to the edit-a-thon, technology needs, etc.) and whether this should be an individual or group assignment. We believe our dialogue exemplified Diaz and Mandernach's (2017) intentional relationship-building as well as Ivey's (2003) four essential behaviors for successful librarian-faculty collaboration: a shared, understood goal; mutual respect, tolerance, and trust; competence for the task at hand by each of the partners; and ongoing communication.

An Iterative Collaboration

This first iteration of the assignment in LGBTQ Media Representation had students complete WikiEdu training modules during the first weeks of the semester. Then they were assigned to groups, each of which was responsible for identifying edits they could make to one article related to the course. They had a few weeks to collaborate and collect their planned edits, which they would then make to Wikipedia during regular class time at the edit-a-thon. In addition to connecting students with a broader Wikipedia editing community, the edit-a-thon was beneficial for this first-time assignment as it meant there were librarians with Wikipedia experience available who could help students who may have forgotten elements of their training. Moreover, it gave the edits a sense of purpose as the students were part of an event larger than the class itself.

The lessons learned from the first iteration were useful in updating the assignment for a different course offered in fall 2019, spring 2020, and fall 2020: Technology and Culture. In this course, editing and talking about Wikipedia intersected with several course themes, and so it made sense to develop this into a semester-long project. Students selected an existing article relevant to the course to contribute to or identified a topic/person relevant to the course in which to create a new Wikipedia article. This longer project also made it easier to check students' progress week by week and allowed time for students to review their peers' drafted contributions in the WikiEdu sandbox (along with instructor feedback) before moving their edits to "Live" Wikipedia. In addition, students were required to write weekly summaries of assigned readings using "Wikipedia-style" neutral writing. Many students acknowledged that this type of writing was hard but also helped them learn how to better synthesize things they read (as well as how to paraphrase without plagiarizing). As one student wrote, "The main takeaway I received from contributing to Wikipedia is it has made me an overall better writer. Wikipedia has taught me how to concisely and accurately produce meaningful information based on academic sources." Throughout the iterative collaboration we were also able to connect editing Wikipedia to the course content in a way that helped students connect to core learning objectives in new ways.

Understanding Technology and Culture through Wikipedia

In Technology and Culture, the weekly WikiEdu trainings were scaffolded to connect with course topics. For instance, the discussion of "content gaps" on Wikipedia was covered in the same week the often-forgotten role of women as the earliest computer programmers was discussed (Abbate, 2012). Through our collaboration we found ways to do this better and more robustly over time. Following the fall 2019 semester where students had trouble finding media and images they could use, for example, we decided it would be helpful to reinstate a unit on digital media and copyright that coincided with the WikiEdu module on contributing images and media files. Furthermore, we worked together to find the topics throughout the semester where class discussions could reflect on editing Wikipedia. Early classes, for example, focused on understanding points in history where Internet technologies were developed to serve communal, rather than commercial, goals, yet material infrastructure shapes who actually gets to engage with different Internet technologies (Curran, 2012; Lobato, 2019). A student later reflected that "Wikipedia is one of the ultimate crossroads between technology and culture, as its foundation is built on the mission to provide free information for all through the community." But, another student noted, "Depending on the technology (internet connection and a reliable PC) and sources we have access to, it affects the information we add to the article, and that in turn affects what information the public gets access to." The Wikipedia project made tangible lessons about the importance of understanding the cultural, material, and human infrastructures of digital technologies and critically addressing questions of representation and access to Internet-based media and communication technologies.

Moreover, students connected the work that they did in Wikipedia to topics that were only briefly touched on in class. A discussion on hacking, for example, included the story of Aaron Swartz, who took his own life after being charged with computer fraud and abuse when he downloaded and planned to distribute millions of academic articles from JSTOR for free; the charge could have resulted in millions of dollars in penalties and decades in jail (Gustin, 2013). This served as a chance to talk about how academic publishing works, how knowledge can and should be shared, as well as the students' own privileged access to academic materials they often take for granted. And students articulated these takeaways in their final papers:

What makes this Wikipedia assignment different from other assignments I've had in the past is the impact it has had on how I perceive higher education. It was a refreshing change from the endless cycle of research papers and presentations that leave me feeling drained and unfulfilled. As I've gone through college, I have found myself slowly losing interest in my education and, in turn, taking it for granted. This assignment has changed my perspective entirely, challenging me to let go of my frustrations with academia and instead consider my privilege.

Students were able to not only see their work as having meaning beyond the semester but were also able to better recognize information imbalances, confronting their own information privilege (Booth, 2014).

The course also focused on how power works through historical, material, political, economic, legal, and cultural frameworks culminating in a discussion of trust and information literacy. The students read research on mis- and disinformation online, as well as the intersections of online harassment and "trolling" culture in online spaces (Gray, 2011; Marwick & Lewis, 2017; Phillips, 2015). Students watched misinformation expert Claire Wardle's 2019 TedTalk, in which she summarized her research-driven solutions for transforming the "internet into a place of trust" (Wardle, 2019). The model she described for creating a healthy information commons is in many ways modeled on that of Wikipedia. Similarly, she argued that understanding the underlying architecture of *how* online platforms work is central to rebuilding trust of information—pushing healthy skepticism over knee-jerk distrust. As one student commented, "The amount of research that Wikipedians use helps them sift between fake news and true information." All of this culminated in a key takeaway: understanding how things work is the best way to enact change (focusing on making the world more just and equitable). Or, as Freire (2003) wrote, "To surmount the situation of oppression, people must first critically recognize its causes, so that through transforming action they can create a new situation, one which makes possible the pursuit of a fuller humanity" (Freire [1970], p. 47). In addition to the assignment feeling more meaningful than a traditional course paper, it helped students feel more directly invested in the course content itself. This is seen even more clearly in the ways students connected broader course themes about representation, who is left out and who is included in technology industries and digital spaces, to their own work editing Wikipedia.

Representation and Wikipedia

In bringing Wikipedia into the classroom, we did recognize the well-established drawbacks of Wikipedia, particularly in terms of representation (Davidson, 2017; Gauthier & Sawchuk, 2017). We knew that bullying and harassing behavior from some Wikipedia editors has chased women and members of marginalized groups off the platform (Menking & Erickson, 2015; Wulczyn et al., 2017). Rather than treating these as reasons to avoid the platform, however, these issues were part of the course. For example, while talking about online harassment, we also discussed how using the WikiEdu sandboxes to draft their edits was risk-free space for students to learn how to use Wikipedia without worrying about other editors critiquing their works in progress. This also meant they could refine their edits, guided by their instructor, so they felt more confident in them before changing existing articles.

At the end of the semester, students read about gender disparities in who Wikipedia articles are written about (Adams et al., 2019). And by this point, students were able to critique the norms created by "notability" rules, but they were also empowered to work within the rules of Wikipedia to push back on those norms. As one student wrote, "The quality and depth of content on Wikipedia can be improved by having more women and people of color editing articles, and the same can be said for further inclusion and diversity in other areas of cultural work and study." They also recognized that this was a space they could be part of the change to the culture and perception of Wikipedia.

In this final discussion, students were able to see themselves as shifting whose perspectives are represented in the site, adopting what Lambert (2018) deemed as representational social justice (p. 228). In part because of university/major demographics, half or more than half of the students in the courses were women or nonbinary, and about a third were students of color. Some students made connections between their own subjectivities and the project directly. One student elected to edit an article on LGBTQ+ media representation, focusing on the possibilities of new digital media platforms. In this student's final reflection paper, they wrote, "With more than 70 countries that criminalize LGBTQ+ people and their identities, it is vital to have a tool like Wikipedia that serves as a resource for LGBTQ+ people." In the same class, another student elected to translate an article from English Wikipedia into Spanish, her first language, as the Spanish Wikipedia article had little information on a topic she had researched previously. In her final reflection paper she wrote, "As a Hispanic woman, I feel a responsibility to contribute information from a perspective that is lacking within the overall collaborative space. I can use Wikipedia to showcase how fun research can be."

As Freire (2003) wrote, "Students, as they are increasingly posed with problems relating to themselves in the world and with the world, will feel increasingly challenged and obliged to respond to that challenge . . . the resulting comprehension tends to be increasingly critical and thus constantly less alienated . . . and gradually the students come to regard themselves as committed" (Freire [1970], p. 81). Similarly, speaking of her experiences with engaged pedagogy, hooks (1994) wrote that her students "want an education that is healing to the uninformed, unknowing spirit" and want instructors to address "the connection between what they are learning and their overall life experiences" (p. 19). Later she said, "The academy is not paradise. But learning is a place where paradise can be created. The classroom, with all its limitations remains a location of possibility. . . . This is education as the practice of freedom" (p. 207). Although not all students explained their contributions in relation to their identities, several did elect to create articles for or contribute to articles that actively tried to improve gender and racial representation in what is available on Wikipedia. And the students' reflections on their work further informed our ongoing iteration of the assignment.

Lessons Learned

Bringing Wikipedia into the classroom required some trial and error. Several students in the fall 2019 semester, for example, opted to make new articles for authors read in the course. Despite discussions emphasizing that this was more complex than editing existing articles, students still thought it would be easier. These students ran into problems finding reliable sources to cite (beyond faculty bios on university websites). We identified that this largely stemmed from students being unfamiliar with sources like academic book reviews, which facilitate scholarship as conversation (Rowland et al., 2019). Thus, in spring 2020, short academic book reviews were assigned to be read alongside the selections from academic books assigned in the course. This addition helped put academic conversations in context but also helped students realize what other sorts of information would be useful in creating articles about scholars. Rather than shy away from having students create new articles, the iterative process simply showed what skill sets and knowledge practices students would need before tackling such projects. Indeed, one student in fall 2020 created a new article for a scholar that has thus far met Wikipedia's notability standards. The article was shared with the scholar, who then immediately shared it with her entirely family, much to the delight of the student who had worked so hard on it.

In addition, one student in fall 2019 expressed concern that they did not feel comfortable making contributions to Wikipedia because they weren't an "expert" on the topic. We now know it was important to emphasize that students need not be subject matter experts to identify flaws with existing articles and restructured some of the training activities to emphasize this. The WikiEdu trainings were reorganized for spring 2020 so that students identified the article they were going to edit/create earlier in the semester. For students contributing to existing articles, they did an evaluation exercise, identifying the changes they would make before finalizing that choice. Students creating new articles analyzed similar existing articles, identifying what they would need to do to make a good one. Then each of the weekly trainings and exercises required them to work on the articles they had chosen (e.g., learning to add citations by adding content and a citation to their sandbox for their article). This required reworking the default training timeline offered by WikiEdu and indeed showed some of the limitations of relying on adopting a premade, rather than creating a tailored, scaffolded training structure. Finally, students in fall 2019 were asked to write letters to the next semester's students to give them advice. This helped reinforce that they were part of an ongoing community, but also these notes helped ease students' anxieties about their contributions. Students in spring 2020 wrote similar letters to the next semester's students, but also some wrote to the fall 2019 students thanking them for their advice. This practice continued in fall 2020 as it has proven successful.

Conclusion

On the final day of class for fall 2019/spring 2020/fall 2020, De Voe visited the classes not to "give the library talk" (Eisenhower & Smith, 2009, p. 319) but to discuss her own perspectives on editing Wikipedia as both a librarian and scholar. This culminating moment reminded students that, by editing Wikipedia, they engaged in a scholarly project that reached beyond the bounds of the semester. The students enjoyed hearing someone else place their own experiences using Wikipedia in context. This was followed by a discussion of a reading on how to rebuild academics' trust of Wikipedia (Jemielniak & Aibar, 2016). Students connected their work as part of that broader mission. One student wrote, "I appreciated how Kristina De Voe described Wikipedia as more of an entry point into a subject, as opposed to the ultimate authority on it. If the cultural understanding and expectations of Wikipedia change, as they have for me, perhaps it will become more broadly accepted in academia and positively regarded in popular culture." Similarly, students found that they only really understood how Wikipedia works by actively engaging with it: "It was not until actively participating in the Wikipedia process, that I began to understand who is contributing, how they are going about doing it, and why."

Over the course of four semesters, and two different courses, 98 students have added approximately 73,000 words, 680 references, and 51 commons uploads while editing 56 articles and creating 7 new ones. These edits, as of December 2020, had been viewed 7.5 million times. Adding Wikipedia to these courses served multiple pedagogical purposes, such as integrating course content into tangible real-world actions, improving students' writing skills, engaging in digital and information literacy skills, and creating projects in which students felt invested. As Davidson summarizes, assignments like these are "the ideal way to empower the next generation to use the avalanche of information at their fingertips in a purposive, responsive way to make possible their own future success and, ideally, their contribution to a better society" (2017, p. 97). At the end of the course, most students commented on feeling "proud" of their contributions: "After all of the time I put into this project I have to say that it is one of things I am most proud of doing here at school. I visited and worked on Wikipedia every week for the entirety of the semester, which really made this assignment mean a lot."

In *The New Education*, Cathy Davidson (2017) reviews the Stanford Study of Writing led by Andrea Lunsford, which found that students in the early 2000s felt more invested in writing that had an audience beyond their professor and classmates (pp. 94–95). Wikipedia can provide such an experience; as one student reflected, "Over one million Wikipedians viewed our pages! In just a few months our entire class made an impact. . . . Wikipedia is a true gem as its free information that would otherwise be hidden behind paywalls or for select individuals." In their final reflection papers, regardless of the negative feelings they had around the project at times, nearly all students said the project was unlike anything they have ever done before. In one student's words, "The process of actually editing a live Wikipedia page is not only educational, but gratifying. To be able to pull open Wikipedia and tell your family and friends, 'Yeah, I wrote that!' is a really rewarding and satisfying feeling."

References

Abbate, J. (2012). *Recoding gender: Women's changing participation in computing.* MIT Press.

Adams, J., Brückner, H., & Naslund, C. (2019). Who counts as a notable sociologist on Wikipedia? Gender, race, and the "professor test". *Socius 5*, 1–14. https://doi.org/10.1177%2F2378023118823946.

Art+Feminism (2020). Art+Feminism. www.artandfeminism.org.

Bali, M. (2017). What is open pedagogy anyway? *Year of open.* www.yearo fopen.org/april-open-perspective-what-is-open-pedagogy/.

Booth, C. (2014, December 1). On information privilege. *info-mational.* https://infomational.com/2014/12/01/on-information-privilege/.

Bridges, L. M., & Dowell, M. L. (2020). A perspective on Wikipedia: Approaches for educational use. *Journal of Academic Librarianship, 46*(1), 102090.

Cassell, M. K. (2018). When the world helps teach your class: Using Wikipedia to teach controversial issues. *PS: Political Science & Politics, 51*(2), 427–33.

Curran, J. (2012). Rethinking internet history. In J. Curran, N. Fenton, and D. Freedman (Eds.), *Misunderstanding the internet* (pp. 34–60). Routledge.

Davidson, C. N. (2017). *The new education: How to revolutionize the university to prepare students for a world in flux.* Basic Books.

Davis, L. L. (2018). Wikipedia and education: A natural collaboration, supported by libraries. In M. Proffitt (Ed.), *Leveraging Wikipedia: Connecting communities of knowledge.* ALA Editions.

DeRosa, R., & Jhangiani, R. (2017). Open pedagogy. In E. Mays (Ed.), *A guide to making open textbooks with students* (pp. 7–20). Rebus Community. https://press.rebus.community/makingopentextbookswithstudents/.

Díaz, J. O., & Mandernach, M. A. (2017). Relationship building one step at a time: Case studies of successful faculty-librarian partnerships. *portal: Libraries and the Academy, 17*(2), 273–82. https://doi.org/10.1353/pla.2017.0016.

Eisenhower, C., & Smith, D. (2009). The library as a "stuck place": Critical pedagogy in the corporate university. In M. T. Accardi, E. Drabinski, & A. Kumbier (Eds.), *Critical library instruction: Theories and methods* (pp. 305–18). Library Juice.

Elmborg, J. (2006). Critical information literacy: Implications for instructional practice. *Journal of Academic Librarianship, 32*(2), 192–99. https://doi.org/10.1016/j.acalib.2005.12.004.

Evans, S., Mabey, J., & Mandiberg, M. (2015). Editing for equality: The outcomes of the Art+Feminism Wikipedia edit-a-thons. *Art Documentation: Bulletin of the Art Libraries Society of North America, 34*(2), 194–203.

Fields, E., & Harper, A. (2020). Opening up information literacy: Empowering students through open pedagogy. *Scholarship of Teaching and Learning, Innovative Pedagogy, 2*(1). https://digitalcommons.humboldt.edu/sotl_ip/vol2/iss1/1.

Freire, P. (2003). *Pedagogy of the oppressed* (30th anniversary ed.). Continuum. (Original work published 1970).

Gauthier, M., & Sawchuk, K. (2017). Not notable enough: Feminism and expertise in Wikipedia. *Communication and Critical/Cultural Studies, 14*(4), 385–402.

Giroux, H. A. (1988). *Teachers as intellectuals: Toward a critical pedagogy of learning.* Bergin & Garvey.

Gray, K. L. (2011). Intersecting oppressions and online communities: Examining the experiences of women of color in Xbox Live. *Information, Communication & Society, 15*(3), 411–28.

Gustin, S. (2013, January 13). Aaron Swartz, tech prodigy and internet activist, is dead at 26. *Time.* https://business.time.com/2013/01/13/tech-prodigy-and-internet-activist-aaron-swartz-commits-suicide/.

Hartley, J. (2011). Outlearning. In B. Zelizer (Ed.), *Making the university matter* (pp. 162–72). Routledge.

hooks, b. (1994). *Teaching to transgress: Education as the practice of freedom.* Routledge.

Ivey, R. (2003). Information literacy: How do librarians and academics work in partnership to deliver effective learning programs? *Australian Academic & Research Libraries, 34*(2), 100–13.

Jacobson, T., & Xu, L. (2002). Motivating students in credit-based information literacy courses: Theories and practice. *portal: Libraries and the Academy, 2*(3), 423–41. doi:10.1353/pla.2002.0055.

Jemielniak, D., & Aibar, E. (2016). Bridging the gap between Wikipedia and academia. *Journal of the Association for Information Science and Technology, 67*(7): 1773–76. https://doi.org/10.1002/asi.23691.

Lambert, S. R. (2018). Changing our (dis)course: A distinctive social justice aligned definition of open education. *Journal of Learning for Development, 5*(3), 225–44.

Lobato, R. (2019). *Netflix nations: The geography of digital distribution.* NYU Press.

Marwick, A., & Lewis, R. (2017). Media manipulation and disinformation online. *Data and Society.* https://datasociety.net/output/media-manipulation-and-disinfo-online/.

Menking, A., & Erickson, I. (2015). The heartwork of Wikipedia: Gendered, emotional labor in the world's largest online encyclopedia. *CHI'15: Proceedings of the 33rd Annual ACM Conference on Human Factors in Computing Systems* (pp. 207–10). https://doi.org/10.1145/2702123.2702514.

Phillips, W. (2015). *This is why we can't have nice things: Mapping the relationship between online trolling and mainstream culture.* MIT Press.

Robichaud, D. (2017). Wikipedia edit-a-thons: Thinking beyond the warm fuzzies. *Partnership: The Canadian Journal of Library and Information Practice and Research, 11*(2). https://doi.org/10.21083/partnership.v11i2.3802.

Rowland, N., Knapp, J. A., & Fargo, H. (2019). Learning "scholarship as conversation" by writing book reviews. *Scholarship and Practice of Undergraduate Research, 2*(3). www.cur.org/download.aspx?id=4001.

Snyder, S. (2018). Edit-a-thons and beyond. In M. Proffitt (Ed.), *Leveraging Wikipedia: Connecting communities of knowledge* (pp. 119–32). American Library Association.

Tewell, E. (2016). Putting critical information literacy into context: How and why librarians adopt critical practices in their teaching. *In the Library with the Lead Pipe.* www.inthelibrarywiththeleadpipe.org/2016/putting-critical-information-literacy-into-context-how-and-why-librarians-adopt-critical-practices-in-their-teaching/.

Wardle, C. (2019, April). How you can help transform the internet into a place of trust [Video]. *TED Conferences.* www.ted.com/talks/claire_wardle_how_you_can_help_transform_the_internet_into_a_place_of_trust?language=en.

Wiley, D. (2015, August 3). An obstacle to the ubiquitous adoption of OER in US higher education. *iterating toward openness: pragmatism before zeal.* https://opencontent.org/blog/archives/3941.

Wiley, D., & Hilton, J. (2018). Defining OER-enabled pedagogy. *International Review of Research in Open and Distributed Learning, 19*(4). www.irrodl.org/index.php/irrodl/article/view/3601/4724.

Wulczyn, E., Thain, N., & Dixon, L. (2017). Ex machina: Personal attacks seen at scale. *WWW'17: Proceedings of the 26th International Conference on World Wide Web* (pp. 1391–99). https://doi.org/10.1145/3038912.3052591.

CHAPTER 3

WHERE HISTORY MEETS MODERN: AN OVERVIEW OF ACADEMIC PRIMARY SOURCE RESEARCH-BASED LEARNING PROGRAMS AGGREGATING SPECIAL COLLECTIONS AND WIKIMEDIA

Odin Essers,[1] Henrietta Hazen,[1] and Nicolette Siep[1]

[1] Maastricht University Library

Abstract

At Maastricht University Library, the use of literary sources from its Special Collections by students is promoted and facilitated through the development and organization of specialized research-based learning programs as part of the Wikipedia Education Program. The central aim of these learning programs is to educate students on the social relevance of the Special Collections, such as the Jesuit library, which contains books (on philosophy, history, anatomy, literature, theology, law, and various social sciences) dating back to the beginning of the sixteenth century. In addition, by participating in these programs, undergraduate students from various colleges are given the opportunity to develop their information literacy skills by gaining experience in conducting empirical literature research on primary historical sources and its publication through a popular open-access platform. Evaluations from students indicate that the unique combination of

DOI: https://doi.org/10.3998/mpub.11778416.ch3.en

analyzing historical literature and the publication of their review on a modern open-access platform led to increased motivation, readership, sense of responsibility, and understanding about the importance of open-access knowledge transfer and valorization of information. In addition to the Wikipedia Education Program, Maastricht University has also been involved in a noneducational Wikimedia project: Wiki-Wetenschappers. The aim of this chapter is to provide an overview of the activities, approaches, and evaluation of the Wikipedia Education Program and the Wiki-Scientists project at Maastricht University.

Author Note

Correspondence concerning this article should be addressed to Essers, Odin L. M. J., Maastricht University Library, P. O. Box 616, 6200 MD Maastricht. Email: odin.essers@maastrichtuniversity.nl

Keywords

Wikimedia, Wikipedia, Wikidata, Special collections, Research-based learning, Skills and academic support, Information literacy, Historic books, Academic library courses, Social media, Open access.

Introduction

In recent years, several Dutch universities have been collaborating with Wikimedia Nederland on educational activities as part of the *Wikipedia: Benelux Education Program.* This program is part of a worldwide initiative that encourages academic teachers and students to share their knowledge by contributing to Wikipedia and Wikimedia projects. For example, in 2017 undergraduate students from Utrecht University wrote articles about manuscripts held by the library as part of the minor *Discovery of the Middle Ages: From Parchment to the Internet.* In 2019, students from the University of Amsterdam wrote articles about Dutch or Flemish book printers, publishers, cartographers, and engravers as part of the course *Old Books in a New World.* When developing and implementing these programs, universities often ask for support from experienced Wikipedia editors or the local Wikimedia associations if they want to organize projects or activities. The general mission of this collaboration is to make free, online educational content accessible everywhere.

With two courses and a research project, Maastricht University has been most prolific in its collaboration with Wikimedia Nederland. Alongside the regular curriculum, ambitious and motivated students of Maastricht University can participate in three excellence programs: *Maastricht Research Based Learning (MaRBLe)*, *Honours+*, and *Premium*. The aim of these excellence programs is to offer students extracurricular opportunities that help them to develop their talents, increase their knowledge, and strengthen their resume. Currently, more than 500 students participate in these programs each year (*Excellence Education, 2020*).

The MaRBLe program is offered to third-year undergraduate students during the elective period in order to provide hands-on experience in conducting multidisciplinary scientific research. The number of credits varies from 15 to 18 ECTS,[1] depending on the college that organizes the course. Second- and third-year undergraduate students can enroll in an Honours+ program for additional lectures and projects in order to develop academic skills, expand their knowledge, and build community. Students receive 5 ECTS if they successfully complete the course. Premium is an excellence program for graduate students to additionally work on a three-month group assignment with personal coaching, aiming to bridge the gap between the students' academic and professional life.

Since 2014, Maastricht University Library has been collaborating with Wikimedia Nederland in the development of several educational programs. The first program developed was the MaRBLe course *On Expedition* at the Faculty of Arts and Social Sciences (FASoS). In 2017, the *Honours+* elective course *Historical Book Review* was introduced at the Faculty of Psychology and Neuroscience (FPN). The Maastricht University Library has also been collaborating with Wikimedia Nederland on the research project *Opening up old books: Investigating the botanical archives of Maastricht* at the Maastricht Science Programme (MSP), an internationally oriented Liberal Arts and Sciences program of the Faculty of Science and Engineering (FSE).

Educational Programs

On Expedition

For years now, FASoS students have been participating in the *On Expedition* course. The general aim is to guide students in the selection, analysis, and review of historical travel books from the *Jesuit Library* for their bachelor's thesis. In the first part of this five-month MaRBLe course, students have the opportunity to experience and strengthen their interdisciplinary scholarly research skills through examining literary sources that contain information about trade missions and scientific expeditions and analyzing these sources in terms of identity and concepts such as *othering*, a concept linked to the work of modern theorist Edward Said (Said, 1978). This course consists of lectures, collection tours, presentations, group discussions, skills workshops, and feedback sessions. In 2020, an additional activity was introduced, which consisted of the creation of a vlog series in which one of the students (Hvalić, 2020) shared her thoughts, accomplishments, struggles, and aw-moments throughout the course.

Knowledge valorization or societal outreach is an important aspect of the MaRBLe program. Students present their research results not only to their fellow researchers but also to interested parties outside of the university. They share academic knowledge with nonacademic stakeholders. In the second part of this course, students are given an assignment to disseminate their research results to a wider audience by writing and publishing an article on Wikipedia. Although most students are familiar with Wikipedia, none or only few have experience with creating or editing its content. Therefore, students learn how to write articles for Wikipedia during three instruction classes with a volunteer at Wikimedia Nederland. In the first class meeting, students are introduced to the scope and writing guidelines of the platform; then students start writing their article in a personal Wikipedia sandbox (i.e., a space to experiment with the process of editing Wikipedia). During the second class meeting, students receive feedback on the first draft of their article, which they have to incorporate for the final class meeting. In between the instruction classes, students also receive online feedback from a Wikimedia volunteer in their sandboxes and on their Wikipedia talk pages (i.e., administration pages where editors can discuss improvements to articles or other Wikipedia pages). After the third and last class meeting, students submit their final draft for review. One week later, the course is finalized in online one-on-one sessions in which the students are taught how to add their articles to Wikipedia. Additional information about this MaRBLe course, including the program, handy links (e.g., tutorials and cheat sheets), guidelines, contact information, and links to contributions, sandboxes, and talk pages are published on a dedicated Wikipedia project page (*FASOS Marble Spring*, 2020). Students are graded on three different outputs: their thesis proposal, a Wiki article on the book of choice, and their bachelor's thesis. All outputs are evaluated with a pass or a fail that is based on peer and individual supervisor feedback, forms, and checklists. A Wikimedia volunteer pays special attention to the structure and encyclopedia-style writing of the Wiki article and the selection and citation of references.

In sum, an important objective of the *On Expedition* course is to encourage students to analyze, write, and present information about literary sources to a global audience using the popular open-access platform Wikipedia. Contributing to Wikipedia gives students a sense of ownership and responsibility for their work that lasts long after the course has ended. In addition, students practice writing from a neutral point of view. The encyclopedia-style writing is challenging as Wikipedia policy states that any material or quotations challenged or likely to be challenged, anywhere in the article, require citations. Strict adherence to referencing and citing primary sources in this course is an academic skill students will benefit from in the rest of their academic career.

Historical Book Review
During the *Historical Book Review* elective course of the FPN Honours+ program, students write Wikipedia articles on original, strange, or unusual psychology (related) books from the Special Collections that were published before 1920. The course consists of five class meetings during which the students are taught how to write a book review

article for Wikipedia. Furthermore, students participate in a guided Special Collections tour, either on location or in the form of a livestream. During this tour, students are shown examples of psychology classics and other collection highlights held by the University Library.

During the first class meeting, students are introduced to the Special Collections and learn how to search for primary sources within these collections using the online library catalog. Students pitch and discuss their book of choice during the second class meeting, followed by a training session in specific discipline database search. During the third class meeting, students are instructed about the scope and writing guidelines of Wikipedia by a Wikimedia volunteer. Students present the results of a deep reading analysis of their book, for example, in the form of an argument map, during the fourth class meeting. In the fifth and last class meeting, students showcase their Wikipedia articles with brief presentations of their book reviews, offering room for peer review and general feedback from the instructors. Following this final meeting, students have time to finalize their Wikipedia book review and add it to their personal sandbox. A Wikimedia volunteer gives feedback via the talk pages. Detailed information about this course is centrally structured in a dedicated Wikipedia project page (FPN Historical Book Review, 2020). Students are graded on two outputs: the presentation of the results of the deep reading exercise and the Wikipedia book review. Since the aim of the Historical Book Review course is to write a book review, special attention is paid to the historical context and layout of the book (e.g., context, time frame, book reception, intro sentence, and headers).

Opening Up Old Books

Opening up old books: Investigating the botanical archives of Maastricht is an intermediate-level research project within the MSP of the FSE. In this project, students study historical plant books from the Special Collections. During this four-week, full-time project, students are asked to analyze historical botanical books in the context of contemporary science. The aim of this project is to conduct a comparative analysis between the contents of an interesting, important, or peculiar book from plant biology and current knowledge on the book's topic. In addition, students write a book review article for Wikipedia. At the end of this course, both the outcome of the comparative analysis and the book review are published on Wikipedia.

In January 2019, thirteen students participated in this new project, which was developed by an evolutionary biologist from the FSE, the University Library, and a Wikimedia volunteer. During this course, the students worked on a comparative analysis of four botany textbooks from the Special Collections dating from the nineteenth to the twenty-first century, resulting in a forty-five-page report. At the start of the project, the students formed three groups; each group selected a post-Linnaean botanical book from the Special Collections, the oldest one dating back to 1821. Students used a personal Wikipedia sandbox for writing sections of the book review and then merged their individual contributions using a group sandbox. After having completed this merger, a Wikimedia volunteer provided in-depth feedback, with a focus on meeting the Wikipedia quality standards and layout guidelines. All the Wikipedia articles have a similar structure: short introduction, context, content, literary styles, reception and impact, gallery, references, and an info box. Information about the project was published on a dedicated Wikipedia project page (*MSP*, 2019). The instructors assessed the quality of the Wikipedia articles on three levels: contents, referencing, and structure. Grading was done on a Likert-type scale, ranging from very poor to excellent.

A feedback session indicated that it was an interesting experience for everyone involved for several reasons. First, the MSP program was established in 2011 and does not have big historical collections of books to study. They were therefore eager to use books from the Special Collections. Furthermore, the library skills training sessions were evaluated as particularly essential because searching for old books is different from navigating modern literature. Students also indicated that they were excited and eager to physically touch and browse through these old, historical, literary sources and that they really got an understanding about how knowledge evolved. For example, they had great fun laughing at the idea that bacteria were once thought to be plants.

In conclusion, all students were highly motivated by the combination of discovering and examining old books, learning about Wikipedia, and improving their literature search skills. All students passed the project with high results.

Impact in and beyond the Classroom

The collaboration between college staff (teachers, researchers), university library employees (curators, information specialists), and Wikimedia volunteers resulted in engaging and comprehensive courses. Evaluation of these courses suggests a valuable impact on multiple levels, both inside and outside the classroom. An important aim for the developers of these courses was to improve the academic information literacy skills of students, such as searching and analyzing historical information sources, communicating academic knowledge to a public audience, practicing encyclopedia-style writing, and referencing and citing literary sources. Surprisingly, practical implementation and hands-on experience with these courses suggest that the realized impact was much broader.

An additional impact of these courses relates to a unique element that differentiates them from other academic courses: the course results in the publication of the student's work on an open-access platform. For many students, this is the first time that they expose and demonstrate their academic knowledge and skills to a general audience. Feedback from the students indicates that the prospect of this outcome results in increased motivation, readership, and a sense of responsibility and ownership for "their" Wikipedia article throughout the course. Students also indicate that this course contributed to their understanding about the importance of open-access knowledge transfer and valorization of information. For example, by contributing high-quality, scholarly articles to Wikipedia they can contribute to a positive image of Wikipedia as a legitimate information source freely accessible to everybody in the world. The hands-on experience of contributing to these processes resulted in a feeling of personal gratification and proudness.

In addition to the actual course activities, the library contributed by scanning the images and other relevant information from the books students selected. All of the public domain images that were scanned for these courses are accessible on Wikimedia Commons. By doing this, visibility and usability have increased. This shows in the analytics of file usage in other Wikis. Images that are still under copyright are listed to be undeleted when they become public domain. Maastricht University Library recently decided that all scanned, copyright-free images from the Special Collections should be available on *Wikimedia Commons* (2020), and in Wikidata as Linked Open Data.

Limitations and Future Recommendations
Although evaluation of the Wikipedia Education Program courses suggests a valuable impact on multiple levels, there are also areas of improvement. First, past experiences in the course Historical Book Review indicate that many students struggle with finding relevant information about the historical context of the book. Students tend to primarily search for references and texts directly linked to the book title. Future courses should focus on training students to find relevant information that is not directly linked to the book title. Second, some of the articles written by the students remain unpublished. The final draft of an article is generally graded when it is still in the student's sandbox. Sometimes only a few minor adjustments have to be made in order to publish the article. For future courses, it is paramount that all articles are published if they meet the course criteria and Wikipedia's policies and guidelines. Third, not all the books or authors students selected are suitable for a Wikipedia article. Some books are relatively unknown and did not receive a lot of media attention. The effort and time students invested in researching these books is not always visible. Future courses could benefit from identifying poorly covered topics and contribute to filling Wikipedia's knowledge gaps. Last, not so much an area of improvement as an observation, these courses and projects fit better with smaller classes. Maastricht University uses a problem- and research-based learning approach working in small groups of ten to fifteen students. In bigger classes it is difficult to monitor students' work and provide feedback. Universities with a more traditional mode of learning should take this into account.

Noneducational Wikimedia Project

The Wiki–Scientists Project

From late 2018 to October 2019, Maastricht University participated in the *Wiki-Scientists project* (translated from Dutch; *Wiki-Wetenschappers*, 2019) of the *Dutch Foundation for Academic Heritage* (SAE). The SAE is a network of Dutch universities that supports these universities' heritage and cultural collections. With the *Wiki-Scientists project* the SAE aimed to construct a publicly and centrally accessible overview of biographical information on Dutch professors and prominent scientists. Currently, four Dutch universities have an online Album Academicum, but a national overview did not yet exist. With the construction of this overview, the SAE wished to meet the need for a central access point to the distributed information sources held by the various Dutch university libraries and heritage institutions. In order to obtain this goal, it was proposed to collect all available biographical information of prominent Dutch scientists since 1575 and enter them into Wikidata. Furthermore, the intention was to construct this database in such a way that it could be optimally used and easily accessed by a general audience. In order to achieve the goals of the *Wiki-Scientists project*, two Wikimedians-in-residence were appointed. They made the biographical data structurally available on Wikidata.

At Maastricht University, data of all deceased professors has been processed, mapped, and linked to existing items in Wikidata, including first and last name, profession, date/place of birth, date/place of death, sex/gender, education and university, employer, position, and academic degree. All professors received a persistent identifier and all items have been assigned one or more citations. If possible, data is linked to the Virtual International Authority File (VIAF). The list is periodically updated by bots. Information and a current overview of Maastricht professors is available on Wikidata and the renderings of the Maastricht project data in Scholia (*Scholia: Maastricht University*, 2020). By participating in the *Wiki-Scientists project*, we have been able to contribute to a visible, usable, and sustainable heritage of prominent scientists in the Netherlands.

Conclusion

In recent years, the love-hate relationship that teachers and researchers had with Wikipedia is changing for the better. More and more academics see the benefits of Wikipedia, Wikidata, and other Wikimedia project websites. With the collaborations and projects described in this chapter, Maastricht University Library has contributed to a better understanding of how Wikipedia and Wikidata can be deployed within an academic context and what the advantages are for students and others interested in contributing. Maastricht University Library serves as an inspiring example for other teaching librarians in the Netherlands. In the years to come, the library will continue its collaboration with Wikimedia Nederland as part of the Wikipedia Education Program, for the three courses described above, and for new courses with a focus on legal history, medical history, and the history of science. Furthermore, Maastricht University Library aims to provide better access to its collections by optimizing object registrations in line with innovative developments based on linked, open-access data. The library has recently started a pilot project to link its Golden Age of Illustration data to Wikidata. These courses, projects, and initiatives are in line with the library's long-term ambition to contribute to building an extensive digital infrastructure in the form of a sustainable distributed digital network, based on linked (open) data.

Note

1 ECTS is an abbreviation for European Credit Transfer System. One ECTS is equal to twenty-eight hours of study.

References

Excellence Education. (2020). Maastricht University. Retrieved September 29 from https://edlab.nl/excellence/.

FASOS Marble Spring. (2020). Wikipedia. Retrieved September 29 from https://en.wikipedia.org/wiki/Wikipedia:Benelux_Education_Program/Maastricht_University#See_also.

FPN Historical Book Review. (2020). Wikipedia. Retrieved November 25 from https://en.wikipedia.org/wiki/Wikipedia:Benelux_Education_Program/ Maastricht_University/FPN_Historical_Book_Review_Spring_2020.

Hvalić, J. (2020). Exploring the Special Collections. Retrieved September 29 from www.youtube.com/watch?v=L5v6Pxp6WwU&t=31s.

MSP. (2019). Wikipedia. Retrieved November 25 from https://en.wiki pedia.org/wiki/Wikipedia:Benelux_Education_Program/Maastricht_ University/MSP_January_2019.

Said, E. (1978). *Orientalism.* Pantheon Books.

Scholia: Maastricht University. (2020). Scholia. Retrieved November 25 from https://scholia.toolforge.org/organization/Q1137652.

Wiki-Wetenschappers. (2019). SAE. Retrieved November 25 from www.acad emischerfgoed.nl/projecten/wiki-wetenschappers/.

Wikimedia Commons. (2020). Wikimedia. Retrieved November 25 from https://commons.wikimedia.org/wiki/Main_Page.

CHAPTER 4

LEARNING DESIGN TO EMBED DIGITAL CITIZENSHIP SKILLS IN THE UNDERGRADUATE CLASSROOM: A COLLABORATION AMONG INSTRUCTOR, ACADEMIC LIBRARIAN, AND WIKIPEDIAN

Crystal Fulton,[1] *Rebecca O'Neill,*[2] *and Marta Bustillo*[1]

[1] University College Dublin, [2] Wikimedia Community Ireland

Abstract

A collaboration among an instructor, librarian, and Wikipedia was initiated to help second-year undergraduate students at University College Dublin, Ireland, increase their digital citizenship skills through publishing in Wikipedia. The collaboration brought together diverse relevant expertise to design and deliver an effective learning experience. Integrating Wikipedia into the classroom experience gave students firsthand involvement with the research and scholarly communication process.

The chapter is divided among three perspectives, reflecting academic, library, and Wikipedia perspectives on the implementation of the collaborative authorship project:

DOI: https://doi.org/10.3998/mpub.11778416.ch4.en

1. Deeper learning through learning design in the classroom using Wikipedia—an academic's perspective.
2. Using Wikipedia to teach critical thinking and academic integrity—a librarian's perspective.
3. Enabling university students to write and publish collaboratively with Wikipedia—a Wikipedian's perspective.

Students engaged enthusiastically with Wikipedia. Challenges included supporting students in implementing new learning, such as academic integrity skills. The partnership among academic staff, the library, and Wikipedia suggests a potential framework for learning design (Boling, 2010), which may help others apply a similar experiential approach to learning.

Keywords

Collaborative authorship in higher education, Digital citizenship, Experiential learning, Wikipedia.

Developing Students' Digital Citizenship Skills

The development of a range of digital literacies plays a significant role in students' abilities to participate successfully in the workplace and wider society. The European Union (EU) (Carretero Gomez et al., 2017, pp. 8–9) has classified five areas of digital competence as foundational to digital citizenship information and data literacy:

- Information and data literacy
- Communication and collaboration
- Digital content and creation
- Safety
- Problem Solving

While university students may be assumed to possess these critical skills for active and full participation in higher education, researchers (e.g., Head & Eisenberg, 2011; Martzoukou et al., 2020) have observed gaps in students' information skills and a reliance on Internet search engines to find information. A survey based on the EU's five areas of digital competencies revealed that higher education students perceived their digital skills to be lacking in some areas (Martzoukou et al., 2020). Educators have long expressed concern about levels of digital skills among the "Google Generation." For example, Ercegovac (2008) reported that students possessed technical skills but lacked skills that would define them as information literate, such as approaches to information searching, evaluation, critical thinking, and using information ethically.

Wikipedia in Higher Education

Increasingly, Wikipedia has come to play a role in education as a free encyclopedia providing information with an error rate close to that of *Britannica* (Giles, 2005). Further, Wikipedia has become a household word among the general public as one of the most popular sources of information in multiple subject contexts. However, Wikipedia has another role to play in the development of digital literacies among students, offering a valuable learning environment in which to develop multiple competencies that lead to digital citizenship and social engagement (Fulton, 2019). While the appropriateness of using Wikipedia is often a source of debate in higher education, research has shown that both students and academics refer to the online encyclopedia for information (Knight & Pryke, 2012). Student editors are not commonplace in Wikipedia (Obregón-Sierra & González-Fernández, 2020). However, introducing students to a deeper engagement with the encyclopedia as editors and creators of content has significant potential for digital skills development. The relationship between student editors and Wikipedia also has reciprocal benefits. Student editing of Wikipedia can have a long-lasting impact on the encyclopedia itself with increased page views and editing activity in the Wikipedia community (Zhu et al., 2020). Ross (2020), a champion for the *Wikipedia Education* program, has applauded its *Wikipedia Student Program* for supporting this impact:

> The work students are doing isn't just an "academic exercise;" it has an audience, and it matters enough that people are both reading it and building on it (para 4).
> Importantly, understanding this impact can increase the meaning of social participation for students.

A Collaborative Partnership to Embed Digital Competencies

THE COURSE

The focal point for the collaborative initiative was an information literacy course, *DigiComp: Core Competencies for Digital Citizenship*, which
has long been taught (under various titles) as part of the second-year
undergraduate program in the School of Information and Communication Studies in the College of Social Sciences & Law. The course
focuses on students' development as digital citizens and, to this end,
has proactively supported students as they developed critical thinking
skills essential for full social participation after university.

The course challenges students to engage with an array of digital
skills noted in the EU's classification of essential digital competencies
for digital citizenship (Carretero Gomez et al., 2017). In particular, students learn a variety of skills to help them locate, organize, manage,
use, and create information for not only the academic setting but also
for their future careers and workplaces. The course is organized around
the university's twelve-week trimester, with topics covered as follows:

- Super Searchers: The Characteristics of Effective Searchers and
  Users of Information
- Discerning Factual Information from Fake News, Disinforma-
  tion, & Misinformation
- Engaging with Information and Academic Integrity
- Acknowledging the Work of Others Appropriately
- Digital Bibliographic Skills
- Developing Successful Digital Search and Evaluation Strategies
- Effective Collaborative Authoring in Wikipedia
- Organizing Information
- Bibliographic Control vs. Miscellany
- Expanding Citizenship: Information Published by Government
- Selecting and Utilizing Channels of Communication Effectively

Students examine a range of pathways to information through formally structured literature channels, as well as informal channels,
including user-generated content, learning how to select pathways to

information and apply appropriately to problem-solving. Evaluating information is emphasized, enabling students to identify fake news, misinformation, and disinformation. Learning is mapped to various areas of these information literacies with deeper engagement weekly in particular topics to scaffold overall learning over the twelve-week course.

At the end of the course, students reflect on their learning journey. They submit a reflection in which they critically analyze their learning. Importantly, they must identify what they have learned, report emotions attending this learning, relate their new knowledge to previous knowledge, validate and integrate these perspectives such that they challenge their previously held assumptions and approaches to their studies, and plan for future use of their newly acquired skills. The reflection helps to embed skills acquisition further, by encouraging students to review their learning holistically and to understand what it is they have learned and why.

The Collaboration

A collaboration among Wikipedia, academic staff, and the library to help second-year undergraduate students at University College Dublin become digital creators through publishing in Wikipedia began with the common objective to help students develop core digital competencies for digital citizenship. The course instructor had long liaised with the library to deepen student learning of information skills, with the college liaison librarian visiting the classroom to help teach particular information skills, such as referencing. The instructor and the Wikipedian met as the Wikipedian began working with the encyclopedia in Ireland and the Wikipedian gave a guest lecture to the class, and from there the librarian's involvement in the course continued to grow. Alongside the involvement of Wikipedia in the classroom, the assessment for the course evolved to provide students not only the experience of locating and evaluating information but also to apply their developing information skills experientially in the "real-world" setting of the encyclopedia. The course combines classroom instruction, guest instruction, problem-solving exercises and activities, e-tutorials to help reinforce concepts and various information skills, a wide array of literature and resources to support information-seeking skills, visits to libraries, and other online and offline institutions that house information along with working in teams to write and publish collaboratively with Wikipedia. This opportunity to apply learning directly further supports students' involvement with the research and scholarly communication process.

As common goals for information literacy became evident, a more formal collaborative partnership among the instructor, librarian, and Wikipedian was established. The collaboration brings together diverse, relevant expertise to design and deliver an effective learning experience. From guest visits, we have moved to a deeper engagement with student learning so that partners work collaboratively in considering course content and scaffolding learning across the course. As a result, students find they are introduced to key concepts and practical application systematically. Their work then culminates in an edit-a-thon, in which the collaborators work with the students to finalize details of historical portraits and publish this work to Wikipedia.

Perspectives on Learning Design and Outcomes

The expertise each partner brings to the course is significant, both overlapping and complementary to the overarching goal of information literacy. This section explores the roles of the instructor, librarian, and Wikipedia collaborators in developing and engaging with learning design for increased achievement of competencies among students as follows:

1. Deeper learning through learning design in the classroom using Wikipedia—an academic's perspective.
2. Using Wikipedia to teach critical thinking and academic integrity—a librarian's perspective.
3. Enabling university students to write and publish collaboratively with Wikipedia—a Wikipedian's perspective.

This approach provides a unique examination of our collaboration and input into helping students develop their literacy skills, creating what Boling (2010, p. 2) refers to as a learning design case, that is, "a description of a real artifact or experience that has been intentionally designed." Our learning design is rooted in our collaborative perspectives on digital competencies and the process of acquiring this learning. Our partnership is also reflective, in which we are constantly "observing and mentally storing episodic memories" to improve on our application of collaborative teaching and to create "precedent," that is, a proactive, continuous gathering of knowledge to apply now or in future learning and our practice (Boling, 2010, p. 4).

(1) Deeper learning through learning design in the classroom using Wikipedia—an academic's perspective

After many years of working with students to develop their information skills, the instructor adopted an experiential learning approach using Wikipedia to embed fundamental information skills and theoretical principles into the course, DigiComp. Incorporating Wikipedia into the classroom was a first in higher education in Ireland—considered bold, if not controversial in 2011. Our collaboration supported students' development of these essential citizenship skills from different perspectives. The course coordinator/academic instructor provided the course framework and grounded the work in the academic context; the librarian brought practical tools and digital skills training, which augmented course content; and the Wikipedian provided context for writing for Wikipedia and offered essential skills training.

In class, instruction was provided by each team member. For example, students learned about formal and informal channels to information during the course, and importantly the role of factual information and tools, such as encyclopedias, in solving problems. The Wikipedian reinforced this by explaining standards for content development in the online encyclopedia. Similarly, students learned about evaluating and attributing information sources appropriately. The librarian reinforced this learning with instruction around critical thinking and academic integrity. Students then put their learning into action, setting up Wikipedia accounts, locating and verifying information appropriate for an encyclopedia, and referencing their work in an article. Students ran individual plagiarism checks using a tool called Earwig, which assesses Wikipedia articles for copyright violations, as well as the plagiarism tool, Urkund, in the learning management system (LMS) Brightspace. Throughout this process, students had exemplars, in the form of full articles, which were published in Wikipedia, as well as support from people in the Wikipedia community who could answer questions and note points that required further editing attention.

Learning culminated in an end-of-course Wikipedia Edit-a-thon, an editing workshop during class, bringing all instructors and students together. The Wikipedian also ran mini advanced lessons, such as adding visual content to articles, during the edit-a-thon. The edit-a-thon provided students an opportunity to ask residual questions, offer peers feedback, and to wrap up their work. Having experienced collaborative authorship firsthand, students then wrote a reflection about their learning over the course, detailing their application of learning in Wikipedia and relating this learning to plans for future learning and the workplace. This reflective piece was significant for helping students review and deepen their learning around literacy skills further.

(2) Using Wikipedia to teach critical thinking and academic integrity—a librarian's perspective

Critical thinking and academic integrity are foundational skills undergraduate students must develop in order to succeed at university and later in their working careers (Shavelson et al., 2019; Tremblay et al., 2012). Yet librarians often find themselves teaching these skills in a vacuum: a lecturer calls them into their classroom to "do the library session" without explicitly integrating the session's learning outcomes into the wider module. Such one-shot sessions often fail to provide students with the information and digital literacy skills they require for academic success and responsible citizenship (Mays, 2016). In contrast, by introducing critical thinking and academic integrity in the context of collaborative authorship for a Wikipedia entry, students are no longer expected to develop these skills in the abstract: they become active researchers involved in a scholarly conversation with their peers, develop critical thinking skills while evaluating the quality of the sources selected for their projects to prepare biographies for individuals who were significant in Irish History, and adhere to academic integrity principles in order to have their Wikipedia entries accepted. Collaborating with the instructor and the Wikipedia representative gives the librarian greater influence over the introduction of critical thinking and academic integrity skills.

The library component for this learning experience involved three interventions: an academic integrity session, a critical thinking session, and a short introductory session on finding relevant library resources for the specific Wikipedia biographical articles the students were editing. The academic integrity session was developed as part of a university-wide plagiarism prevention effort with contribution from UCD Library (University College Dublin Library, 2019). The session was designed by members of the library and included a class discussion about the nature of plagiarism; giving students a set of specific scenarios and asking them to decide whether they constituted plagiarism (University College Dublin Library, 2013); and providing practical strategies to avoid plagiarism such as paraphrasing exercises and citation exercises using the APA referencing style (Collery, 2014).

As Biando Edwards (2018) identified, students often lack the ability to approach information in a critical manner and librarians are particularly well placed to impart this knowledge in the classroom (pp. 288–93). The critical thinking workshop was designed to provide students with the necessary tools to evaluate the academic quality of the sources they found for their Wikipedia entries and apply critical reading and writing skills to their collaborative work. The workshop used elements from both the Society of College, National and University Libraries (SCONUL)'s *Seven Pillars of Information Literacy Core Model* (SCONUL Working Group on Information Literacy, 2011) and the Association of College & Research Libraries *Framework for Information Literacy for Higher Education* (ACRL, 2016) to focus on the evaluative aspect of information literacy. It also introduced John McManus' *SMELL* test for analyzing the validity of news media reports (McManus, 2013). SMELL stands for Source, Motive, Evidence, Logic, and "Left Out," prompting students to search beyond the surface of news reports to uncover potential manipulations of facts or evidence. The short introduction to library resources was an opportunity to highlight specific materials of relevance to the various Wikipedia entries and to reinforce the use of techniques such as paraphrasing and correct referencing in plagiarism prevention.

Overall, the three library interventions constituted a much more effective contribution to the learning outcomes of the module than is usually provided by a catch-all, one-shot library session. The collaboration with the course instructor and the Wikipedia representative provided the librarian with a greater understanding of the specific aims of the module and the learning needs of the students, particularly given the challenges in developing students' academic integrity skills that were uncovered during the implementation of the Wikipedia component of the module. It was also an exciting opportunity to position academic integrity and critical thinking skills in the broader context of digital competencies for successful citizenship in the real world. However, the three interventions also posed questions about the scalability of this approach to other modules and student groups, given the workload involved and the existing constraints on the librarian's time.

(3) Enabling university students to write and publish collaboratively with Wikipedia—a Wikipedian's perspective

The first introductory Wikipedia lecture gave students an overview of Wikipedia and the wider ecosystem of Wikimedia projects, with a focus on the media repository, Wikimedia Commons. The session ranged from the origins of Wikipedia to the basics of setting up an account, finding the user sandbox in which students can make some initial test edits, and making those first few edits to a Wikipedia article. Suitable and unsuitable sources for citations were also covered, as well as the basics regarding copyright in relation to adding photographs or other media to Wikipedia articles. This was followed up later with the second session, in which students raised questions that were answered, usually with live demonstration, for the benefit of the whole class. Queries ranged from simple technical questions regarding editing articles to more nuanced discussions about appraising sources or conflicting historical narratives.

The longest-lasting impact that writing Wikipedia articles has for any student is the knowledge that their work has life beyond the traditional essay. The information they gathered has been added to the largest encyclopedia ever written, instead of languishing in an essay that only themselves and their lecturer will read. This has been one of the main rallying calls for many Wikipedia-based education programs across the world (Wikimedia Education, 2019).

By editing Wikipedia, students are enabled to use their access to university library resources in order to free information from paywalled and specialized information repositories. They are taking this information, to which most people outside of educational institutions do not have free access, and adding it to "the sum of all human knowledge." In their research, they access a wide and varied corpus of information, from newspapers to dictionaries of national biography, many of which they are using for the first time. In exploring what it means to be able to draw on resources, such as paywalled journals, expensive academic publications, and specialized materials, the students are experiencing their library collections in a new and pragmatic way.

In recruiting student editors to contribute to Wikipedia internationally, we come closer to bridging gaps in representation regarding gender, geography, language, sexuality, or nationality on Wikipedia. In this case, working with students in Ireland, they are confronted with a platform that has a number of recognized gaps in knowledge and that is making a concerted effort to map all of these gaps as part of a wider movement strategy (Zia et al., 2019). One nuance of editing content relating to Ireland on English-language Wikipedia is the issue of being a nondominant culture within the Anglophone world. Many of the histories of Ireland have been historically dominated by the narratives from the United Kingdom and the United States.

From the simple problem of historic figures being misidentified as British, rather than Irish, to misconceptions about the impact of historic moments within a specific Irish context, Wikipedia can act as a clearing house for these issues. This is best illustrated with an example.

In 2019, the students focused on famous Irish sportspeople. As a number of these people competed in the Olympic Games of the early twentieth century, the students were confronted with periods in history where Irish people competed first under the British flag, followed by a period in which Irish athletes were forced to participate as part of the British team with some bringing their own Irish flags to fly in protest, and finally a period after Irish independence during which some Irish nationalistic athletic associations refused to allow their members to participate in the Olympic Games at all. This engagement with the historical record provides a new and more nuanced way for students to engage with issues of identity, nationhood, and representation through the individual experiences of those from a tumultuous period in Irish history.

Students also encountered the often-frustrating lack of source material regarding the history of women in many walks of life, from politics to science. They discovered that women's biographic entries in works like the Dictionary of Irish Biography (DIB) are subentries in articles about their fathers, brothers, or husbands rather than entries in their own right. One example was the Olympic fencer Shirley Armstrong, whose husband's entry in the DIB barely makes mention of her, despite her being only one of two Irish women selected to take part in the 1960 Rome Olympics and her long and storied career as a fencer and trainer. Encountering these issues themselves, rather than having them explained as an abstract idea through a lecture, makes the challenges around representation more tangible for students.

By teaching the next generation the importance of verifiable and reliable information sources, we are not only fostering good digital citizenship but we are also equipping students with the critical tools to find, assess, and analyze sources and facts. While these skills can be fostered through lectures and information seeking and evaluation exercises, Wikipedia offers a unique peer-review environment in which the students have their additions to articles quickly accepted or rejected by the community. By experiencing the sometimes highly exacting demands of fellow editors to adhere to Wikipedia editing guidelines and policies, students are exposed to an assessment of their work unlike anything within traditional academia. In some cases, when students have not adhered to Wikipedia guidelines and conventions, they have had all of their edits removed or reverted, and in an extreme example, a group of students were blocked from editing Wikipedia owing to persistent copyright infringement. In this case, the students continued to add the same content to an article and, despite repeated warnings, attempted to add the same content again and were blocked from any further editing. The real-world consequence of being blocked from editing had an impact on the students, which felt far more immediate than a low-grade or critical feedback from a lecturer. It was also something from which I or their lecturer could not shield them or afford them any special dispensation.

Outcomes and Learning Design

Students engaged enthusiastically with Wikipedia and valued the opportunity to participate in an activity they could list on their curricula vitae (CVs). While students embraced collaborative authoring in Wikipedia, their participation was not without challenges. For instance, some students found academic integrity, considered a highly important area of learning for students in the university, complex and sometimes difficult to put into practice, even with training. While students received instruction about plagiarism and how to avoid it, there have been occasions where students found their work deleted by editors because it was not properly cited; in these cases, the sandbox in Wikipedia can help students manage their work while they make necessary modifications. Ongoing iterations of the course have involved increasing learning support to help students avoid plagiarism. The collaboration among Wikipedia, the library, and the instructor has facilitated a coordinated approach to topics, such as academic integrity, which utilizes in class instruction, problem-solving around scenarios, and use of Wikipedia's plagiarism detector. Additionally, student tutors from other program levels in the school meet with the second-year students outside class instruction hours to help embed team collaboration and literacy skills.

The collaboration has provided new insights into the needs of students regarding the development of digital literacy skills. From an academic perspective, the collaboration has highlighted the different facets of instruction and learning, which can be brought together to support student learning. Academic libraries have also long offered instruction and assistance to students as part of their development of core literacy skills and competences. Higher education instruction continues to help students acquire learning and critical thinking skills that will serve them in the workplace. Bringing together these often parallel efforts provides students with an opportunity to excel in their development holistically. Currently, University College Dublin's Library is developing a programmatic approach to teaching academic integrity to students across the university, and the experience of this collaboration among Wikipedia, the librarian, and the instructor will feed into the planning for that project. Collaborating with a partner external to the university, such as Wikipedia, has enabled the bringing together of parallel efforts toward digital citizenship development. The Wikipedia Education Program has a history of working with students and instructors, providing guidance for becoming and teaching others to become an editor of the encyclopedia (Wikipedia Education, 2020). Having a Wikipedia champion present during learning provided our students with direct access to expert knowledge about the workings of the online encyclopedia and deeper sense of involvement with Wikipedia.

The collaboration offers a potential framework for incorporating learning design that utilizes partnership and collaboration to help others apply a similar approach to learning. Collaborating does not necessarily mean developing teaching and learning materials from scratch. Existing courses may already involve excellent learning opportunities for students. Adding Wikipedia to the mix enhances the desired learning acquisition among students, critically through provision of experiential learning. Students can access assistance and advice from a professional in the field, apply learning immediately through Wikipedia, and reflect immediately throughout the process of learning, in keeping with Kolb's (2014) experiential learning process.

References

Association of College & Research Libraries. (2016). *Framework for information literacy for higher education.* Chicago, IL: Association of College & Research Libraries. Retrieved from www.ala.org/acrl/sites/ala.org.acrl/files/content/issues/infolit/framework1.pdf.

Biando Edwards, J. (2018). Added value or essential instruction? Librarians in the twenty-first-century classroom. *Reference & User Services Quarterly, 57*(4), 285–93. Retrieved from https://ucd.idm.oclc.org/login?url=https://www-proquest-com.ucd.idm.oclc.org/docview/2057223238?accountid=14507.

Boling, E. (2010). The need for design cases: Disseminating design knowledge. *International Journal of Designs for Learning, 1*(1), 1–8. https://doi.org/10.14434/ijdl.v1i1.919.

Carretero Gomez, S., Vuorikari, R., & Punie, Y. (2017). DigComp 2.1: The digital competence framework for citizens with eight proficiency levels and examples of use. *European Commission, EU Science Hub.* Retrieved from http://publications.jrc.ec.europa.eu/repository/bitstream/JRC106281/web-digcomp2.1pdf_(online).pdf.

Collery, J. (2014). Practical paraphrasing exercise [Unpublished educational resource]. Dublin: University College Dublin Library.

Ercegovac, Z. (2008). Is the Google generation information literate? A case study of secondary school students. *Proceedings of the American Society for Information Science and Technology, 45*(1), 1–3. http://doi:10.1002/meet.2008.1450450359.

Fulton, C. (2019). The use of collaborative open-access publishing via Wikipedia in university education to embed digital citizenship skills. *Netcom, 33*(33–1/2), 9–22. http://doi:10.4000/netcom.3893.

Giles, J. (2005). Internet encyclopaedias go head to head. *Nature, 438*, 900–1. www.nature.com/articles/438900a/

Head, A. J., & Eisenberg, M. B. (2011). How college students use the Web to conduct everyday life research. *First Monday, 16*(4). https://doi.org/10.5210/fm.v16i4.3484.

Knight, C., & Pryke, S. (2012). Wikipedia and the university, a case study. *Teaching in Higher Education, 17*(6), 649–59. http://doi:10.1080/13562517.2012.666734.

Kolb, D. A. (2014). *Experiential learning: Experience as the source of learning and development.* 2nd ed. Pearson Education.

Martzoukou, K., Fulton, C., Kostagiolas, P., & Lavranos, C. (2020). A study of higher education students' self-perceived digital competences for learning and everyday life online participation. *Journal of Documentation, 76*(6), 1413–58. Retrieved from: http://doi.org/10.1108/JD-03-2020-0041.

Mays, D. (2016). Using ACRL's framework to support the evolving needs of today's college students. *College & Undergraduate Libraries, 23*(4), 353–62. https://doi-org.ucd.idm.oclc.org/10.1080/10691316.2015.1068720.

McManus, Jo. (2013, February 7). Don't be fooled: Use the SMELL test to separate fact from fiction online. *MediaShift*. Retrieved from: http://medi ashift.org/2013/02/dont-be-fooled-use-the-smell-test-to-separate-fact-from-fiction-online038/.

Obregón-Sierra, Á., & González-Fernández, N. (2020). Wikipedia at the Spanish faculties of education. The vision of university students. *Alteridad (Cuenca, Ecuador), 15*(2), 218. http://doi:10.17163/alt.v15n2.2020.06.

Ross, S. (2020). Research quantifies Wiki Education's impact to articles. *Wiki Education*. Retrieved from https://wikiedu.org/blog/2020/09/17/research-quantifies-wiki-educations-impact-to-articles/.

SCONUL Working Group on Information Literacy. (2011). *The SCONUL seven pillars of information literacy core model for higher education*. Society of College, National and University Libraries (SCONUL). Retrieved from: www.sconul.ac.uk/sites/default/files/documents/coremodel.pdf.

Shavelson, R. J., Zlatkin-Troitschanskaia, O., Beck, K., Schmidt, S., & Marino, J. P. (2019). Assessment of university students' critical thinking: Next generation performance assessment. *International Journal of Testing, 19*, 337–62. https://doi.org/10.1080/15305058.2018.1543309.

Tremblay, K., Lalancette, D., & Roseveare, D. (2012). Assessment of higher education learning outcomes. *Design and implementation: Feasibility Study Report, Vol. 1*. Retrieved from www.oecd.org/education/skills-beyond-school/AHELOFSReportVolume1.pdf.

University College Dublin Library (2013): *Scenarios: Plagiarism or not?* [Unpublished educational resource]. University College Dublin Library.

University College Dublin Library. (2019). Academic integrity—referencing, citation & avoiding plagiarism. Retrieved from https://libguides.ucd.ie/academicintegrity.

Wikimedia Education. (2019). Reasons to use Wikipedia. Retrieved from https://outreach.wikimedia.org/wiki/Education/Reasons_to_use_Wikipedia.

Wikipedia Education. (2020). Wikipedia: Education program/educators. Retrieved from https://en.wikipedia.org/wiki/Wikipedia:Education_program/Educators.

Zhu, K., Walker, D., & Muchnik, L. (2020). Content growth and attention contagion in information networks: Addressing information poverty on Wikipedia. *Information Systems Research, 31*(2), 297–652. http://doi.org/10.1287/isre.2019.0899.

Zia, L., Johnson, I., Mansurov, B., Morgan, J., Redi, M., Saez-Trumper, D., & Taraborelli, D. (2019). Knowledge Gaps—Wikimedia Research 2030. http://doi.org/10.6084/m9.figshare.7698245.v1.

CHAPTER 5

AUTHENTIC LEARNING IN CULTURAL ANTHROPOLOGY: EDITING WIKIPEDIA FOR REAL-WORLD IMPACT

Jessica L. Lott[1] and Jennifer L. Sullivan[2]

[1] Northern Kentucky University, [2] Upstate Medical University

Abstract

Jennifer L. Sullivan (academic librarian) and Jessica Lott (anthropology professor) are invested in pedagogical approaches that help learners apply course content to their everyday lives. With this goal in mind, we created a flexible Wikipedia-based assignment for an upper-level anthropology course, Gender, Sex, and Sexuality: A Global Perspective, as a way to teach information literacy skills in a real-world setting while also enriching course content. As the course's culminating assignment, learners researched an information gap on Wikipedia addressing gender. Learners were also asked to use their experience on Wikipedia to reflect on the significance of the documented gender bias in Wikipedia.

This chapter discusses the advantages of Wikipedia as a platform for cultivating authentic information literacy practices. In particular, we address ACRL's Framework for Information Literacy in Higher Education, information literacy as a social justice imperative, and disciplinary information literacy. We taught this assignment four times over the period summer 2017–summer

DOI: https://doi.org/10.3998/mpub.11778416.ch5.en

2020 and draw from our experiences collaborating on this assignment. We hope that learning from our successes and failures will inspire those who wish to adapt it for their instruction.

Keywords

Active learning, Wikipedia, Information literacy, Social justice, Gender, Teaching methods, Instruction, Collaboration, Cultural anthropology.

Introduction

How can we empower our learners to share their work in a meaningful way and position our learners' hard work to make a difference outside of the classroom? In 2017, Jessica (anthropology professor) and Jennifer (academic librarian) set out to address these questions in Jessica's upper-level anthropology course at Southern Methodist University (SMU), a private research university in Dallas, Texas, United States. We asked learners in our class to contribute to a Wikipedia article as the culminating class assignment. We loved that the assignment motivated learners to deeply engage with information literacy and cultural anthropology because they valued Wikipedia as a public resource and felt responsible for adding accurate content.

Jessica's course, *Gender, Sex, and Sexuality: A Global Perspective*, fulfilled an information literacy requirement in the university curriculum, so we pursued and won a stipend funded through the university library. The stipend was created by the SMU Libraries to encourage faculty/librarian partnerships in assignment design and implementation. The faculty member received a one-time stipend of $1,000. While the librarian did not receive a stipend, they enjoyed an enhanced reputation at the library, increased recognition on campus, and opportunities to collaborate with additional faculty members.

In this chapter, we will share our process of collaborating to develop and implement an assignment asking learners to contribute content to a Wikipedia page. We begin by situating our work in the literature on Wikipedia in higher education and on librarian-faculty collaboration. We go on to illustrate why editing Wikipedia provides unique opportunities for teaching information literacy and contextualize our assignment in terms of social justice and feminist pedagogy. We conclude with a discussion of lessons learned and possibilities for modifying this assignment for other course contexts. It is our sincere hope that by sharing our journey, we can offer a tangible approach for those who wish to use Wikipedia in the classroom but have yet felt equipped to try.

Literature Review

Editing Wikipedia in Higher Education Classrooms
Many educators in higher education have implemented Wikipedia editing assignments in their courses. Case studies using this approach have been published in a variety of fields, including kinesiology and physical education (Kingsland & Isuster, 2020); political science, women's studies, communication (Carver et al., 2012); medicine (Azzam, 2017; Murray et al., 2020); health science (Dawe & Robinson, 2017); chemistry (Walker & Li, 2016); history (Chandler & Gregory, 2010; Edwards, 2015; Nix, 2010; Pollard, 2008; Watts, 2012); athletic training (Camihort, 2009); sociology (Konieczny, 2012, 2016; Wright, 2012); law (Witzleb, 2009); and economics (Freire & Li, 2016). However, we are unaware of any published case studies from anthropology. As we will discuss, the context of cultural anthropology encourages learners to take a global, contextual approach to Wikipedia pages that may not be found across disciplines. This context also attunes learners to various social inequalities and a social justice approach, perspectives they can apply as they identify inequalities in information and how they manifest on Wikipedia.

Collaboration between Librarians and Faculty
Collaboration between faculty and librarians can have a substantial impact on learners' information literacy skills. Including a librarian in the classroom yields increased levels of critical information literacy, digital literacy, research skills, and technical capabilities for learners (Koziura et al., 2020). Moreover, working together in both the planning and implementation of an assignment enables a greater level of

strategic and holistic instruction (Junisbai et al., 2016). Feminist pedagogy, furthermore, suggests that as faculty-librarian partnerships develop over time, librarian time in the classroom (even as a one-shot) can be increasingly effective (Kingsland, 2020). Instruction at this level can create learners who have increased fluency in producing and consuming information that lasts beyond graduation and creates socially responsible and engaged citizens.

While collaborating may seem like a daunting and time-consuming undertaking, it does not have to be. In fact, a pragmatic implementation imparts valuable information literacy skills with only a moderate level of librarian input with assignment design and pedagogy. A couple of strategically placed, hands-on library sessions accrue the greatest gains in learner outcomes. Moreover, the addition of a librarian into the planning and implementation of a course can reduce the burden on faculty by supporting and implementing a share of the discipline-based research goals (Junisbai et al., 2016).

Effective information literacy instruction is ideally embedded within the context of a discipline, since each discipline has its own research paradigms and modes of thought (Grafstein, 2002). Disciplinary information literacy requires participation from the learners, the librarian, and the professor. Learners must critically engage with a variety of kinds of information in different formats. The librarian elevates classroom learning by incorporating fundamental ideas of information literacy, and the professor provides curricular assignments that deepen interaction with disciplinary scholarship. In our collaboration, we worked together to develop learning outcomes that incorporated specific information learning skills within the context of anthropology.

The Assignment

As a culminating assignment for Jessica's upper-level anthropology course, *Gender, Sex, and Sexuality: A Global Perspective*, learners identified an information gap on a Wikipedia page dealing with gender, completed research to address the gap, composed text to add to their chosen article, and published their work. Learners were also asked to reflect on their experience on Wikipedia to discuss the significance of the documented gender bias on the platform (Maher, 2018) in a reflection essay.

Though this project was the culminating assignment, it was a semester-long project. We identified six learning outcomes for this assignment, based on defined information literacy objectives. We utilized these learning outcomes to create our assignment and assessment, an approach known as backward design (Wiggins & McTighe, 2005). The assignment included professor-led discussions, two librarian-led sessions, a librarian-led working session, learner reading outside of class, and the research and writing for the Wikipedia page that learners completed outside of class. By weaving the assignment throughout the course, we helped learners see connections between course content and online knowledge production. See Appendix for the full lesson plan, including learning outcomes.

Wikipedia and the Framework for Information Literacy in Higher Education

In 2016, the Association of College and Research Libraries (ACRL) revamped its information literacy standards to reflect today's more complicated and nuanced information landscape, where much information access occurs in an unfettered, increasingly data-driven online environment. The revised framework better allows users to address the information issues we face today. It defines information literacy as a "set of integrated abilities encompassing the reflective discovery of information, the understanding of how information is produced and valued, and the use of information in creating new knowledge and participating ethically in communities of learning" (ACRL, 2015, p. 8). Information literacy is no longer defined as a set of concrete skills to be learned; instead, it is a network of interrelated core concepts and understandings that inform our ideas around and use of information. Its goal is to help users successfully adapt to and navigate information presented in a variety of contexts and formats.

The learning goals of the new Information Literacy Framework include a combination of two important elements: knowledge practices (the demonstrated ways in which learners can increase their understanding of the core concepts) and dispositions (the affects, attitudes, and values we bring to knowledge seeking and use). In our research, we focused on two frames: Authority Is Constructed and Contextual and Scholarship as Conversation.

Authority Is Constructed and Contextual

Authority Is Constructed and Contextual is the recognition that information may be presented formally or informally and through various media types, as well as that authority is based on the information needed and the context in which it is created (ACRL, 2015). Expert searchers approach authority with an attitude of informed skepticism and the recognition that biases exist that privilege some sources over others, especially in the areas of gender, sexual orientation, and cultural orientation.

Engaging in the knowledge practices defined under each section of the Framework paves the way for embodying the dispositions that prime our learners to successfully work in a global society. For example, practice in the Authority Is Constructed and Contextual frame allows for learners to become more comfortable having an openness to new ideas, perspectives and worldviews, the motivation to seek authority from nontraditional sources, and the recognition that frequent self-evaluation is necessary to carry out these dispositions. This frame is ideal to teach in the context of Wikipedia for two reasons: the neutrality pillar and the dynamic structure of Wikipedia's platform.

Wikipedia has five pillars, or guidelines, that Wikipedia editors must adhere to. Here, we focus on the pillar "Wikipedia is written from a neutral point of view" ("Wikipedia," 2020a, para. 2). This pillar requires authors to maintain an objective stance and to include multiple points of view. Maintaining an objective stance was a novel and challenging experience for most of our learners, who were accustomed to writing thesis-driven essays. Neutrality (as Wikipedia labels it) required them to continuously check their own biases to be sure they were covering all points of view.

Anthropological course work can position learners to utilize the pillar of neutrality. Our course, for example, centered on global perspectives on gender. Learners were then prepared to include multiple points of view when writing about a non-Western culture for Wikipedia. For instance, a learner in our course who wrote about polygamy in Afghanistan discussed the issue in terms of practical reasons for the practice, cultural belief, historical context, and local and global politics. Several of our learners stated that this project broadened their awareness of their own biases and thus made it possible to ensure that they were seeking out sources that presented viewpoints different from their own.

Scholarship as Conversation

Scholarship as Conversation refers to the idea that discourse among scholars occurs over time, and new insights and discoveries occur because of the presence of competing ideas and differing perspectives (ACRL, 2015). These conversations are clearly seen on an article's talk page.

Every article on Wikipedia has a talk page where the article's content is discussed. Through examination of talk pages, our learners saw the peer-review process in action. Effective communication on these talk pages is a critical component of maintaining the growth of Wikipedia as a viable, volunteer-driven, open resource. The transparency of the discourse on the talk pages allowed us to discuss academic writing with our learners, as they were able to see comments and discussion around topic content and scope (Dowell & Bridges, 2019). When learners engaged in the talk pages of their chosen articles, they participated in peer review. As editors, it allowed them to "see themselves as contributors to scholarship rather than only consumers of it" (ACRL, 2015, para. 10).

Our learners were also required to review each other's writing through an in-class, peer-review exercise. This provided an avenue for learners to gain the knowledge practice to "critically evaluate contributions made by others in participatory information environments" (ACRL, 2015, para. 11).

Disciplinary Information Literacy: Working with Information in Cultural Anthropology

A discipline-based approach to teaching information literacy, where responsibilities for teaching are shared between faculty and librarians, provides a holistic, rich experience for learners (Grafstein, 2002; Junisbai et al., 2016). This approach allows learners to develop subject-specific content knowledge and research practices within that subject. This area is where Jessica's disciplinary knowledge and expertise became an invaluable part of information literacy instruction.

Cultural anthropologists gather information through ethnographic fieldwork, typically living with a group of people whose lives are different than their own (American Anthropological Association, n.d.). The American Library Association (2008) developed disciplinary information literacy standards based on the ACRL Framework described above. Importantly, these disciplinary standards are intended for use with research and writing about human subjects. Information literate learners in anthropology understand how the validity of evidence is assessed and original solutions are proposed (Grafstein, 2002).

Cultural anthropology seeks to understand human cultures and lifeways across the globe. There is an emphasis on understanding diverse points of view, so information must be understood in its appropriate cultural context (American Library Association, 2008). By writing about a culture different from one's own for a public audience, learners practice this element of disciplinary information literacy and experience the challenges of communicating these nuances.

Information Literacy as Social Justice

Libraries have a long-held connection to social justice. In fact, the American Library Association (2019) included many values associated with social justice as "library core values," such as unfettered access to ideas; freedom for all people to form, to hold, and to express their own beliefs; respect for the individual person; democracy; diversity; social responsibility; intellectual freedom; education and lifelong learning; and serving the public good. Moreover, information literacy education was proclaimed a human right in 2005 (IFLA, 2015) and is considered an important prerequisite for democracy (Obama, 2009).

While the *Framework for Information Literacy in Higher Education* does require taking a critical approach toward information literacy, both in its knowledge and dispositions objectives, it stops at learners acknowledging biases in bodies of knowledge. In response, Laura Saunders (2017) at Simmons College proposed a new frame: Information Social Justice. The Information Social Justice frame asserted that in order to most effectively understand and use information, "users must be able to examine and interrogate the power structures that impact that information and analyze the ways that information can be used to both inform and misinform" (Saunders, 2017, p. 67). Our project—through readings, class discussions, self-reflections, and the editing of Wikipedia—helped our learners, and ourselves, develop several of the knowledge practices and dispositions that serve this proposed frame by both exposing and expanding the dynamic, multifaceted nature of the information landscape, and thereby reinforcing the importance that we all employ empathy, critical scrutiny, and self-reflection when engaging with information. Our learners gain critical information literacy fluency when they can recognize where injustice occurs in a presentation of information and feel empowered with skills to effect change.

Information Literacy as Social Justice in Cultural Anthropology

Contemporary cultural anthropology closely interrogates social inequalities on local, national, and global scales. Anthropologists research from the "ground up," analyzing rich detail of lived experiences within larger social and cultural contexts. Many cultural anthropologists align themselves with those who are oppressed (Kirsch, 2018; Singer & Baer, 2018). Gender inequality is often an important element of these analyses of social inequalities.

Our focus on information literacy as social justice strengthened the disciplinary goals that Jessica already had for her course. Jessica asked learners to think deeply about gender inequality—how it emerges, how it perpetuates, and possibilities for mitigating it—as a key course goal. Through the Wikipedia editing assignment, learners expanded on this theme by experiencing how information creation and information access are also shaped by global and gendered inequalities.

Gender Bias on Wikipedia
We employed feminist pedagogy when we asked learners to interrogate gender bias as a social justice issue on Wikipedia (Accardi, 2013; Hoodfar, 1992). We introduced learners to the information gaps that exist on Wikipedia (and, more broadly, in the literature) and asked them to use their experiences on the platform to reflect on these inequalities. Here, we unpack some of the issues around gender bias on Wikipedia.

The guidelines for knowledge production in English-language Wikipedia, while necessary, often perpetuate a gender bias in what is considered notable and publishable. This is evidenced most conspicuously in the "notability" pillar (discussed previously as an example of the frame Authority Is Constructed and Contextual). This pillar—a crucial part of how Wikipedia can minimize editors' explicit biases—is especially problematic for women based on the verifiability requirement, which states that for an article to exist, the topic must have received significant coverage in reliable sources that are independent of the subject (Harrison, 2019). Perhaps most famously, Donna Strickland, a Nobel Prize winner in physics, was not granted her own Wikipedia page, even though her male collaborators were, as she had not received enough media coverage to satisfy the verifiability requirement (Koren, 2018).

Wikipedia's structure also contributes to gender bias on the platform. Wikipedia's foundational infrastructures, policies, and technologies were built in a male-dominated culture that excluded women. Unfortunately, this led to a pervasive culture where women were faced with multiple barriers for contributing, both due to comparatively fewer technological skills and female editors' adversarial experiences with pushback from the Wikipedia community (Ford & Wajcman, 2017).

The demographics of the editor population are another likely contributor to Wikipedia's inherent biases. Over 85 percent of Wikipedia's 40 million editors are white men ("Wikipedia," 2020b). This narrow demographic comprises a large portion of the editor population, so their interests and worldviews influence what does and does not get covered (Wagner et al., 2016). The topics receiving the most coverage on Wikipedia tend to be narrow: war, sports, and video games (Carleton et al., 2017).

Empowering Learners

After spending the semester discussing inequality and issues of social justice, learners can feel helpless in the face of pervasive structural issues. However, developing skills to communicate about gender inequality for a broad audience empowers learners in a variety of ways. Some learners told us that this skill equipped them to push back against gender inequality in their lives and their activism. The assignment also allowed learners to "talk back" in a small way by helping to address the gender gap in Wikipedia. They also participated in "public anthropology" by translating anthropological research for the public, in service of the common good (Borofsky, 2008). By editing Wikipedia, learners supported diverse voices on a widely read public platform.

Advice and Recommendations

Since we found this project so rewarding, we have taught this assignment four times over three years. Each time, we solicit learner feedback and work to improve the assignment. Here, we share some of what we learned in this process as well as ideas for how to adapt this assignment for different contexts.

It is important to consider how assignment information is presented to learners. We found that it is best to provide a list of pages that learners can research. When we provided cross-cultural examples, learners researched more diverse topics instead of choosing topics close to their own lives. We also found that it is best to only give learners an abbreviated assignment overview at the beginning of the semester. Too much information up front leads to information overload, causing confusion (Bawden & Robinson, 2009). Jessica found that learners are less overwhelmed if scaffolding assignments are distributed through-out the semester. Jessica also reiterates the assignment's goals often, so learners continue to connect their work with course goals. We also would like to experiment with an infographic to streamline communi-cation about steps of the assignment.

In early versions of this assignment, Jennifer's visits to the classroom focused on how and why we were using Wikipedia in class. However, there are other powerful approaches that librarians can take. The initial librarian visit could begin by facilitating a critical discussion of Wiki-pedia as a source before delving into the mechanics of the project. The librarian can also guide learners through information literacy frames that we focus on in the project, using some of the activities developed by the Private Academic Library Network of Indiana (PALNI) (2020). The assignment could also require a visit with a librarian.

The first time we taught this assignment, we had a learner who did not participate, though he was otherwise active in class. We suspected that he was simply too anxious about sharing his writing to engage. Jessica came to realize this was a stumbling block and started telling learners that some nervousness is a normal part of the research pro-cess. In the future, we will draw from Carol Kuhlthau's (1991) founda-tional work, "Inside the Search Process," to normalize anxiety as part of the process to show how meeting with a librarian can help them move past this stage.

This assignment can be modified for a variety of courses. Jessica has since modified the assignment for a lower-level class by offering more professor support, decreasing the required number of citations, and having learners work in pairs. As an alternative, learners could also add citations to an undercited page, rather than write new text (Oliver, 2015). These pages can be found in Google by using the query: "needs additional citations" site:en.wikipedia.org and a topic. For example, "needs additional citations" site:en.wikipedia.org anthropology will provide a list of Wikipedia articles on anthropology that require more citations. Another option is to use the Citation Hunt tool (*Citation Hunt*, n.d.), which pulls up a random snippet in a Wikipedia article that needs a citation. If a learner wants to address the snippet, they click on the "I Got This" button, which directs them to the Wikipedia page where they can add a citation. In upper-level courses, the assignment might be used as a springboard for a traditional research paper. Learners could also reflect on how their paper differs from the Wikipedia page, engaging in critical thinking skills around bias and different styles of writing.

Developing, implementing, and iterating this assignment has been an edifying and enjoyable experience. The assignment has reinforced feminist pedagogy and social justice themes present in Jessica's course, and we have learned from each other's approaches and knowledge bases. We hope that our discussion is a resource for those who want to teach using Wikipedia but who have had more questions than solutions. As with any high-impact classroom activity, there are bound to be hiccups. However, working through the challenges has been beyond worth it for this assignment, as it has been an important learning opportunity for everyone involved: faculty, librarian, and learners alike.

References

Accardi, M. T. (2013). *Feminist pedagogy for library instruction*. Library Juice Press.

ACRL. (2015). Framework for information literacy for higher education. www.ala.org/acrl/sites/ala.org.acrl/files/content/issues/infolit/framework.pdf.

American Anthropological Association. (n.d.). What is anthropology? Advance your career. www.americananthro.org/AdvanceYourCareer/Content.aspx?ItemNumber=2150.

American Library Association. (2008, February 6). Information literacy standards for anthropology and sociology students. *Association of College & Research Libraries (ACRL)*. www.ala.org/acrl/standards/anthro_soc_standards.

American Library Association. (2019). Core values of librarianship. *Advocacy, Legislation & Issues*. www.ala.org/advocacy/intfreedom/corevalues.

Azzam, A. (2017). Embracing Wikipedia as a teaching and learning tool benefits health professional schools and the populations they serve. *Innovations in Global Health Professions Education.* https://dx.doi.org/10.20421/ighpe2017.01.

Bawden, D., & Robinson, L. (2009). The dark side of information: Overload, anxiety and other paradoxes and pathologies. *Journal of Information Science, 35*(2), 180–91. https://doi.org/10.1177/0165551508095781.

Borofsky, R. (2018). Public anthropology. In H. Callan (Ed.) *The international encyclopedia of anthropology.* John Wiley & Sons. https://onlinelibrary.wiley.com/action/showCitFormats?doi=10.1002%2F9781118924396.wbiea1899.

Camihort, K. M. (2009). Students as creators of knowledge: When Wikipedia is the assignment. *International Journal of Athletic Therapy and Training, 14*(2), 30–34. https://doi.org/10.1123/att.14.2.30.

Carleton, A., Musselman, C. A., Rust, A., Suiter, G. K., & Thorndike-Breeze, R. (2017). Working Wikipedia: A year of meaningful collaboration. *Double Helix, 5.* https://wac.colostate.edu/docs/double-helix/v5/carleton.pdf.

Carver, B. W., Davis, R., Kelley, R. T., Obar, J. A., & Davis, L. L. (2012). Assigning students to edit Wikipedia: Four case studies. *E-Learning and Digital Media, 9*(3), 273–83. https://doi.org/10.2304/elea.2012.9.3.273.

Chandler, C. J., & Gregory, A. S. (2010). Sleeping with the enemy: Wikipedia in the college classroom. *History Teacher, 43*(2), 247–57.

Citation Hunt. (n.d.). Retrieved December 17, 2020, from https://citationhunt.toolforge.org/en?id=b001095b.

Dawe, L., & Robinson, A. (2017). Wikipedia editing and information literacy: A case study. *Information and Learning Science, 118*(1/2), 5–16. https://doi.org/10.1108/ILS-09-2016-0067.

Dowell, M. L., & Bridges, L. M. (2019). A perspective on Wikipedia: Your students are here, why aren't you? *Journal of Academic Librarianship, 45*(2), 81–83. https://doi.org/10.1016/j.acalib.2019.01.003.

Edwards, J. C. (2015). Wiki women: Bringing women into Wikipedia through activism and pedagogy. *The History Teacher, 48*(3), 409–36. JSTOR.

Ford, H., & Wajcman, J. (2017). 'Anyone can edit', not everyone does: Wikipedia's infrastructure and the gender gap. *Social Studies of Science, 47*(4), 511–527. https://doi.org/10.1177/0306312717692172

Freire, T., & Li, J. (2016). Using Wikipedia to enhance student learning: A case study in economics. *Education and Information Technologies, 21*(5), 1169–81. http://dx.doi.org/10.1007/s10639-014-9374-0.

Grafstein, A. (2002). A discipline-based approach to information literacy. *Journal of Academic Librarianship, 28*(4), 197–204.

Harrison, S. (2019, March 26). How the sexism of the past reinforces Wikipedia's gender gap. *Slate Magazine*. https://slate.com/technology/2019/03/
wikipedia-women-history-notability-gender-gap.html.

Hoodfar, H. (1992). Feminist anthropology and critical pedagogy: The
anthropology of classrooms' excluded voices. *Canadian Journal of
Education/Revue Canadienne de l'éducation, 17*(3), 303–20. https://doi.
org/10.2307/1495298.

IFLA. (2015). Beacons of the information society: The Alexandria proclamation on information literacy and lifelong learning. www.ifla.org/
publications/beacons-of-the-information-society-the-alexandria-procla
mation-on-information-literacy.

Junisbai, B., Lowe, M. S., & Tagge, N. (2016). A pragmatic and flexible approach to information literacy: Findings from a three-year
study of faculty-librarian collaboration. https://doi.org/10.1016/j.
acalib.2016.07.001.

Kingsland, E. (2020). Undercover feminist pedagogy in information literacy:
A literature review. *Evidence Based Library and Information Practice, 15*(1),
126–41. https://doi.org/10.18438/eblip29636.

Kingsland, E. S., & Isuster, M. Y. (2020). A different ball game: Physical education students' experiences in librarian-led Wikipedia assignments. *Journal of
Academic Librarianship, 46*(1). https://doi.org/10.1016/j.acalib.2019.102089.

Kirsch, S. (2018). *Engaged anthropology: Politics beyond the text.* University of
California Press.

Konieczny, P. (2012). Wikis and Wikipedia as a teaching tool: Five years later.
First Monday, 17(9). https://doi.org/10.5210/fm.v0i0.3583.

Konieczny, P. (2016). Teaching with Wikipedia in a 21st-century classroom:
Perceptions of Wikipedia and its educational benefits. *Journal of the Association for Information Science & Technology, 67*(7), 1523.

Koren, M. (2018, October 2). One Wikipedia page is a metaphor for the Nobel
Prize's record with women. *The Atlantic.* www.theatlantic.com/science/
archive/2018/10/nobel-prize-physics-donna-strickland-gerard-mourou-
arthur-ashkin/571909/.

Koziura, A., Starkey, J. M., & Rabinovitch-Fox, E. (2020). Teaching Wikipedia:
A model for critical engagement with open information. In A. Clifton and
K. Davies Hoffman (Eds.), *Open pedagogy approaches.* Milne Publishing.
https://milnepublishing.geneseo.edu/openpedagogyapproaches/chapter/
teaching-wikipedia-a-model-for-critical-engagement-with-open-infor-
mation/.

Kuhlthau, C. C. (1991). Inside the search process: Information seeking from
the user's perspective. *Journal of the American Society for Information Science, 42*(5), 12.

Maher, K. (2018, October 18). Wikipedia is a mirror of the world's gender biases. *Wikimedia Foundation.* https://wikimediafoundation.org/news/2018/10/18/wikipedia-mirror-world-gender-biases/.

Murray, H., Walker, M., Dawson, J., Simper, N., & Maggio, L. A. (2020). Teaching evidence-based medicine to medical students using Wikipedia as a platform. *Academic Medicine, 95*(3), 382–86. https://doi.org/10.1097/ACM.0000000000003085.

Nix, E. M. (2010). Wikipedia: How it works and how it can work for you. *The History Teacher, 43*(2), 259–64.

Obama, B. (2009). Presidential proclamation national information literacy awareness month. https://obamawhitehouse.archives.gov/the-press-office/presidential-proclamation-national-information-literacy-awareness-month.

Oliver, J. T. (2015). One-shot Wikipedia: An edit-sprint toward information literacy. *Reference Services Review, 43*(1), 81–97. https://doi.org/10.1108/RSR-10-2014-0043.

PALNI. (2020). *LibGuides: Framework for information literacy for higher education.* https://libguides.palni.edu/c.php?g=185459&p=1224981.

Pollard, E. A. (2008). Raising the stakes: Writing about witchcraft on Wikipedia. *The History Teacher, 42*(1), 9–24.

Saunders, L. (2017). Connecting information literacy and social justice: Why and how. *Communications in Information Literacy, 11*(1), 55–75. https://doi.org/10.15760/comminfolit.2017.11.1.47

Singer, M., & Baer, H. (2018). *Critical medical anthropology.* Routledge.

Wagner, C., Graells-Garrido, E., Garcia, D., & Menczer, F. (2016). Women through the glass ceiling: Gender asymmetries in Wikipedia. *EPJ Data Science, 5*(1), 5. https://doi.org/10.1140/epjds/s13688-016-0066-4

Walker, M. A., & Li, Y. (2016). Improving information literacy skills through learning to use and edit Wikipedia: A chemistry perspective. *Journal of Chemical Education, 93*(3), 509–15. https://doi.org/10.1021/acs.jchemed.5b00525.

Watts, L. S. (2012). Writing radical lives: Undergraduates publishing activist biographies on Wikipedia. In C. Wankel & P. Blessinger (Eds.), *Increasing student engagement and retention using online learning activities: Wikis, blogs and Webquests.* Emerald Group Publishing.

Wiggins, G. P., & McTighe, J. (2005). *Understanding by design.* ASCD.

Wikipedia: Five Pillars. (2020a). In Wikipedia. https://en.wikipedia.org/w/index.php?title=Wikipedia:Five_pillars&oldid=991092342.

Wikipedia: Who Writes Wikipedia? (2020b). In Wikipedia. https://en.wikipedia.org/w/index.php?title=Wikipedia:Who_writes_Wikipedia%3F&oldid=992703476.

Witzleb, N. (2009). Engaging with the world: Students of comparative law write for Wikipedia. *Legal Education Review, 19*(1, 2), 83–98.

Wright, E. O. (2012). Writing Wikipedia articles as a classroom assignment. *ASA Newsletter* (*Teaching Sociology*).

Appendix: Wikipedia Editing Assignment

In this assignment, we asked learners in an upper-level cultural anthropology course to add to an existing article on Wikipedia. In developing the assignment, we drew from the templates laid out by Wiki Education and some of the resources they created to provide resources for learners in the class (Wiki Education, 2017).

Since the course was *Gender, Sex, and Sexuality: A Global Perspective*, we focused on pages that addressed gender or sexuality in some way. However, since there is a dearth of information about the Global South in English-language Wikipedia (Salvaggio, 2015), most cultural anthropology courses have the potential to contribute to an instance of information inequality on Wikipedia.

Learning Outcomes

We used the frames in the ACRL Framework for Information Literacy for Higher Education to organize learning outcomes for this project. Table 1 lists our learning outcomes with the information literacy frame that they are meant to develop. The table also shows how elements of our assignment address our learning outcomes. Depending on your course, you may wish to focus more on some frames and less on others. This is part of what makes this assignment flexible.

Assignment

In this assignment, we ask learners to research and write a contribution to an existing Wikipedia page about gender or sexuality. Learners also submit an annotated bibliography and write a short reflection essay at the end of the semester. This project is spread out over the

Table 1 Learning Outcomes and Assignment Design

Learning Outcome	Class Discussion	Learners Identify Research Gap and Choose Article	Learners Research and Write Drafts	Peer Review and Professor Review	Interact with Wikipedians	Annotated Bibliography	Reflection Paper
Articulate how knowledge is produced on a popular, participatory online platform (Wikipedia) IL Frame: Authority Is Constructed and Contextual	X	X			X		X
Locate relevant and trustworthy sources of information, both through the university library and online. IL Frame: Authority Is Constructed and Contextual	X		X			X	X

(Continued)

Table 1 Continued

Learning Outcome	Class Discussion	Learners Identify Research Gap and Choose Article	Learners Research and Write Drafts	Peer Review and Professor Review	Interact with Wikipedians	Annotated Bibliography	Reflection Paper
Write collaboratively with others, both in person and in a digital space. This includes giving and receiving feedback in a productive and respectful manner. IL Frame: Scholarship as Conversation		X	X	X			X
Write in accordance with style guide and informational framework of a specialized platform. IL Frame: Information Creation as Process		X	X	X			X

Learning Outcome	Class Discussion	Learners Identify Research Gap and Choose Article	Learners Research and Write Drafts	Peer Review and Professor Review	Interact with Wikipedians	Annotated Bibliography	Reflection Paper
Define and recognize bias in information and remove it from their research and writing. IL Frame: Information Has Value	X		X	X	X		X
Identify when a piece of writing does not adequately address issues of gender and/ or sexuality. IL Frame: Research as Inquiry	X	X					X

semester, and learners practice writing in drafts. Below is an example of the assignment introduction that we give to learners early in the semester:

> This semester, you will learn to edit Wikipedia! You will be adding a section or more to a Wikipedia page related to gender or sexuality, working toward the goal of making your changes "live" to the site. This project will be completed piece by piece throughout the semester. You will have the professor and librarian Jennifer L. Sullivan to support you through this process.

By the end of the semester, your writing should meet Wikipedia's guidelines and should cite at least 4 authoritative sources. Your grade on this project will be based on a final packet, with an annotated bibliography, reflection essay, and final contribution to Wikipedia. By going through this process and adding to an article on Wikipedia, you will help to close information gaps on the platform.

We progressed through the following steps in our semester-long project. These steps are scaffolded and introduced as we move through the semester:

- Discussion of information bias
- Students choose Wikipedia page
- Introduction to Wikipedia and introduction to searching with Jennifer (librarian)
- Draft of writing for peer review (in class)
- Draft of writing for professor review
- Make writing live to Wikipedia (in-class with Jennifer—librarian)
- Continued edits and interacting with Wikipedia editors
- Final packet submitted to professor consisting of a short reflective essay, annotated bibliography, and best draft of their writing (as determined by the learner)

The first step—discussion of information bias—will likely vary from class to class. Jessica used this time to set up the relationship between information bias and course content. Jennifer made the inspired suggestion of using an article from *The Atlantic* titled "This Article Won't Change Your Mind" as assigned reading for this day of class (Beck, 2017). Building on this reading, Jessica led a discussion of the cultural life of ideas and what kinds of information are appropriate or convincing in what situation. This can easily bridge to a discussion of information privilege and why we are editing Wikipedia in our course. The professor can introduce this link even earlier, if desired, on the first day of class. Any first-day activity that asks students to think about the nature of information in the course discipline will work. Jessica has asked students about truth and belief (Jenks, 2016) or practiced data collection (Keys, 2000) to meet this goal.

Assessment

Learners often have a flash of anxiety when they first find out about this assignment, since they assume their grade will be based on how Wikipedians judge their writing. However, learning goals for this project emphasize the research process and contextualizing research experience as part of larger bodies of work. So, our approach was to award points for tasks that supported these goals. For example, we awarded points for a reflection essay, completing WikiEdu trainings, participating in peer review and professor review drafts, interacting with Wikipedians, and an annotated bibliography.

Another common challenge is assessing the final student writing. Learners are used to meeting word count or page length parameters in their writing, but those measures are not necessarily useful when writing for Wikipedia (Blumenthal, 2018, May 1). We have used benchmarks such as number of citations to signal length requirement to students. It is also important to clarify how writing will be assessed; Wiki Education (2017, November 14) provides sample rubrics to draw from. Some criteria we have used in our rubric are "conformed to Wikipedia style" and "added a significant new idea."

Different Semester Lengths

We have taught this assignment in both abbreviated and full-length semesters. We have had best success with courses lasting a month or more, though the overall context of your course is important to consider. We reflect upon some of our experiences below.

A fifteen-week class meets Wiki Education's requirements for full enrollment and support in their program. This is a helpful resource and a good reason to use this assignment in a longer semester. Moreover, learners have more time to research and write in this format. We have found, however, that in these longer semesters, learners' efforts typically are spread over more courses and professors only see them a few times a week, so communication can be more difficult.

We originally developed the assignment for use in a one-month summer course. This worked well: students expected an intensive experience and Jessica was able to address student questions face-to-face quickly. In the one-month format, learners researched and drafted their contribution to a Wikipedia page during the first full week of class, worked through drafts the second week, made work live to Wikipedia in the third week, and submitted their final reflection paper on the last week of class.

Resources

Teaching and Learning Wikipedia

Art+Feminism. (n.d.). Get started: Learn to edit! *Art + Feminism*. https://artandfeminism.org/resources/getting-started/quick-guides-for-editing/.

This is a quick guide for editing Wikipedia—great for an overview or to plan an edit-a-thon.

Blumenthal, H. (2018, May 1). Assessing Wikipedia contributions. *Wikiedu*. https://wikiedu.org/blog/2018/05/01/assessing-wikipedia-contributions/.

This blog post lays out guidelines for grading learner contributions to Wikipedia.

Citation Hunt. (n.d.). https://citationhunt.toolforge.org/en?id=b001095b.

Citation Hunt finds ideas in Wikipedia that are tagged "citation needed." This can be used as part of an assignment.

Education/Reasons to use Wikipedia—Outreach Wiki. (n.d.). https://outreach.wikimedia.org/wiki/Education/Reasons_to_use_Wikipedia.

This is a discussion of some of the benefits and drawbacks of teaching with Wikipedia.

Wiki Education. (2017, November 1). Teach with Wikipedia. *Wiki Education*. https://wikiedu.org/teach-with-wikipedia/.

Learn how the Wikipedia Education Foundation can support your teaching.

Wiki Education. (2017, November 2017). Wiki Education classroom program example grading rubric. *Wikimedia Commons*. https://commons.wikimedia.org/wiki/File:Wiki_Education_Classroom_Program_example_grading_rubric.pdf.

Sample rubrics for assessing learner writing and references for Wikipedia writing.

Wikimedia Education. (n.d.). https://outreach.wikimedia.org/wiki/Education.

This is a hub for all things Wikipedia in Education.

Readings and Activities

Beck, J. (2017). This article won't change your mind. *The Atlantic.* www.
theatlantic.com/science/archive/2017/03/this-article-wont-change-
your-mind/519093/.
This reading asks students to think about the social life of information.

Jenks, A. (2016). First day activity: Ten things you believe to be true. *Society for Cultural Anthropology.* https://culanth.org/fieldsights/first-day-
activity-ten-things-you-believe-to-be-true.
This first-day activity asks students to consider what is true and what they
believe.

Keys, G. (2000). Doing ethnographic research in the classroom: A simple
exercise for engaging introductory students. In P. C. Rice & D. W. McCurdy
(Eds.), *Strategies in teaching anthropology* (pp. 164–66). Prentice Hall.
Students take turns pretending to be an alien from outer space who is inter-
viewing an American about eating habits in this first-day activity.

PALNI. (2020). LibGuides: Framework for information literacy for higher
education. https://libguides.palni.edu/c.php?g=185459&p=1224981.
PALNI has gathered activities and ideas for teaching information literacy
frameworks.

Salvaggio, E. (2015). Theories: Wikipedia and the production of knowledge.
Wikimedia. https://upload.wikimedia.org/wikipedia/commons/1/1a/The
ories_Wikipedia_and_the_production_of_knowledge.pdf.
This document provides topics and discussion questions for discussing Wikipedia as knowledge production.

SECTION 2
PRACTICAL
APPLICATIONS
OUTSIDE THE
CLASSROOM

CHAPTER 6

DO BLACK WIKIPEDIANS MATTER? CONFRONTING THE WHITENESS IN WIKIPEDIA WITH ARCHIVES AND LIBRARIES

Kai Alexis Smith[1]

[1] Massachusetts Institute of Technology

Abstract

Wikipedia is in the top ten of the most visited websites in most places in the world and makes up the backbone of the Internet's information ecosystem. Despite the global presence of the website and its sister projects, the knowledges of the African diaspora, in particular the Caribbean, are poorly represented. This chapter introduces and outlines Black-led projects, campaigns, and initiatives both within and outside of the formal networks of the Wikipedia communities and the Wikimedia Foundation. The history and value of Black encyclopedic sources are explored and frame the important work by projects like Black Lunch Table, WikiNdaba, Ennegreciendo Wikipedia, and AfroCROWD, which were started to help these editors and bridge content gaps.

In June 2020, the Wikimedia Foundation released a statement in support of Black Lives highlighting the support they provide to U.S.-based projects. This was followed with criticism from the community on missed opportunities

DOI: https://doi.org/10.3998/mpub.11778416.ch6.en

to acknowledge the work and networks outside the United States of on-wiki communities, information activists, academics, independent scholars, and communities who often go unrecognized. This chapter explores how the system of white supremacy is a part of libraries and archives and Wikipedia; how Black-led shared knowledge information activists are circumventing the system; and suggestions for a more inclusive path forward.

Keywords

Black Wikipedians, White supremacy, Wikipedia, Libraries and archives.

Introduction

> There is no way to talk about liberational value if you don't address the needs communities are facing. LGBT and black and indigenous communities— we need to have them as central. We need to center on justice and not be afraid of politics. Archives have never been neutral—they are the creation of human beings, who have politics in their nature. Centering the goals of liberation is at the heart of the issue.—Jarrett Drake ("Archives Have Never Been Neutral," 2017, para. 7)

"While we are in the same STORM, we are not the same BOAT" (Barr, n.d.). Some, especially Black and Indigenous people, are facing other storms on top of two pandemics: systemic racism and COVID-19. Just a week after George Floyd's death on June 3, 2020, the Wikimedia Foundation's executive director Katherine Mayer and the chief operating officer Janeen Uzzell released a statement titled, "We Stand for Racial Justice" where the Foundation committed to supporting Black community members, readers, and editors and the movement for Black Lives (Maher & Uzzell, 2020). However, editors, especially Black editors, have been critical of the statement since they had not received this kind of public support prior to global protests for Black lives and in light of other corporations and institutions capitalizing on releasing statements tied to the Black Lives Matter movement. There were questions surrounding this statement: Will systemic change be addressed in the foundation and the Wikipedia movement? Will Black

Wikipedians be a part of shaping a plan for change? Is this simply performative or will there be action?

In their statement, Mayer and Uzzell (2020) highlighted campaigns, specifically *AfroCROWD*, *Black Lunch Table*, and *Whose Knowledge?*—three U.S.-based campaigns and affiliates that have a proximity to the Foundation. In the past, the Foundation had been critical of these groups through grant evaluations. These groups still are grant funded, but now their works are publicly promoted with the Foundation's backing. The statement also focused on the lived experiences of Black people in the United States and while the aim of it was to be supportive and inclusive of all, the statement potentially alienated other members of the Black diaspora. By excluding Black Wikipedian communities outside of the United States, who are not affiliated with the Foundation, they further marginalized the community that they desired to support.

There is a great deal of work to be done addressing white supremacy in libraries and archives. Librarians and archivists partially contribute to inequities in source materials and by defining authority. Black-led projects have been doing important and critical work around information activism connected to the African diaspora in Wikipedia. Where there is no content, some of these projects are creating it and opening conversations around authority of sources including marginalized communities' definition of what an authoritative source is.

Roots in White Supremacy: Libraries and Archives

The roots of many professions in the United States are in white supremacy. Librarianship in the United States is no different. Many library scholars, such as Hathcock (2015), Bourg (2014), Espinal (2001), Galvan (2015), Hall (2012), and Honma (2005), have documented and highlighted this in literature. Scholar and activist April Hathcock (2015) described the invisible normativity of whiteness in librarianship's origins as "a fundamental role in the profession from the start. Public libraries in the U.S. developed initially as sites of cultural

assimilation and 'Americanization' of immigrants needing to learn the
mores of white society (Hall, 2012; Honma, 2005). Given the historical context, white normativity continues to be a hallmark of modern
librarianship" (para. 4).

Although the way knowledge is organized is often perceived as neutral, classification systems are heavily biased. Sociologist Chris Bourg
(2018) added, "Our classification systems are also not neutral. We use
subject headings that center the straight, white, male, European experience; and are often racist and dehumanizing" (para. 36). Recent literature,
for example, has established and documented that Melville Dewey, often
called the "father of modern librarianship" and creator of the Dewey
Decimal Classification System, had a history of antisemitism, racism,
and misogyny (Blakemore, 2018; Flood, 2019; Ford, 2018; Gooding-
Call, 2019; Lindell, 2019; Oster, 2019). The earliest iterations of his
classification system had his bigotry woven into it, and the system is
still used to organize information throughout the English-speaking
world. Similarly, the Library of Congress Classification system, which
was mainly adopted by large academic libraries, did not include any
Black, Indigenous, and People of Color (BIPOC) when it was created.
In the 1930s and 1940s, librarians and information activists like Alfred
Kaiming Chiu and Dorothy Porter began to change these systems to
make the works of BIPOC content creators more visible in the systems
designed to erase them (Liu, 2000; 裘开明_百度百科 (Qiú kāimíng_
bǎidù bǎikē), n.d.; Nunes, 2018).

Black Scholars Building Encyclopedic Knowledge

Before Dorothy Porter, a librarian, bibliographer, and curator at Howard University who started identifying white supremacy in the Dewey
Decimal system in the 1930s and 1940s, Black information activists
helped pave the way for her important work. In the early 1900s, sociologist, journalist, and activist W. E. B. Du Bois took a different route
to changing the system. Instead of trying to change the popular encyclopedia of the day, the *Encyclopaedia Britannica*, "Du Bois sought to
publish nothing less than the equivalent of a black *Encyclopaedia Britannica*, believing that such a broad assemblage of biography, interpretive

essays, facts, and figures would do for the much denigrated black world
of the twentieth century what Britannica and Denis Diderot's *Ency-
clopedie* had done for the European world of the eighteenth century"
(Gates & Appiah, 2007). He envisioned a four-volume, two-million-
word Encyclopedia Africana, which would be a comprehensive knowledge of the history, cultures, and institutions of the people of African
descent. The announcement of this project celebrated the fiftieth anniversary of the Emancipation Proclamation and the "tercentenary of the
Landing of the Negro" (Du Bois, 1909a). In a letter to Dr. Edward W.
Blyden, a leading Pan-Africanist and scholar of Islam in Africa, Du
Bois wrote that although the advisory board would consist of eminent
"white scholars" that the "real work I want done by Negroes" (Du Bois,
1909b). In 1909, Du Bois invited over sixty Black scholars to participate in the project and wrote to at least fourteen white scholars for
"co-operation and advice."

Du Bois' idea was first materialized by historian Carter G. Woodson who founded the Encyclopedia of the Negro with support from
the Phelps-Stokes Fund. However, Woodson's work did not deter Du
Bois' attempts. Through the 1930s and 1940s he worked to secure
funding and build his editorial structure while arguing with Woodson
who claimed that Du Bois stole the idea from him and was critical
of Du Bois for only wanting Black scholars to contribute to the encyclopedia. In the beginning, Du Bois struggled to get his vision off the
ground and published parts of it in journals. It wasn't until 1960, when
the president of Ghana, Kwame Nkrumah, invited him to move to the
country and fund the project, that he started writing the encyclopedia on African soil (Gates, 2000). In 1962 at a conference to launch
the encyclopedia, Du Bois expanded on his grand visionary project,
"The encyclopedia hopes to eliminate the artificial boundaries created
on this continent by colonial masters. Designations such as 'British
Africa,' 'French Africa,' 'Black Africa,' 'Islamic Africa' too often serve to
keep alive differences which in large part have been imposed on Africans by outsiders. The encyclopedia must have research units throughout West Africa, North Africa, East, Central and South Africa which
will gather and record information for these geographical sections of

the continent. The encyclopedia is concerned with Africa as a whole"
(p. 216). Du Bois died before he could see the work through to completion. Committed to the dream, the Secretariat for the Encyclopedia
Africana published three volumes throughout the 1970s and 1980s.

The project was revived in the 1970s by three young scholars at the
University of Cambridge. All from different places in the Black world,
these three scholars included an African American, Henry Gates, Jr.;
a Nigerian, Wole Soykinka; and a Ghanaian British, Kwame Appiah.
They expanded on Du Bois' vision to include scholars not only from the
African continent but also from the diaspora. In 1999, Perseus Books
and Microsoft Corporation funded and published the 2.5 million word
project including the work of about 400 scholars on CD-ROM and the
five-volume paper version *Africana: The Encyclopedia of the African
and African American Experience* (Appiah & Gates, Jr., n.d.).

Doing the Work, but Is It Our Responsibility?

Black people are often expected to do race labor for friends and or
family and even be the Black expert on anti-racism in their workplace
(Buckingham, 2018; Nichole, 2020). This work is exhausting. Author
Alanah Nichole (2020) wrote, "You don't pay Black people enough—or
at all—for the emotional labor and anti-racism work that some of you
are asking for" (para. 1). Changing systems, removing gatekeepers and
barriers, and eradicating white supremacy is not the responsibility or
work of Black people. It is the responsibility of those that benefit and
have the privilege and power from those systems. Participation in such
work is optional and often strategic to preserve mental and physical
health. Black Wikipedia editors and organizers choose to organize in
the community around this work even though it is not their responsibility, and they should not be expected to do this work.

Black women face both marginalization and tokenization in white
spaces like Wikipedia; however, they are often at the forefront of
organizing projects and communities platforming BIPOC voices in the
Wikipedia movement. After experiencing erasure and systemic disparities on Wikipedia, these leaders still decided to organize, fill gaps by

creating knowledges, and partnering with libraries and archives in different ways. The following groups are a small sum of all of the projects and leaders in the movement to shape a more inclusive Wikipedia.

Black Lunch Table

Artists and educators Jina Valentine and Heather Hart founded Black Lunch Table (BLT) in 2014. They attended an artists' retreat and quickly realized that they were the only Black people there, so they decided to sit with one another at lunch, which inspired the name Black Lunch Table (H. Hart, personal communication, August 25, 2020). They came to editing Wikipedia in the late 2000s, but Hart was briefly deterred when an article she wrote about a musician was speedily deleted (H. Hart, personal communication, August 25, 2020). Valentine and Hart did not try again until around 2014 when they contacted well-known artists to make them aware that they had no presence on the Wikipedia. Valentine and Hart further educated and encouraged the Black arts community around the impact of editing. Soon after, they hosted their first BLT edit-a-thon at the Studio Museum in Harlem, and they have been organizing these events ever since. Hart and Valentine understand the lack of visibility in Wikipedia is not the only place where Black artists' stories are not readily accessible. To add breadth and depth to oral histories, they decided to interview and document the work of Black artists through their creation of BLT and a partnership with the University of North Carolina Chapel Hill. Hart and Valentine have partnered with both museums and libraries nationally and abroad.

Wiki Indaba

In 2013, Wiki Indaba started as the first Wikipedia regional conference on the continent of Africa (D. Ndubane, personal communication, September 18, 2020). This conference is an official Wikimedia-funded conference that aims to build community around African Wikipedians and to increase growth and coverage of African Wikimedia Projects. Now it has grown to include other African countries and the African diaspora. While the conference itself doesn't partner with libraries and archives, the affiliates do run partnered programs, which include

Wikimedia South Africa, Wikimedia Community User Group Ghana, Open West Foundation, Wikimedia Community User Group Nigeria, and Wikimedia Community User Group Uganda (D. Ndubane, personal communication, October 15, 2020).

Ennegreciendo Wikipedia/Noircir Wikipedia/Blackening Wikipedia

Wikipedians AfricanadeCuba and Galahmm founded a global campaign that has Wikipedia projects in English and French, which started in 2018, and in Spanish and Catalan, which launched in 2019. In French, the project is referred to as *Noircir Wikipedia*, in Spanish as *Ennegreciendo Wikipedia*, in Catalan as Trobades Ennegrint Viquipèdia, and in English as *Blackening Wikipedia*. All four projects work to increase and improve references, articles, and information about African and Afro-descendant diaspora culture on Wikipedia. Blackening Wikipedia is multilingual and aims to organize all over the diaspora.

AfroCROWD

In 2015, lawyer and activist Alice Backer was recruited by a Wikipedian at a Global Voices Summit, an international, multilingual volunteer community. This Wikipedian shared with Backer his cognizance of the white-centric homogenous community that existed then and still does now (A. Backer, personal communication, August 29, 2020). After attending a BLT edit-a-thon, Backer was inspired and started AfroCROWD in an attempt to bring Black voices into the movement and diversify content on the platform.

With the initial intention to organize in local Black communities, Backer learned access to technology and space was not equitable. However, libraries often provided computer rooms for community-organized events. Backer started having AfroCROWD events at the Brooklyn Public Library. Backer is currently taking a step back and allowing the executive director to steer the campaign. She still edits but enjoys the freedom from the stress of dealing with of the bureaucracy of Wikipedia and the Foundation's grants committee (A. Backer, personal communication, August 29, 2020).

BIPOC in the Built

While working with communities in the art, architecture, and planning professions across multiple U.S. institutions, Kai Alexis Smith, author of this chapter, noticed the lack of visibility of BIPOC contributors connected to the built environment in Wikipedia content and the lack of secondary source material of BIPOC individuals that didn't work at large institutions or firms and/or weren't "big names" in the profession. In summer 2020, Smith partnered with the student chapter of National Organization of Minority Architects and student group of the Department of Urban Studies and Planning's Students of Color Committee with support from the School of Architecture and Planning at Massachusetts Institute of Technology to launch the first *BIPOC in the Built* edit-a-thon. Inspired by Porter, Du Bois, and Gates, Jr., Smith is building a coalition of practitioners, scholars, and librarians around ways to fill these gaps with contributions to Wikipedia. Smith educates and organizes around this campaign in the United States and abroad.

The Future Is Black

Search engines and other technologies also create barriers to sources in libraries and archives, and equitable access to information in person and online. Digital access is lauded as the great equalizer, but it simply emphasizes the problem of unequal access. Many sources are behind paywalls, and computer scientist and digital activist Joy Buolamwini and cofounder and codirector of the UCLA Center for Critical Internet Inquiry Safiya Umoja Noble (2018) both document that the algorithms behind commercial search engines like Google are biased and reinforce racism (Lee, 2020; Tucker, 2017). This extends to the technology used to create content added to Wikipedia, Wikidata, and WikiCommons.

Cofounder of Wikipedia Jimmy Wales said the aim of Wikipedia is to provide access to the sum of all human knowledge ("Wikipedia," 2020). Wikipedia is a community-based platform created in Western society, which is organized and governed with white supremacy.

Westernized people designed the systems that govern Wikipedia; therefore, Wikipedia is flawed and a reflection of society. Wikipedia inherently has white supremacy woven throughout its systems and governance. "While we try to be neutral our work on Wikipedia will always involve bias. Bias can appear in many areas like Wikipedia's policies, practices, content, and participation," qualitative research analyst Jackie Koerner (2019) wrote in the article entitled " Wikipedia Has a Bias Problem," Bias leads to barriers to inclusion. These barriers mean imbalanced participation and distorted knowledge. Most recognizable barriers relate to contributor retention, emerging communities, and content exclusion" (p. 4). In essence, Wikipedia has the same problems experienced in the fields of librarianship and archival science.

Wikipedia was not designed for Black people and they were not involved in its creation. In fact, the system of white supremacy is working the way it was designed, to marginalize dissenting opinions that are critical of the Wikipedia platform. Some examples of this include the exclusion of sources from African, Black, and Indigenous communities that are deemed authoritative by these very communities. Wikipedia relies on Western media sources that often negatively document Black people, exploiting and profiting off of their suffering (Kulaszewicz, 2015; Sancto, 2018). Western news sources also have origins in white supremacy (Gonzalez & Torres, 2011; Mathis, 2018). There is often the rapid deletion of articles on Black topics (D. Cuba, personal communication, September 11, 2020). This creates a barrier for editors learning to contribute to the Wikipedia platform and often deters them from the desire to continue contributing.

There is much more to be done both by accomplices or collaborators for Black Wikipedians and information equity in libraries and archives in general. This brings us back to what the Wikipedia Foundation can do to provide equitable solutions for Black editors on Wikipedia. The Foundation periodically surveys contributors, among other things, to measure gender ("Community Insights/2018 Report—Meta," n.d.). However, the survey does not identify race, ethnicity, or people from marginalized communities within the Wikipedia community. Therefore, there is no data to show how editors from Africa and the African diaspora are represented among those who make the encyclopedia.

A low-stakes way to support Black lives is to measure race and ethnicity among the community as they do gender.

Another idea for change is to update Wikipedia's Five Pillars policy, which have not been changed since the platform was founded. If the community and the Foundation are committed to change and not claiming neutrality, they can benefit from the principles of the Design Justice Network, a community of design practitioners and community organizers that work in social justice ("Design Justice Network," n.d.). The principles would be one framework that could be used to revise the pillars of Wikipedia and invite BIPOC into the room to redesign this community encyclopedia. Educator and founder of Design Justice Network Sasha Costanza-Chock (2020) advocates for design liberation and exclaimed that concepts can help people "move beyond the frames of social impact design or design for good or human centered design to challenge people working on design processes to think about how good intentions are not enough to make sure design processes and practices are really tools for liberation. And to develop, together, principles that might help practitioners avoid what is often an unwitting production of existing equalities" (Guzman, 2020, para. 8). More examples include decentering Western white sources as the only "authoritative" sources and inviting BIPOC to the table to reimagine the sources they deem authoritative for usage in Wikipedia and for the Foundation to support more Black leaders and information activists in their efforts to make Wikipedia more equitable through grant funding.

Conclusion

Black people live with a cognitive dissonance within the diaspora between burning the house (system) down or grabbing a hose and putting the fire out (Belafonte, 2008). Within Wikipedia, libraries, and archives, personal values and behaviors have to match. Prior to COVID-19 and during the pandemic, Black Wikipedian leaders, organizers, and information activists are partnering, organizing within, and creating new knowledge resources to make information more equitable and accessible through Wikipedia, libraries, and archives. We are at a pivotal time in history as we live through two pandemics that are colliding to impact civil rights and change information systems and hopefully global systems as we know them. Author Arundhati Roy (2020) framed this moment and a pathway forward.

"Nothing could be worse than a return to normality. Historically, pandemics have forced humans to break with the past and imagine their world anew. This one is no different. It is a portal, a gateway between one world and the next. We can choose to walk through it, dragging the carcasses of our prejudice and hatred, our avarice, our data banks and dead ideas, our dead rivers and smoky skies behind us. Or we can walk through lightly, with little luggage, ready to imagine another world. And ready to fight for it" (para. 46 and 47).

There is a preference for the latter. The intention of this chapter is to be a catalyst with which to spark and continue thought that leads to action around organizing priorities within Wikipedia, and libraries and archives that include Black people.

References

Appiah, K. A., & Gates, Jr., H. L. (n.d.). Africana. *Archive NY Times*. Retrieved October 15, 2020, from https://archive.nytimes.com/www.nytimes.com/books/first/a/appiah-africana.html.

"Archives have never been neutral": An NDSA Interview with Jarrett Drake. (2017, February 15). National Digital Stewardship Alliance—Digital Library Federation. http://ndsa.org//2017/02/15/archives-have-never-been-neutral-an-ndsa-interview-with-jarrett-drake.html.

Barr, D. (n.d.). We are not all in the same boat. We are all in the same storm. Latest news from Damian Barr. Retrieved October 15, 2020, from https://www.damianbarr.com/latest/tag/We+are+not+all+in+the+same+boat.+We+are+all+in+the+same+storm.

Belafonte, H. (2008). Harry Belafonte reflects on working toward peace. *Santa Clara University*. www.scu.edu/mcae/architects-of-peace/Belafonte/essay.html.

Blakemore, E. (2018, August 22). The father of modern libraries was a serial sexual harasser. *HISTORY*. www.history.com/news/the-father-of-modern-libraries-was-a-serial-sexual-harasser.

Bourg, C. (2014, March 4). The unbearable whiteness of librarianship. *Feral Librarian*. https://chrisbourg.wordpress.com/2014/03/03/the-unbearable-whiteness-of-librarianship/.

Bourg, C. (2018, February 12). Debating y/our humanity, or Are Libraries Neutral? *Feral Librarian*. https://chrisbourg.wordpress.com/2018/02/11/debating-y-our-humanity-or-are-libraries-neutral/.

Buckingham, D. (2018). Invisible labor: A mixed-method study of African American women and their emotional labor in the academy. Electronic Theses and Dissertations. https://egrove.olemiss.edu/etd/849.

Community Insights/2018 Report—Meta. (n.d.). Retrieved October 15, 2020, from https://meta.wikimedia.org/wiki/Community_Insights/2018_Report.

Design Justice Network. (n.d.). Design Justice Network. Retrieved October 15, 2020, from https://designjustice.org/designprinciples.

Du Bois, W. E. B. (1909a). Notes on Encyclopedia Africana letterhead, ca. 1909. UMass Amherst. http://credo.library.umass.edu/view/full/mums312-b002-i197.

Du Bois, W. E. B. (1909b, August 9). Letter from W. E. B. Du Bois to Charles W. Eliot, August 9, 1909. UMass Amherst. http://credo.library.umass.edu/view/full/mums312-b002-i196.

Espinal, I. R. (2001). A new vocabulary for inclusive librarianship: Applying whiteness theory to our profession. [The Power of Language/ El Poder de la Palabras: Selected Papers from the Second REFORMA National Conference] REFORMA, Englewood, CO .

Flood, A. (2019, June 27). Melvil Dewey's name stripped from top librarian award. *The Guardian*. www.theguardian.com/books/2019/jun/27/melvil-deweys-name-stripped-from-top-librarian-award.

Ford, A. (2018, June 1). Bringing harassment out of the history books. *American Libraries Magazine*. https://americanlibrariesmagazine.org/2018/06/01/melvil-dewey-bringing-harassment-out-of-the-history-books/.

Galvan, A. (2015, June 3). Soliciting performance, hiding bias: Whiteness and librarianship. *In the Library with the Lead Pipe*. www.inthelibrarywiththeleadpipe.org/2015/soliciting-performance-hiding-bias-whiteness-and-librarianship/.

Gates, H. L. (2000, March). W. E. B. Du Bois and the Encyclopedia Africana, 1909–63. *Annals of the American Academy of Political and Social Science, 568*, 203–19.

Gates, H. L., & Appiah, K. (2007, September 15). W.E.B. Du Bois and the making of the Encyclopedia Africana, 1909–1963. www.blackpast.org/

african-american-history/w-e-b-dubois-and-making-encyclopedia-afri
cana-1909–1963/.

Gonzalez, J., & Torres, J. (2011). *News for all the people: The epic story of race and the American media* (1st Edition). Verso.

Gooding-Call, A. (2019, April 3). Classism, sexual misconduct, racism . . . the life of Melvil Dewey. *Book Riot*. https://bookriot.com/life-of-melvil-dewey/.

Guzman, R. L. (2020, May 6). Episode 66 Dad & Society [Audio podcast]. Retrieved from https://listen.datasociety.net/episodes/design-justice/transcript.

Hall, T. D. (2012). The black body at the reference desk: Critical race theory and black librarianship. In A. P. Jackson, J. Jefferson, & A. Nosakhere (Eds.), *The 21st-century Black librarian in America: Issues and challenges.* Scarecrow Press. http://public.ebookcentral.proquest.com/choice/public fullrecord.aspx?p=928524.

Hathcock, A. (2015, October 7). White librarianship in Blackface: Diversity initiatives in LIS. *In the Library with the Lead Pipe*. www.inthelibrarywith theleadpipe.org/2015/lis-diversity/.

Honma, T. (2005). Trippin' over the color line: The invisibility of race in library and information studies. *InterActions: UCLA Journal of Education and Information Studies, 1*(2). https://escholarship.org/uc/item/4nj0w1mp.

Koerner, J. (2019). Wikipedia has a bias problem. In J. Reagle & J. Koerner (Eds.), *Wikipedia@20: Stories of an incomplete revolution.* MIT Press.

Kulaszewicz, K. (2015). Racism and the media: A textual analysis. *Master of Social Work Clinical Research Papers*. https://sophia.stkate.edu/msw_papers/477.

Lee, J. (2020, February 8). When bias is coded into our technology. *NPR.Org*. www.npr.org/sections/codeswitch/2020/02/08/770174171/when-bias-is-coded-into-our-technology.

Lindell, K. (2019, September 27). The name "Dewey" is synonymous with libraries. So why did librarians strike it from an award? *Slate Magazine*. https://slate.com/human-interest/2019/09/melvil-dewey-american-li brary-association-award-name-change.html.

Liu, M. (2000). The history and status of Chinese American in librarianship. *Library Trends, 49*(1), 109–37.

Maher, K., & Uzzell, J. (2020, June 3). We stand for racial justice. [Blog]. *Wikimedia Foundation*. https://wikimediafoundation.org/news/2020/06/03/we-stand-for-racial-justice/.

Mathis, J. (2018, October 30). Journalists of color were right about Trump. Why didn't we listen? *The Week*. https://theweek.com/articles/804633/journalists-color-right-about-trump-why-didnt-listen.

Nichole, A. (2020, June 4). For white people considering anti-racism, when your Black friends and colleagues have had enough. *Technical.ly Baltimore*.

https://technical.ly/baltimore/2020/06/04/alanah-nichole-anti-racism-baltimore-social-media-shops-resources/.

Noble, S. U. (2018). Algorithms of oppression. https://nyupress.org/97814 79837243/algorithms-of-oppression.

Nunes, Z. C. (2018, November 26). Remembering the Howard University librarian who decolonized the way books were catalogued. | *History* | *Smithsonian Magazine*. www.smithsonianmag.com/history/remembering-howard-university-librarian-who-decolonized-way-books-were-cata logued-180970890/.

Oster, M. (2019, June 25). US library group expunges Dewey name from medal over anti-Semitism, misogyny. *The Times of Israel*. www.timesofis rael.com/us-library-group-expunges-dewey-name-from-medal-over-an ti-semitism-misogyny/.

Roy, A. (2020, April 3). The pandemic is a portal. *Financial Times*. www.ft.com/content/10d8f5e8-74eb-11ea-95fe-fcd274e920ca.

Sancto, R. (2018, June 26). How the media profits from Black bodies. *Shout Out UK*. www.shoutoutuk.org/2018/06/26/how-the-media-profits-from-black-bodies/.

Tucker, I. (2017, May 28). "A white mask worked better": Why algorithms are not colour blind. | *Technology* | *The Guardian*. *The Observer*. www.theguardian.com/technology/2017/may/28/joy-buolamwini-when-algorithms-are-racist-facial-recognition-bias.

Wikipedia:Prime objective. (2020). In Wikipedia. https://en.wikipedia.org/w/index.php?title=Wikipedia:Prime_objective&oldid=980667607.

裘开明_百度百科 (Qiú kāimíng_bǎidù bǎikē). (n.d.). Baidu. Retrieved October 15, 2020, from https://baike.baidu.com/item/%E8%A3%98%E5 BC%80%E6%98%8E.

CHAPTER 7

WP:CATÉGORIE IS ... LIAISON LIBRARIAN CONTRIBUTION TO LOCAL QUÉBÉCOIS LGBTQ+ CONTENT IN FRANCOPHONE WIKIPEDIA

Michael David Miller[1]

[1] McGill University

Abstract

Liaison librarians have unique roles in their institutions and in their greater communities. They often support and collaborate with professors and students in their subject areas and, of equal importance, have a special knowledge of resources available in their assigned liaison areas. This chapter will explore how a liaison librarian with subject responsibilities can contribute to closing gaps and community building through Wikipedia and the Wikimedia projects. It will describe the author's contribution, as a liaison librarian, in addressing the Québécois LGBTQ+ gap in the Francophone Wikipedia project, WikipédiaFR. The author will also discuss how Wikipedia can be used as a tool for community building and raising awareness about the Québec LGBTQ+ culture and history gap in WikipédiaFR. The contribution events and their format, les soirées contributives, hosted at the Bibliothèque à livres ouverts du Centre Communautaire LGBTQ+ de Montréal, that sought to improve and create local LGBTQ+ Wikipedia content en français will be discussed. Additionally, the author will share thoughts on existing and not existing in Wikipedia for local LGBTQ+ communities.

DOI: https://doi.org/10.3998/mpub.11778416.ch7.en

Keywords

LGBTQ+, Queering Wikipedia, Liaison librarianship.

Introduction

The cultural capital of Wikipedia is such that existence within it denotes a level of power and importance. The phenomenon of considering something or someone truly significant or insignificant, through its presence or absence on Wikipedia, can be a damaging one.

—Kelly Doyle (Minding the Gaps, Ch. 5, *Leveraging Wikipedia: Connecting Communities of Knowledge*)

Communities must be represented in the world's premier information source—and more importantly in their native language. Kelly Doyle (2018) reminds us that Wikipedia is power, existing or not existing in Wikipedia is a cultural statement, and she alludes to Wikipedia having authority—if your community exists in it, it is important; if it does not exist in it, it is not important. Take the francophone nation of Québec as an example. Québec is Canada's only francophone, or French-speaking, province, with a population of 8.5 million people out of an estimated 38 million people in all of Canada (Statistique Canada, n.d.). Of Canada's 10.9 million francophones, 7.8 million (71 percent) live in Québec (Quéméner et al., 2019). On October 14, 2020, 1.37 percent of articles in the WikipédiaFR were linked to *Québec's Wikipedia Portal*, 9.03 percent were to the U.S. portal, and 16.97 percent to France's portal—this showed a possible underrepresentation of content about Québec. This representation may look bleak, but back in 2016, the Fondation Lionel Groulx, a historical society that focuses on Québec's history, reported that approximately 5,000 WikipédiaFR articles were about Québec (Pierre Graveline, 2016). Today there are more than 30,000 articles about the *Je me souviens*, Québec, province (*Portail:Québec—Wikipédia*, 2020).

Wikipedia content is a reflection of the interests of the thousands of volunteers who contribute to it each month. That is to say, the more

Table 1 Francophone Population and Number of Articles by Wikipedia Portals in WikipédiaFR as of October 14, 2020

Country	Number of Francophones	Number of Articles in Portal	Percentage out of 2,259,644 Articles (%)
France	66,060,000	383,510	16.97
Congo-Kinshasa	42,533,000	4,382	0.19
Algeria	13,804,000	11,360	0.05
Morocco	12,729,000	7,825	0.35
Cameroun	10,006,000	10,808	0.48
Belgium	8,678,000	42,181	1.87
Côte d'Ivoire	8,259,000	3,897	0.17
Québec	7,833,000	30,195	1.34
Tunisia	6,081,000	7,721	0.34
Switzerland	5,734,000	26,767	1.18
Canada (excluding Québec)	3,149,000	36,217	1.60
United States	2,127,000	204,745	9.06

Québécois that contribute to WikipédiaFR, the better Québec's coverage will be. This also applies to LGBTQ+ content. With more LGBTQ+ Québécois contributing to WikipédiaFR the better this local culture will be represented. Table 1 shows the top ten countries with Francophone populations, the total Francophone population, and the specific articles in their associated country profiles in comparison to the overall number of articles in WikipediaFR. In this table, the United States was added for comparison purposes and Québec was removed from the Canadian numbers, as this chapter's focus is on this Canadian province. In addition to what appears to be a small number of articles for Québec, an argument can be made that most Francophone countries have local cultural content gaps. WikipédiaFR notability policies are not favorable to local cultures and histories and tend to favor their national counterparts, due primarily to the criteria on a credible source ("Wikipédia," 2020a, 2020b). A future research project on what constitutes a "credible" source in WikipédiaFR could help explain the low levels of articles about countries other than France. One thing is for sure, Québec LGBTQ+ newspapers, magazines, and other media publications are not considered "national" sources.

Francophone Wikipedia and LGBTQ+ Content: Wikipédia and la francophonie

WikipédiaFR is the fifth largest language Wikipedia with over 2.2 million articles as of December 2020. Understanding the geographic reach of the Francophone world helps understand the emphasis of this chapter on the geographic distribution of articles in the WikipédiaFR. In 2018, the *Organisation internationale de la Francophonie (OIF)* estimated that there were 300 million francophones spread across 106 countries and territories (Quéméner et al., 2019, p. 87). Total 235 million of the 300 million francophones use French on a daily basis (Quéméner et al., 2019, p. 88). A little over 59 percent of these daily users are in Africa and the Middle East, 33.4 percent in Europe, 7 percent in the Americas, and 0.3 percent in Asia and Oceania (Quéméner et al., 2019, p. 38).

In September 2018, the Wikimedia Traffic Analysis Report showed that WikipédiaFR received 636 million page views that month (Wikimedia Foundation). In addition, the most recent 2013 Edits Per Wikipedia Language report breaks down the provenance of WikipédiaFR editors: 80.1 percent from France, 5.5 percent from Belgium, 4.5 percent from Canada (including Québec), 1.7 percent from Switzerland, and 1.2 percent from the United States (Wikimedia Foundation, 2013).

LGBTQ+ Francophone Content

As of October 24, 2020, of the 2.2 million articles in WikipédiaFR, 10,294[1] are in the LGBTQ+ Category *Catégorie:Lesbiennes, gays, bisexuels et transgenres* and 5,353[2] are in the *Catégorie:LGBT par pays* (translation:

Table 2 Number and Percentage of Articles by Country Portals in WikipédiaFR

Catégorie	Number of Articles	Percentage out of 5,330 *LGBT par pays* articles (%)	PetScan Permalink
LGBT par pays	5,353	100	https://petscan.wmflabs.org/?psid=17963101
LGBT en France	883	16.44	https://petscan.wmflabs.org/?psid=17967595
LGBT au Congo-Kinshasa	No category	0	No permalink
LGBT en Algérie	6	0.09	https://petscan.wmflabs.org/?psid=17967596
LGBT au Maroc	13	0.24	https://petscan.wmflabs.org/?psid=17967597
LGBT au Cameroun	4	0.08	https://petscan.wmflabs.org/?psid=17967598
LGBT en Belgique	43	0.79	https://petscan.wmflabs.org/?psid=17967599
LGBT en Côte d'Ivoire	2	0.04	https://petscan.wmflabs.org/?psid=17967607
LGBT au Québec	152	2.85	https://petscan.wmflabs.org/?psid=17967611
LGBT en Tunisie	15	0.26	https://petscan.wmflabs.org/?psid=17967612
LGBT en Suisse	54	1.03	https://petscan.wmflabs.org/?psid=17967613
LGBT au Canada*	150	2.78	https://petscan.wmflabs.org/?psid=17967614
LGBT aux États-Unis	2,117	39.53	https://petscan.wmflabs.org/?psid=17967615
LGBT au Royaume-Uni	342	6.32	https://petscan.wmflabs.org/?psid=17967618

* Excluding Québec

LGBT by country). There are ninety-nine subcategories associated with the *Catégorie LGBT par pays* of which eighty-six are about specific countries. The *Catégorie LGBT au Canada* is divided into subcategories, which includes, as a subcategory, the *Catégorie LGBT au Québec*.

The previous table (Table 2) is a breakdown of LGBTQ+ content as of October 24, 2020, in the WikipédiaFR based off of country or region using the Wikimedia Foundation Labs' PetScan Tool[3] that provides the number of articles associated to a category as well as the number of articles associated to a category's subcategories. The depth of analysis goes as deep as the eleventh subcategory. After the eleventh subcategory, the number of results ceased to increase.

This data indicate that there is possible underrepresentation of Francophone countries and an overrepresentation of the United States in LGBTQ+ country-specific information in the WikipédiaFR. As mentioned earlier in this chapter, however, the content of Wikipedia reflects the interests of its contributors; perhaps there is more interest in creating Francophone LGBTQ+ content related to France and the United States. Librarians and other organizers can help build interest in creating Wikipedia content about underrepresented topics by hosting events and other activities to train and onboard new editors; in the next section, the author will discuss his role in hosting such an event.

Where It All Started

My passion for this project started in August 2017 in Montréal, the Francophone province of Québec's largest, and Canada's second largest, city. Montréal celebrated its 375th anniversary, Canada celebrated its 150th, Wikimania and the WikiConference North America were *en ville*, and it was the month of the world's largest Francophone LGBTQ+ Pride celebration, Fierté Montréal (Tourisme Montréal, 2019). During a *Wikipédia aime les bibliohtèques* event, in a moment of introspection, I wondered if my intersecting identities—a gay, cisgender, néo-Québécois, originally from Michigan, and born of a Korean mother who was adopted by my white American grandparents—were represented in Francophone Wikipedia (WikiédiaFR).

Mado Lamotte: La reine du Québec

That very same summer of 2017 I found myself considering Québébcois LGBTQ+ cultural icons, particularly *Drag Queens*. In a world before *Rita Baga*—a finalist in the 2020 *Canada's Drag Race*—the most well-known Drag Queens from Québec were Mado Lamotte and Michel Dorion. Lamotte and Dorion helped bring drag culture to mainstream Québécois culture. They both own Drag Queen cabarets, *Le Cabaret Mado* and *Le Bar le Cocktail*, respectively, that offer a performing stage to Montréal's Drag Queens.

Lamotte is a household name in Québec society via her appearances on many Québec television programs and is also known internationally, notably in Francophone Europe. Lamotte has produced large public shows such as *Mado's Got Talent* at the *Festvial Juste pour rire/Just for Laughs Festival* and what was reported to be the world's largest outdoor Drag Queen show, *Mascara*, at the *Festival Divers/Cité* (Montreal Gazette, 2014). Dorion is well known thanks to her personifications of Célion Dion, her organization of the *Illusions* drag show at Fierté Montréal, and thanks to her numerous appearances in Québec media.

Despite the wide notoriety of these people, locations, and events in Québec, Lamotte was the only one with a Wikipedia page on WikipédiaFR in August 2017. Michel Dorion was absent, as was Rita Baga and Barbada de Barbades the Drag Queen who brought Drag Story hour to Québec public libraries (Simard, 2019). Learning of these absences moved the author to get involved with Wikipedia to help contribute to addressing this culture gap.

Catégorie:LGBT par pays > LGBT au Canada > LGBT au Québec

The first step in the project was to identify how many LGBTQ+ articles already existed in WikipediaFR. Thankfully, the WikipédiaFR's *Catégorie* classification system already had established categories in this area. The WikipediaFR *Catégorie* system finds itself somewhere between the ultraconservative Library of Congress Classification System and the pure freedom of #HashTags ("Aide:Catégorie," 2020). The category that provides a portrait of Québec specific LGBTQ+ articles in WikipédiaFR is the *Catégorie:LGBT au Québec*, a subcategory of *Catégorie:LGBT au Canada*, which is also a subcategory of *Catégorie:LGBT par pays* (translation: LGBT by country). The category system, much like our library classification systems, functions in an arborescence hierarchy.

While exploring the *Catégorie:LGBT par pays*, it was discovered that many of the Québécois LGBTQ+ community's cultural icons, places, and historical events were absent from the *Catégorie:LGBT au Québec*. This content gap was addressed through the professional expertise of the author's role as a librarian, allowing him to leverage his library's collections, and those of others, to contribute to Wikipedia and develop relationships with the LGBTQ+ community of Montréal, and more largely, Québec.

Wikipédia et la communauté LGBTQ: visible et vivante

Five contribution activities were organized as a next step to addressing the Québécois LGBTQ+ gap in WikipédiaFR. The series was entitled "Wikipédia et la communauté LGBTQ+: visible et vivante" (translation: Wikipedia and the LGBTQ+ Community: Visible and Vibrant) and ran from October 2017 to May 2018. This was made possible thanks to a partnership between *la Bibliothèque à livres ouverts du Centre communautaire LGBTQ+ de Montréal* (translation: The Open Book Library of the LGBTQ+ Community Centre of Montréal), *le Café des savoirs libres* (translation: The Free Knowledge Café), and Wikimedia Canada. The goal of these activities was to empower the Québec LGBTQ+ community to write about its culture, history, artists, and public figures in the WikipédiaFR project. This was done by using the LGBTQ+ community center's position in the LGBTQ+ community, along with its library's resources, the resources of other libraries, and the expertise of librarians and Wikipedia volunteers. These activities provided an opportunity for seasoned and perspective Wikipedians to meet notable Québécois LGBTQ+ artists and authors and to learn

Figure 1 Rita Baga (Drag Queen) and participants at the contribution event, April 11, 2018.

Attribution: Lëa-Kim Châteauneuf, CC BY-SA 4.0, https://creativecommons.org/licenses/by-sa/4.0, via Wikimedia Commons.

more about their art and other work in a conference-style format that was inspired by the conference-contribution activities developed at the Cinémathèque québécoise (2020).

The five activities were broken up into four parts:

1. Introduction of the project and discussion about the Québécois LGBTQ+ gap
2. Presentation from an invited guest
3. A workshop on contributing to Wikipedia and to library resources
4. Open time to contribute to WikipédiaFR

The contribution activities focused on local Québec Queer history, spaces, and culture. Participants wrote new articles, created Wikidata entries, and added photos to Wikimedia Commons about the following topics: Parc de l'espoir, Barbada de Barbades, Rita Baga, Kevin Lambert, and important police raids in Queer spaces that helped change LGBTQ+ rights in Québec. We also had the founder of the *Bibliothèque à livres ouverts*, Benoît Migneault, as an invited guest. During this event, we created a Wikidata entry and uploaded photos of him to Wikimedia Commons. Future plans include an article for Migneault once he meets notability criteria.

These events were also used to discuss libraries in general. Participants were encouraged to obtain library memberships with *Bibliothèque et Archives nationales du Québec* (BAnQ), Québec's National Library and Archives, as well as with the *Bibliothèques de la Ville de Montréal* or another local public library. BAnQ proved to be an important resource for historical newspapers, magazines, and government publications on historical LGBTQ+ people, places, and events in Québec because of its digitization projects on Québec heritage newspapers (BAnQ, 2020). I was also able to use important resources available through the McGill University Library: the *Archives of Gender and Sexuality* from Gale and *LGBT Thought and Culture* from Alexander Street Press, to supplement the resources from BAnQ and the public libraries (Miller, 2020). This access allowed me to prepare "press dossiers" before the events that were shared with participants to help in the creation and editing process.

WP:Catégorie est . . . la conclusion

Librarian involvement in Wikipedia and the Wikimedia Projects is an opportunity to engage with their local communities and help close gender, LGBTQ+, and local history and culture gaps. As information professionals working in academic settings, we have privileged access to our own intuition's resources and to an important network of colleagues in national, research, public, and specialized libraries. We can and should be leveraging our own library's collections and working with colleagues in other institutions to help make the information on Wikipedia more robust and accurate because it is the most used source of information that our patrons, colleagues, friends, family, and acquaintances use.

Wikipedia can be intimidating on first approach. It is an ecosystem where there is no formal authority, contributors need to learn a Wikipedia contributor culture and its rules, as well as learn the technical aspects of contributing. There is a learning curve, but a learning curve that all librarians can easily overcome and help others overcome and engage in their local communities in a way that empowers them to tell their stories. It can also be a space that feels unsafe and hostile for LGBTQ+ contributors, but there is hope. The Wikimedia Foundation has positioned itself as an ally to the LGBTQ+ community. On December 8, 2020, Maggie Dennis (2020), vice president of Community Resilience and Sustainability, speaking on behalf of the Wikimedia Foundation, wrote "to restate, reinforce, and firmly assert [the Wikimedia Foundation's] commitment to supporting the LGBTQIA+ volunteers in [the] movement, as well as others who face exclusion and hostility on the basis of identity factors."

Earlier we saw that the U.S. LGBTQ+ category in WikipédiaFR represents 39.53 percent of all country-specific LGBTQ+ content. It would be interesting to know if this larger representation is also present in transcontinental languages such as Portuguese, Spanish, or Russian, or even in more continental languages such as Dutch, German, or Italian. Perhaps this is simply a phenomenon in the WikipédiaFR, but it is possible it is generalized in other language Wikipedias. A future research project could provide some important insight behind what appears to be an overrepresentation of U.S. LGBTQ+ culture in Francophone Wikipedia.

Wikipedia and the Wikimedia sister projects are trying to create a world in which everyone can share in the sum of human knowledge. Local Queer history and culture has a place in the sum of all human knowledge but is often absent, underdeveloped, or subject to strict rules on notability. However, what is beautiful with Wikipedia is that the content and rules of the project reflect the interest of its contributors. The more people from the LGBTQ+ community that contribute to Wikipedia, in all of its language versions, the more we can close the LGBTQ+ gap at a local level and contribute to change the rules that can often make certain gap-closing contributions difficult. That is exactly the aim of this project: to emphasize local Queer Québécois context in WikipédiaFR.

Notes

1 Source: https://petscan.wmflabs.org/?psid=17961118.

2 Source: https://petscan.wmflabs.org/?psid=17963101.

3 WMF Labs PetScan Tool: https://petscan.wmflabs.org.

References

Aide:Catégorie. (2020). In Wikipédia. https://fr.wikipedia.org/w/index. php?title=Aide:Cat%C3%A9gorie&oldid=174771503.

BAnQ. (2020). BAnQ numérique. http://numerique.banq.qc.ca/.

Cinémathèque Québécoise. (2020). GLAM Cinémathèque Québécoise. *Wikipédia.* https://fr.wikipedia.org/w/index.php?title=Wikip%C3%A9dia: Cin%C3%A9math%C3%A8que_qu%C3%A9b%C3%A9coise&ol did=172573673.

Dennis, M. (2020, December 8). Community Resilience and Sustainabil-ity/2020 December Foundation commitment of support for LGBT+ vol-unteers. *Wikimedia Meta-Wiki.* https://meta.wikimedia.org/wiki/Com munity_Resilience_and_Sustainability/2020_December_Foundation_ commitment_of_support_for_LGBT%2B_volunteers.

Doyle, K. (2018). Minding the gaps: Engaging academic libraries to address content and user imbalances on Wikipedia. In M. Proffitt (Ed.), *Leveraging Wikipedia: Connecting communities of knowledge.* ALA Editions. https:// mcgill.on.worldcat.org/oclc/1004555519.

Miller, M. D. (2020). LGBTQ+ studies guide. *McGill University Library.* https:// libraryguides.mcgill.ca/LGBTQ/primarysources.

Montreal Gazette. (2014, May 6). Drag star Mado Lamotte quits Divers/Cité, pulls plug on Mascara to launch stand-up comedy show. *Montreal Gazette.* https://montrealgazette.com/entertainment/drag-star-mado-lamotte-quits-diverscite-pulls-plug-on-mascara-to-launch-stand-up-comedy-show.

Pierre Graveline. (2016, January 22). Le Québec, parent pauvre de Wikipédia. *Le Devoir.* www.ledevoir.com/opinion/idees/460859/le-quebec-parent-pauvre-de-wikipedia.

Portail:Québec—Wikipédia. (2020, December 13). https://fr.wikipedia.org/wiki/Portail:Qu%C3%A9bec.

Quéméner, F., Wolff, A., & Organisation internationale de la francophonie. (2019). La langue française dans le monde: 2015–2018. http://banq.pret numerique.ca/accueil/isbn/9782072786853.

Simard, V. (2019, August 16). Une "Heure du conte" pas comme les autres. *La Presse+*. https://plus.lapresse.ca/screens/d6f0bca3-d12d-4231-a416-1ca4d fb16ce4__7C___0.html.

Statistique Canada. (n.d.). Estimations de la population, trimestrielles [Data set]. *Gouvernement du Canada.* https://doi.org/10.25318/1710000901-FRA.

Tourisme Montréal. (2019, May 22). The history of Pride in Montréal. www. mtl.org/en/experience/history-pride-montreal.

Wikimedia Foundation. (2013, September). Wikimedia traffic analysis report—page edits per Wikipedia language—breakdown. https://stats. wikimedia.org/wikimedia/squids/SquidReportPageEditsPerLanguage Breakdown.htm#errata.

Wikimedia Foundation. (2018, September). Wikimedia traffic analysis report—page views per Wikipedia language—breakdown. https://stats. wikimedia.org/wikimedia/squids/SquidReportPageViewsPerLanguage Breakdown.htm.

Wikipédia:Notoriété. (2020a). In Wikipédia. https://fr.wikipedia.org/w/index.php?title=Wikip%C3%A9dia:Notori%C3%A9t%C3%A9&ol did=175169233.

Wikipédia:Sources fiables. (2020b). In Wikipédia. https://fr.wikipedia.org/w/index.php?title=Wikip%C3%A9dia:Sources_fiables&oldid=174363769.

CHAPTER 8

AFRICAN ACADEMIC LIBRARIES PARTNERING WITH WIKIMEDIA PROJECTS: VALUES AND BENEFITS

Adaora C. Obuezie[1] and Millie N. Horsfall[2]

[1] Nnamdi Azikiwe University, [2] University of Port Harcourt

Abstract

Wikimedia as a foundation is the mother of all Wikis. "It supports hundreds of people around the world in creating the largest free knowledge projects in history" (Wikimedia foundation, https://wikimediafoundation.org). Its resources give benefits that can emerge from the collaboration of librarians and Wikimedia. However, despite the rich contents and vast availability of information on Wikimedia, many scholars refute the credibility of Wikimedia contents. This chapter addresses the benefits and values of African academic libraries partnering with Wikimedia projects and gives a brief definition on the concepts of Wikimedia and Wikipedia. How academic libraries directly improve Wikimedia resources for a reliable information; particularly, it highlights the need to rightly posit librarians as custodians of knowledge, relating the campaigns of 1Lib1Ref and other related projects where librarians in Africa through the African Library and Information Associations and Institution (AfLIA) collaborated with Wikipedia to add reliable sources, edit articles, and write stories to promote the quality, authority, and reliability of intellectual contents in Wikipedia.

DOI: https://doi.org/10.3998/mpub.11778416.ch8.en

It demonstrates the engagement of academic libraries in the development of information resources to aid access to information for all citizens through linking of institutional repository materials to wiki articles in line with the UNESCO policy of ensuring public access to information (UNESCO, 2017). It also discusses challenges associated with the use of Wikimedia resources in some institutions and draws conclusion that Wikipedia promotes discoverability of library resources, librarians improve the reliability of its contents as an important tool to leverage on, in pursuit of academic endeavors, thus providing an interception between Wikipedia and academic libraries.

Keywords

Academic Libraries and Wikipedia, AfLIA, Librarians, Wikimedia, Wikipedia + AfLIA partnership, WikiAfLibs, 1Lib1Ref.

Introduction

Wikimedia provides vast amounts of information resources on any subject matter and is widely used by students, scholars, researchers, and lecturers, yet its resources are not given wide acceptance in academia. In academia, Wikipedia is often treated with negligence and is mostly rejected, citing a lack of authority. However, librarians in Africa cannot afford to neglect the information provided by Wikipedia and its relevance to research, teaching, and learning because Wikipedia has been posited in many studies as a starting point for almost every type of research, as each online query gets results from Wikipedia (O'Neal, 2006).

Before discussing the emerging relationship between African libraries and Wikipedia, it's important to have a basic understanding of Wikipedia and its foundation. First, the *Wikimedia Foundation* is a charitable organization with headquarters in San Francisco, California. The Wikimedia Foundation was founded in 2003 by Jimmy Wales as a way to fund Wikipedia and its sister projects through a non-profit means (Neate, 2008). The *Wikimedia Movement*, often referred to as *Wikimedia*, is the global community of contributors to Wikimedia Foundation projects (Wikipedia, 2021). *Wikipedia* is the free-access, free content, Internet encyclopedia, supported and hosted by the Wikimedia Foundation. Wikipedia operates on five principles called the *Five Pillars*: (1) the identity of Wikipedia as an encyclopedia; (2) adherence to the neutral point of view; (3) free content that anyone can use, edit, and also distribute; (4) respect and civility must exist among Wikipedia editors; and (5) Wikipedia has no firm rules (Otis, 2020). Librarians and other new editors are introduced to Wikipedia with trainings on the five pillars. The five pillars are fundamental principles that guides Wikipedia: - they summarize and provide an understanding of what Wikipedia is in five key points to Wikipedia editors. Information on who can edit, how to edit, collaboration, what Wikipedia is not, the type of contents to add, type of resources to work with, copyright law, online etiquette, and the ruling pattern of Wikipedia forms the content of the five pillars. These make it very essential for new editors, including librarians, to be educated on the five pillars for a smooth sail in the Wikipedia world especially during editing activities.

Wikipedia and Librarians in Africa: Brief History and Future Directions

Wikipedia has become an important source of free knowledge around the globe. In Nigeria, the New Readers Outreach Survey (2016) found that 23 percent of the total population was aware of Wikipedia and 43 percent of those were students (Wikimedia, 2020). Despite this awareness and use, Africa, a continent that is rich in cultures, languages, and music, lacks adequate representation of Wikipedia editors. This gap can be filled by librarians.

Information literacy strives more in the absence of language barriers and this is of high relevance in providing free access to information for all—which is the key aim of libraries and Wikipedia. Hence, in order to fill the existing gap, there is a need for partnerships between African libraries and Wikipedia projects to provide authoritative and reliable resources for the Wikipedia users. These partnerships will transform and encourage a wider acceptance of Wikipedia through

Figure 1 Editing Wikipedia at the Federal University of Agriculture, Abeokuta, Attribution: Kaizenify, CC BY-SA 4.0. < https://creativecommons.org/licenses/by-sa/4.0>, via Wikimedia Commons.

community outreach and trainings as well as nurture librarians and library educators with prerequisite skills to actively be involved in a collaborative and free knowledge space such as Wikipedia, contributing to knowledge, and accurately amplifying Africa's voice (AfLIA, 2019, 2020f; Lubbock, 2018).

The Wikimedia User Group Nigeria (WUGN), managed by Olushola Olaniyan as the president, has been engaging Nigerian librarians in Wikipedia campaign activities such as a maiden campaign, called Wikipedia for Librarians, which kicked off on April 16, 2019, at Federal University of Agriculture, Abeokuta, to train librarians on how to edit and contribute to Wikipedia and sister projects in various tertiary institutions in Nigeria (Wikipedia, 2019). WUGN also established a Wikimedia Fan Club in 2017. The club targets Nigerian students, to help them better understand the edits in Wikipedia and also change the negative narratives and myths against the use of Wikipedia for learning purposes. Wiki Fan Clubs have successfully been established in up to seven Nigerian universities, including: - Lagos State University;

University of Ilorin, Kwara State; University of Ibadan, Oyo State; Ekiti State University; Federal University of Agriculture, Abeokuta, Ogun State; University of Nigeria, Nsukka; and Nigeria Institute of Journalism (Wikimedia, 2021).

Academic libraries in reciprocation have initiated and executed activities that have led to progress in the Wikimedia movement, such as in the case of Nnamdi Azikiwe University Library, University of Nigeria, Nsukka. At this university, Dr. Ngozi Osadebe facilitated an Art + Feminism Wikipedia Edit-A-Thon in 2017. Art + Feminism Edit-A-Thons target the underrepresentation of women in the arts on Wikipedia both in contributing to Wikipedia and the amount of content. Editors for the event were recruited and trained from the underrepresented group to fill the existing gap by editing, writing articles, and adding content on relatable materials in Wikipedia (University of Nigeria Library, 2017). Another way that libraries are introducing staff members and the public to the Wikimedia world is through the #1Lib1Ref campaign. On February 6, 2020, WUGN partnered with the Kenneth Dike Library, University of Ibadan, to improve references on Wikipedia (Wikipedia, 2020). These partnerships benefits libraries and Wikipedia and are good steps taken toward promoting a shared mission: to get more diversified and knowledgeable editors who add credible edits and move the Wikimedia movement forward by increasing visibility and free access to information.

Librarians in Africa can help improve Wikipedia by adding materials related to specific topics where information is lacking. Each library holds books containing information that cannot be found on Wikipedia. Moving the information from the book into Wikipedia is an important first step to building and improving articles that relate to the different language Wikipedias. Wikipedia articles include links designed to guide the user, information seeker, or researcher to related pages/resources with additional information (Lally & Dunford, 2007; Stvilia, et al., 2008). Citations from verified materials, such as books, journals, web pages, online newspapers, and institutional repositories, can be added for further details and in consideration for proper citation/referencing of the intellectual output of researchers.

Articles are only as good as their editors, hence the involvement of librarians as editors in Wikipedia continually improves the quality of citations and the myriad of content presently accessible in the Wikipedia domain. The ten simple rules involved in editing Wikipedia state that you need to have an account;, learn the five pillars that was discussed earlier as the basic principles of Wikipedia:- be bold, that is, having confidence in the edits you are about to make; be aware of your audience, this means that you have to bear in mind the users of the content you are creating or editing, which will guide you in the language and construct of your work; avoid infringement of copyright; make reliable citations; avoid promoting self, which falls in line with conflict of interest; editing on the subject you are knowledgeable on will help you in sharing your expertise; write neutrally; and ask for help whenever it is needed. It is worthy of note that the talk page is always available for discussion and clarity instead of making intentional errors that may register your username as a vandal (Logan, et al., 2010). Edits are monitored by advanced editors, reviewers, and administrators—especially during edit-a-thon-campaigns—and the editors will revert any edits that do not meet editorial criteria. Editors may sometimes be restricted from editing to prevent vandalism, if previous wiki activities by such editor is perceived to be disruptive. Criteria for accessing edits are determined by the project leader and jury of any campaign or contests completed. Criteria may be based on quality or quantity of edits, contents added, articles written or translated, and citations made, among other criterion depending on the scope of the project. Materials that do not meet the Wikipedia standards for quality, notability, or sourcing, normally gets deleted or removed.

AfLIA and Wikimedia Partnerships

The African Library and Information Associations and Institutions (AfLIA) partnered with the Wikimedia Foundation for the first African Librarians Week, May 24–30, 2020. The event was titled, 'Promoting African Scholars to the World' and the hashtags #AfLibWk and #1Lib1Ref (1Librarian + 1Reference) were used to promote the week-long event. The event aimed to build librarian awareness of Wikipedia,

Figure 2 #1Lib1Ref Campaign, January 2020.
Attribution: Kaizenify, CC BY-SA 4.0. < https://creativecommons.org/licenses/by-sa/4.0>, via Wikimedia Commons.

add citations to articles on Wikipedia, and fill gaps in online knowledge. Library and information professionals from across Africa came together to add accurate and reliable sources to Wikipedia articles, which created the opportunity to amplify stories of African cultures, heroes/heroines, and innovations by Africans in African languages (AfLIA, 2020a). As Felix Nartey, Wikimedia Foundation coordinator of the event, said, "The library community is an important ally for Wikipedia and our mission to ensure every human can freely share in the sum of all knowledge. By training librarians in Africa to contribute knowledge to Wikipedia, we're improving the encyclopedia's global representation and diversity, and we're developing local leaders in Africa for future initiatives that improves public knowledge online using reliable sources" (AfLIA, 2019).

The partnership, according to AfLIA Human Capacity Development & Training Director, Dr. Nkem E. Osuigwe, "will be a great opportunity for African librarians to collaborate creatively with Wikipedia to drive inclusiveness and more open sharing of knowledge on the global platform" (AfLIA, 2019). The week-long event hosted 241 editors who actively participated in the event out of the record number of 844 editors on the AfLibWk dashboard. In the end, 660,539 words were added with 27,846 edits made on 3,946 articles and 10,055 missing references were added. The edited articles gained over 33.6 million views during the African librarians' week campaign. Most articles about Africa in English and French Wikipedia were edited, though edits on English Wikipedia constituted 96 percent of the overall contribution made during the campaign. However, other local African-language Wikipedias, user groups, and communities, such as Igbo, Hausa, among others, were discovered in the process by African librarians. Librarians from the five regions of Africa; North, East, Central, West, and Southern Africa, from different library types were represented. At the end of the campaign, the top fifty contributors were awarded a certificate of contribution, while the top five also received a prize from AfLIA during the AfLIA 2021 conference in Accra, Ghana. African countries with the most editors, most edits/references added, and most innovative publicity about African librarians on social media were each awarded a plaque (AfLIA, 2020b).

After the AfLib week, AfLIA received a grant from the Wikimedia Foundation to hire a Wikipedian-in-Residence (WIR) and a curriculum development consultant (CDC). In August 2020, Alice Kibombo emerged as the WIR and in September Prof. Rosemary Shafack as the CDC (AfLIA, 2020c, 2020d, 2020e). Both appointees are librarians from Africa who are knowledgeable on the best integration of Wikipedia into African library system. The grant forms further partnership between the Wikimedia Foundation and AfLIA to collaborate in the Wikipedia in African Libraries Project to produce a suitable curriculum for training over 300 African library and information science professionals of at least ten LIS professionals each from thirty African countries (AfLIA, 2020c).

Prof. Rosemary M. Shafack, the appointed curriculum development consultant (CDC) for the Wikipedia in African Libraries' project is a professor of library and information science and the director of the University of Buea Library and Information Services. Her many years of experience in curriculum development as a university teacher is evident in her positions and involvements in many teaching modes. As the CDC and alongside the WIR, she will adapt the OCLC existing curriculum on Wikipedia + Libraries: Better Together, used to train American public librarians, to design an instructional module that will be suitable for training African librarians who will participate in the pilot testing and the two different cohorts of the Wikipedia in African Libraries project. This curriculum will equip participants with the skills to aid different user communities in using Wikipedia for learning, give life to their individual stories, and create contents in their native languages (AfLIA, 2020e).

The Wikipedian-in-Residence, Alice Kibombo is a practicing librarian at Goethe-Zentrum, Kampala, a member of Wikimedia Community User Group Uganda, and has coordinated many Wikimedia campaigns and projects locally and internationally. The WIR was signed to facilitate the WikiAfLibs training and work remotely with Prof. Rosemary Shafack, the CDC for the success of the project. Future participants will have three opportunities to partake in the course, that is, in the pilot testing or in any of the two cohorts. The pilot aimed to test the adapted curriculum took place from November 16 to December 20, 2020. The first cohort will be admitted from February to April, 2021, and second cohort from May to July, 2021 (AfLIA, 2020d, 2020g). Benefits of the course include training of librarians on how to assist their users to use Wikipedia, to create the opportunity for global communities to amplify their stories, and to nurture Wikipedia community and African libraries' relationships, leading to future collaborations and mutual benefit (AfLIA, 2020f). As she said in her tweet discussion with AfLIA on August 29, 2020, "It has the potential to positively influence information creation and dissemination in a number of ways . . . for starters, individuals will be in a position to identify and create content that would fill knowledge gaps." This surely is a mutual benefit to AfLIA and Wikipedia.

Moving Forward: Challenges and Opportunities
Wikipedia is a multilingual online encyclopedia, which maintains an open collaboration with the community of volunteer editors using a

wiki-based editing system. In African countries, this presents librarians with the challenge of locating the various language communities. As a result, some librarians may be working solo or struggle to engage with the Wikipedia community. Finding editors who speak the same language or librarians willing to join the movement and finding resources written in local languages can be a tedious task.

Librarians need to raise awareness on the relevance of Wikipedia in teaching, learning, and research. This awareness would expose the values and positive features of Wikipedia, which would help clear existing misconceptions surrounding Wikipedia. Librarians could learn from Wikipedia user groups, such as Wikimedia Nigeria, and local language hubs, which are creating awareness and collaborating effectively.

Wikipedia is a starting point for research and is often the top result in Google searches (OCLC, 2020). Wikipedia articles can link to external library resources such as institutional repositories. This creates visibility to not only the institutional repository and library holdings, but also the author of that intellectual work, which would in turn bring maximum impact to publications and improve the library's profile.

Wikipedia also gives room for amplification of stories that are not available on the open web (OCLC, 2020). Libraries, as a powerhouse of knowledge, hold a lot of stories, pertaining to histories, cultures, and indigenous knowledge that may not be in existence or openly accessible online. Librarians can write articles based on their frequently asked questions, reference queries, notable personalities, and burdening issues in their present environment with links to verifiable resources to back up the stories.

Using Wikipedia to teach research improves best practices such as proper and enhanced use of Wikipedia for research, learning, literature review, contribution to knowledge, coding, online etiquette, citation, and, above all, copy-right, among others (Hoeck & Hoffmann, 2013; Kalaf, 2018). Students being taught the dynamics of Wikipedia articles would take them into the world of critical thinking, reading, and deep research skills, because the hyperlinks that lead to different information would equip their flexibility in online navigation, intensify their literature search skills, as well as improve their source evaluation. An online

Wiki Edu handbook on evaluating Wikipedia is available to aid any user in the rudiments for evaluating the quality of articles, be able to recognize biases in any article, and develop strong habit in evaluating the resources being used while researching (Wikimedia Commons, 2016). Contributors can be identified by their username, which directs you to their user pages for further assessment. The progress of each article can be monitored and the article talk page is a good avenue to access the editing history, including the controversies surrounding any article.

Conclusion

Academic libraries in Africa partnering with Wikimedia projects is a relevant collaboration. It equips library professionals with the skills to freely add reliable contents to the free online encyclopedia as well as provide access for digital skills training to the community of librarians. The similarities coexisting in the mission and vision of the two entities necessitated the partnership. Wikipedia is a wonderland of information, therefore active involvement of libraries in editing Wikipedia will encourage proper and enhanced usage of Wikipedia for academic activities. Integration of Wikipedia into academic library services enhances free access to knowledge and encourages the building of further partnerships. The existing partnership serves as a litmus to the high compatibility and relevancy of long-term collaboration. Wikipedia promotes discoverability of libraries' resources and librarians improve the reliability of Wikipedia contents. Using Wikipedia is not something to be ashamed of, but an important tool to leverage on, in pursuit of your academic endeavor. Academic libraries + Wikimedia means sustainability of free knowledge/information and literacy for all.

References

AfLIA, (2019). African librarians invited to contribute knowledge to Wikipedia, through a new Wikimedia/AfLIA partnership. https://web.aflia. net/african-librarians-invited-to-contribute-knowledge-to-wikipedia-through-a-new-wikimedia-aflia-partnership/.

AfLIA, (2020a). All you need to know about the #AfLibWK and #1Lib1Ref Campaign. https://web.aflia.net/all-you-need-to-know-about-the-aflibwk-1lib1ref-campaign/.

AfLIA, (2020b). Recap: #AfLibWk campaign key stats, outcomes and top contributors. https://web.aflia.net/recap-aflibwk-campaign-key-stats-outcomes-and-top-contributors/.

AfLIA, (2020c). AfLIA receives grant from Wikipedia Foundation. https://web.aflia.net/aflia-receives-grant-from-wikimedia-foundation/.

AfLIA, (2020d). AfLIA gets a Wikipedian in residence. https://web.aflia.net/aflia-gets-a-wikipedian-in-residence/.

AfLIA, (2020e). AfLIA signs on a curriculum development consultant: Wikipedia in African Libraries Project. https://web.aflia.net/aflia-signs-on-a-curriculum-development-consultant-wikipedia-in-african-libraries-project/.

AfLIA, (2020f). Wikipedia project for African Librarians: Liberating Knowledge. https://web.aflia.net/wikipedia-project-for-african-librarians-liberating-knowledge/.

AfLIA, (2020g). Wikipedia in African Libraries Course: Call for participants for pilot testing. https://web.aflia.net/wikipedia-in-african-libraries-course-call-for-participants-for-pilot-testing/.

Hoeck, M. V., & Hoffmann, D. (2013). From audience to authorship to authority: Using Wikipedia to strengthen research and critical thinking skills. www.ala.org/acrl/sites/ala.org.acrl/files/content/conferences/confsandpreconfs/2013/papers/VanHoeckHoffmann_FromAudience.pdf.

Kalaf, (2018). A scholar advances academic research by editing Wikipedia. https://wikiedu.org/blog/2018/06/08/a-scholar-advances-academic-research-by-editing-wikipedia/.

Lally, A. M., & Dunford, C. E. (2007, May/June). Using Wikipedia to extend digital collections. *D-Library Magazine*, 13(5/6). ISSN 1082–9873. https://library.educause.edu/resources/2007/1/using-wikipedia-to-extend-digital-collections, www.dlib.org/dlib/may07/lally/05lally.html

Logan, D. W, Sandal, M., Gardner, P. P., Manske, M., & Bateman, A. (2010). Ten simple rules for editing Wikipedia. *30;6*(9). https://pubmed.ncbi.nlm.nih.gov/20941386/.

Lubbock, J. (2018). Wikipedia and libraries. *Journal of National and International Library and*

Information Issues, 28(1), 55–68. https://journals.sagepub.com/doi/10.1177/0955749018794968.

Neate, R. (2008). "Wikipedia founder Jimmy Wales goes bananas". *The Daily Telegraph*. Achieved from the original on November, 10, 2008. Retrieved May 28, 2020, from https://wikimediafoundation.org.

OCLC, (2020). Wikipedia + Libraries: Better together. www.oclc.org/en/member-stories-wikipedia-libraries.html.

O'Neal, Chris., (2006). Using Wikipedia in the classroom: A good starting point. www.edutopia.org/using-wikipedia-classroom.

Otis College LibGuides, (2020). Wikipedia: Strength & weaknesses. https://otis.libguides.com/Wikipedia/strengthsandweaknesses.

Stvilia, B., Twidale, M. B., Smith, L. C., & Gasser, L. (2008). Information quality work organization in Wikipedia. *Journal of the American Society for Information Science and Technology, 59*(6), 983–1001. https://onlineli brary.wiley.com/doi/full/10.1002/asi.20813.

UNESCO, (2017). UNESCO access to information policy. Retrieved from www.unesco.org/new/en/member-states/resources/website-toolkit/unesco-access-to-information-policy/

UNESCO, (2019). Access to Information gets an upgrade in SDG indicators framework.   https://en.unesco.org/news/Access-Information-gets-upgrade-sdg-Indicators-framework.

University of Nigeria Library, (2017). University of Nigeria Library hosts ART+ Feminism Wikipedia "Edit-A-Thon Event". http://libraryunn.blog spot.com/2017/03/university-of-nigeria-library-hosts-art.html.

Wikimedia, (2020). University of Ibadan Wikipedia Edit-a-thon: 1Lib1Ref. Wikipedia: Meetup/Wikimedia Nigeria/UI/1Lib1Ref. https://en.m.wiki pedia.org/wiki/Wikipedia:Meetup/wikimedia_Nigeria/ui/1Lib1Ref.

Wikimedia, (2021). Wikimedia fan club in Nigeria. https://wikimedia<fan_club_in_nigeria

Wikimedia Commons, (2016). Editing Wikipedia brochure (Wiki Education Foundation). https://commons.m.wikimedia.org.wiki/

Wikipedia, (2019). Wikipedia for Librarians. Wikipedia: WikiProject Libraries/Wikipedia for Librarians, Federal University of Agriculture Abeokuta. https://en.wikipedia.org/wiki/Wikipedia:WikiProject_Libraries/Wiki pedia_for_Librarian,Federal_University_of_Agriculture_Abeokuta/.

Wikipedia, (2021). Wikimedia movement. https://en.wikipedia.org/wiki/wikimedia_movement.

CHAPTER 9

ENGAGING STUDENT EMPLOYEE EXPERTISE TO IMPROVE WIKIPEDIA EDIT-A-THONS

Brittany Paloma Fiedler,[1] *Maggie Bukowski,*[1] *Chelsea Heinbach,*[1] *Eduardo Martinez-Flores,*[1] *and Rosan Mitola*[1]

[1] University of Nevada, Las Vegas

Abstract

Since 2007, the University Libraries at the University of Nevada, Las Vegas, has had a student employee peer learning program composed of six to seven undergraduate students. The Mason Undergraduate Peer Research Coaches, known as peer coaches, work within the instruction and outreach department co-teaching library instruction sessions and connecting with students through cocurricular outreach activities. When three librarians decided to plan their first Wikipedia edit-a-thon in 2017, the peer coaches became their collaborators. Since then, the peer coaches have developed lists of resources, identified notable individuals, evaluated Wikipedia pages, and worked with students during the event at orientation, citation, information, creation, and translation stations. They have also engaged in extra projects like creating playlists, designing swag, developing a trivia game, and pop-up tabling. Because of the

DOI: https://doi.org/10.3998/mpub.11778416.ch9.en

collaboration with the peer coaches, the edit-a-thons have developed and grown far beyond initial expectations. In this chapter, we will share the background and institutional context for our university and Wikipedia program; detail the collaborative efforts of library faculty, staff, and peer coaches at each stage; and share reflections and recommendations from the peer coaches themselves.

Keywords

Information literacy, Open pedagogy, Peer learning, Student employees, Student workers, Wikipedia, Wikipedia edit-a-thons

Introduction

> The most rewarding thing about being involved with these amazing events is getting to help students learn a new skill. Editing Wikipedia pages is a good way for students to expand their interest in technology. I have a sense of fulfillment after teaching how to edit, find information, and publish changes that will serve a potentially large number of people.
>
> —Vinicius Passos, Mason Undergraduate Peer Research Coach

Since spring 2018, the University of Nevada, Las Vegas (UNLV) University Libraries has hosted two Wikipedia edit-a-thons each year. These are organized by a planning team of three librarians, one staff member, and seven Mason Undergraduate Peer Research Coaches (known as peer coaches). The planning team is a large group with different backgrounds, ideas, strengths, and areas of expertise. At each edit-a-thon, participants are greeted and registered by a peer coach before they go to the Orientation Station to create an account and learn basic editing. Once participants feel confident, they choose whether to visit the Citation Station to add references, the Information Station to write text and add references, the Translation Station to translate Wikipedia pages between different languages, or the Creation Station to make new pages. Each station has a mix of peer coaches and library faculty and staff offering help and guidance.

The events feature musical playlists, a Wikipedia trivia game, and prizes—all designed and created by peer coaches. They are also responsible for selecting all the source materials and generating lists of Wikipedia pages that participants use (bit.ly/unlvwikipedia). The scope of the events has grown because the peer coaches' roles have expanded. This chapter will provide an overview of UNLV's institutional context, outline how library faculty and staff collaborate with peer coaches at each stage, and share thoughts from the peer coaches themselves.

Institutional Context

UNLV is a public, doctoral-granting research institution with just over 30,000 students enrolled (UNLV, n.d.-b). It is currently ranked the second most ethnically diverse university in the United States for undergraduate students (MacNeil, 2020) with 61 percent of students identifying as racial or ethnic minorities (UNLV, n.d.-a). Although the university doesn't track LGBTQ+ identities, Nevada is ranked third for the highest percentage of LGBTQ+ people in the United States (UCLA School of Law Williams Institute, 2019). In order to increase representation on Wikipedia and to empower and excite UNLV's students, each edit-a-thon focuses on members of different underrepresented groups.

Since 2007 the University Libraries has been home to the Mason Undergraduate Peer Research Coaches, a peer learning program composed of six to seven undergraduate students who work in the library twenty hours or less a week for hourly pay (Rinto et al., 2017). Peer learning can lead to improved classroom experiences for students who may prefer to ask a peer for assistance and can also result in more student-centered library programs when peer leaders are encouraged to share their own thoughts, ideas, and suggestions (Rinto et al., 2017). The peer coaches contribute to the teaching and outreach efforts of the Educational Initiatives department by co-teaching library instruction sessions alongside library faculty and staff and connecting with students through cocurricular learning activities.

In fall 2017, three librarians planned their first Wikipedia edit-a-thon, and the peer coaches became partners in organizing, designing, and working the event. Over the past seven edit-a-thons, a total of 183 editors have added over 22,500 words to Wikipedia on articles about women and nonbinary artists of color and notable members of the LGBTQ+, Latinx, and Indigenous communities.

Preparing for the Edit-a-Thon

It is important to have the entire planning team (which includes three librarians, one staff member, and six to seven peer coaches) together when picking a theme, date, and time to ensure everyone is interested in the topic and that there is enough employee coverage. Over time, library faculty and staff learned that it is hard to sustain excitement for doing the many hours of preliminary work necessary for the edit-a-thon if peer coaches are not able to actually attend. Choosing a theme related to social justice, anti-racist work, and gender equality also increases enthusiasm among all participants.

After a theme and date have been selected, the planning team meets and assigns roles to each member. Usually library faculty and staff communicate with teaching faculty and campus partners, present to classrooms and student organizations, create promotional materials, secure a budget, and coordinate room reservations and technology. Meanwhile, peer coaches research to make a comprehensive list of Wikipedia pages to be created or edited. First, they search the library catalog and pull materials that might encompass the theme. Then they explore the books and identify potential names. Each person's Wikipedia page is categorized into how much work is required to improve it and added to a list in a shared spreadsheet. Organizing the list this way helps to connect edit-a-thon participants with pages that match their editing proficiency.

Usually the peer coaches can complete this work independently, but they occasionally need guidance. Echoing research on peer-assisted learning, the peer coaches usually seek help from one another (Rinto et al., 2017). If the same questions are repeatedly asked and discussed, they loop in library faculty and staff. After a couple of event planning cycles, library faculty and staff discovered that the peer coaches wanted additional group discussions and more opportunities to ask questions, so they built in extra time for this during meetings. For example, during the planning for the Indigenous edit-a-thon, peer coaches identified materials in the collection that were outdated. Library faculty and staff noticed the materials perpetuated the themes of racism, sexism, and colonialism that the team wanted to eradicate from Wikipedia, so they discussed with the peer coaches what to look for in a text to determine whether it was an appropriate source for the event. This led to a broader conversation about why problematic materials are a part of library collections in the first place. Searching for materials reinforces skills the peer coaches already have while discussing and evaluating sources contributes to a more nuanced understanding of the collection. The entire process improves their information literacy expertise, supporting their dual roles as students and employees.

During one event planning meeting, the peer coaches and library faculty and staff had different scopes in mind for the edit-a-thon about Indigenous people. Originally, library faculty and staff thought the event would focus on Indigenous people from what is now the United States, but the peer coaches wanted to include Indigenous people throughout the world. After a discussion about scope, the team expanded the theme to include Indigenous people from all of North and South America. This led to the peer coaches discovering that many robust Wikipedia pages existed on Indigenous people in Spanish that were short or nonexistent in English. As a result, since many of the peer coaches speak Spanish, they developed lists of pages that could be translated and learned about Wikipedia's processes for translation (Wikipedia contributors, 2020). These discoveries greatly increased excitement for the event, and the peer coaches came up with the idea for adding a Translation Station to the edit-a-thon. This is just one of many examples of how their ideas and suggestions improve the events.

After a few edit-a-thons, library faculty and staff recognized it would be beneficial to develop a formal curriculum for editing Wikipedia. Since peer coaches regularly co-teach instruction sessions, they were involved in developing and creating the training. When peer coaches first start working in the Libraries, they go through a comprehensive training program that involves discussions of pedagogy, conducting teaching observations, teaching mock lessons, and finally being assessed when they co-teach. Because of these experiences, senior peer coaches were particularly well-positioned to create a curriculum for Wikipedia edit-a-thon training that included lesson plans, learning activities, and assessment. Two peer coaches worked with a librarian to develop an outline of the training program and then worked by themselves on each lesson plan.

An ongoing challenge of peer coach collaborations is working with their complicated schedules. The peer coaches who created the training could not teach their lesson plans because of scheduling conflicts, so the librarian had to deliver them. Managing student schedules often requires flexibility. While creative problem-solving can help to an extent, honesty, communication, and time are also important factors on how well these kinds of collaborations work.

Along with codeveloping the training program, peer coaches have asked for or been assigned other supplementary projects. These tasks are not event essentials but are instead designed to either utilize their existing strengths or to provide an opportunity for growth. These projects include developing a playlist, designing and making buttons, creating a Wikipedia trivia game, and pop-up tabling. Doing the same kind of work for two similar events each year is monotonous, so offering these other activities keeps team members engaged. It's important to remember that these new ideas require time, energy, and project management, and they don't always work out as planned. Established edit-a-thons could add one or two supplementary projects, but new programs should focus on the essentials.

Debriefing with All Collaborators

A week or two after each edit-a-thon, the planning team meets to debrief. This is particularly important because the team's varied schedules often mean that the only times everyone is together is at the initial planning meeting and at the event itself. The debrief meeting is an opportunity to share the number of participants, the editing statistics, and any particularly inspiring anecdotes. The team reflects on what worked well and what could be improved. Sometimes the issues discussed actually came up before the event, but there wasn't enough time or resources to pre-emptively fix them. By revisiting these, the planning team can evaluate how serious the problems ended up being and then plan appropriately for the next edit-a-thon.

The relationship-building and culture-creating necessary for this kind of collaboration do not happen overnight or even over the course of planning one event. It is ongoing work that begins each time a new peer coach or a new library faculty or staff member starts working in the department. It is also not the most efficient way to organize an outreach program. Having one person in charge who unilaterally makes decisions would be far less time-consuming. However, the edit-a-thons would not be as inclusive or continue to improve as they have without input from each member of the team.

Hearing from the Peer Coaches

Library faculty and staff learn from the peer coaches through the practice of critical reflection. Their feedback informs many aspects of how the department does its work, including the edit-a-thons. Coauthor and peer coach Eduardo recently asked seven peer coaches to reflect on their experiences in helping prepare for and facilitate these events. Four themes emerged: (1) their identities, interests, and experiences at a diverse university influence their relationship with their jobs; (2) planning edit-a-thons utilizes their strengths and increases their skills; (3) their familiarity with Wikipedia as a resource and as a community has grown; and (4) each peer coach faces unique challenges in this work. He also explicitly asked them for what advice they have for other student employees and for librarians who are interested in collaboratively planning a Wikipedia edit-a-thon. We share and summarize their reflections and responses here.

Diversity, Identities, and Interests

All the peer coaches felt the edit-a-thons are important and the focus on underrepresented groups is particularly salient because of UNLV's student population. Many students see themselves in the identities the edit-a-thons have explored. For example, "I am Latinx and I really enjoyed researching and studying about 'my people'. It made me proud to be a member of this community" (E. Rodriguez, personal communication, July 17, 2020). On the other hand, some peer coaches preferred to learn about important people who have different identities than their own. Although none of the peer coaches are Indigenous, two identified the Indigenous edit-a-thon as their favorite because they had an opportunity to learn more about American history. They also understood the importance of approaching the research critically and with care because they did not want to make or perpetuate assumptions. The peer coaches felt that "amplifying marginalized voices is rewarding work" (B. Lopez, personal communication, July 17, 2020) because "Wikipedia is such a widely used site and it's important to make sure that the information on it is diversified" (R. D'Amato, personal communication, July 17, 2020). The peer coaches anticipate that even at predominantly white institutions, edit-a-thons focusing on underrepresented groups would likely help students with marginalized identities feel more welcome and create learning opportunities for others. A case study showing that students who participated in an Art + Feminism edit-a-thon had increased awareness of the gender disparities of Wikipedia supports the peer coaches' beliefs (Vetter & Sarraf, 2019).

Strengths and Prior Knowledge

This project made space for peer coaches to both share their strengths and prior knowledge and improve upon their less practiced skills. For example, B. Lopez (personal communication, July 17, 2020) said, "Bringing all my identities and interests to the table has been a strength. I may not have always been aware that I was bringing them to the table, but adding my perspectives has helped contribute." Three out of seven peer coaches cited their creativity as an important asset. "The librarians we work with encourage us to express our creativity freely because they create a space where our ideas are heard and often implemented, and they also give us the opportunity to lead different parts and roles of the events" (E. Martinez-Flores, personal communication, August 1, 2020). While only one peer coach explicitly mentioned being bilingual as an added skill, the monolingual library faculty and staff would like to emphasize how meaningful it is to work with a largely bilingual team because 79 percent of people in the United States only speak English (U.S. Census Bureau, 2015).

Peer coaches generally felt this work improved their skills in event planning, leadership, technology, and research. Almost every peer coach described increased confidence in teaching, specifically discussing different sources, understanding open access, and utilizing Wikipedia in the research process. "We have done a lot of teaching in this job, but the Wikipedia events have helped me grow as a teacher . . . I really do have more to offer . . . than I ever thought" (E. Martinez-Flores, personal communication, July 28, 2020). They also felt that Wikipedia edit-a-thon instruction is more personal than their other efforts in the classroom and appreciated the opportunity to work one-on-one with other students. "Teaching should be a dialogue, not a monologue" (P. Gutierrez, personal communication, July 17, 2020).

Wikipedia: The Resource and the Community

Although all the peer coaches had experiences as Wikipedia readers, they felt their involvement taught them many things about the website. First, they developed a better understanding of Wikipedia as an important resource. Not only is it a good place to start researching almost any topic, it is also one of the first open-access information sources they have used as university students. "[This event] has expanded my appreciation of information that is offered without a pay wall . . . there can be factual and constructive information . . . free of charge" (V. Passos, personal communication, July 17, 2020). Six out of seven peer coaches discovered the lack of representation on Wikipedia through their research and work. They shared that while it was exciting to improve the pages of talented and notable people from underrepresented groups, it was also disappointing to discover that their contributions were previously unrecognized. Finally, the peer coaches learned about the active editing community that creates Wikipedia. "Editing Wikipedia is really great because you get to be a part of something that helps keep the whole world informed. It's always fun to look at something you edited on the official page and think, 'wow I really did that!'" (E. Martinez-Flores, personal communication, July 28, 2020).

Challenges

The peer coaches felt that there were some challenges both in editing Wikipedia and in planning events. Two peer coaches noted the lack of resources in the Libraries' collections. "The most challenging part for me has been finding sufficient information about certain people . . . It is hard in the sense that sometimes I feel that the person deserves a wiki page, but it is nearly impossible to find more information about their life or works" (D. Ramos-Candelas, personal communication, July 17, 2020). Two peer coaches felt they struggled with the actual writing of information on Wikipedia pages. One peer coach felt their greatest struggle was summarizing sources into their own words while another felt that because the topics are so sensitive they needed to be particularly careful with their word choice and tone. For events, challenges include a lack of routine during planning, the struggle of carrying over editing skills between events, and the difficulty of keeping the edit-a-thons exciting for both peer coaches and participants.

Recommendations

Finally, the peer coaches have edit-a-thon advice. For student employees, they overwhelmingly suggested that they just dive in and not stress about editing Wikipedia. For librarians, they recommended involving student employees from the beginning. The peer coaches felt that librarians should not be afraid to learn alongside their student employees, but a Wikipedia editing teaching plan should be developed in advance. While this seems contradictory, librarians do not need to create the teaching plan from nothing. Find an existing online resource about editing and dedicate adequate time for everyone to learn together (Bukowski & Heinbach, 2020). In fact, one peer coach felt that seeing librarians also in a learning role was an important experience. "I have learned that not knowing something doesn't take my position as an expert or as the teacher away. I appreciated navigating Wikipedia with librarians I consider experts and seeing that they were looking for answers alongside us" (B. Lopez, personal communication, July 17, 2020). Their final piece of advice is "don't forget to ensure your students feel welcome and cared for!" (P. Gutierrez, personal communication, July 17, 2020).

Conclusion

At this point, the edit-a-thons have grown beyond expectations. The program is well-attended, instructors offer extra credit to participating students, and one instructor replaced their traditional research paper assignment with one where students create new pages for women of color artists. The team hopes to expand the program in a few ways. First, library faculty and staff want to grow partnerships with UNLV instructors by bringing Wikipedia into more classes. Additionally, the planning team would like to start a community of practice that regularly edits Wikipedia together. This would help keep skills fresh, increase confidence in Wikipedian identities, and honor the work of the peer coaches through continued use of event materials. The team would also love to involve community partners like regional colleges and nonprofit organizations. Finally, because the peer coaches have developed extensive lists of pages to edit, library faculty and staff plan to share resources through an online edit-a-thon.

There are many possibilities for the future of the team's Wikipedia work, and all of them will include the voices, perspectives, and efforts of peer coaches. The peer coaches share their expertise in very event-specific ways such as editing Wikipedia and teaching others to edit. Preparing for and working the event also contributes to the peer coaches' professional development because they are able to expand their skills in areas such as project management, leadership, research, and information literacy. It is important for academic libraries to create personally and professionally fulfilling student employment opportunities when possible. The success of the program is because of the collaboration and teamwork shared between the peer coaches and library faculty and staff. We are thankful for the time and resources that allow everyone on the team to learn, grow, and work together.

References

Bukowski, M., & Heinbach, C. (2020). Wikipedia edit-a-thon: Teaching yourself. https://guides.library.unlv.edu/c.php?g=1015316&p=7354288.

MacNeil, S. (2020). UNLV again named one of most diverse campuses in country. *Las Vegas Sun*. https://lasvegassun.com/news/2020/sep/14/unlv-again-named-one-of-most-diverse-campuses-us/.

Rinto, E., Watts, J., & Mitola, R. (2017). The Mason undergraduate peer research coach program at the University of Nevada, Las Vegas Libraries. In E. Rinto, J. Watts, & R. Mitola (Eds.), *Peer-assisted learning in academic libraries* (pp. 64–79). Libraries Unlimited.

UCLA School of Law Williams Institute. (2019). LGBT demographic data interactive. https://williamsinstitute.law.ucla.edu/visualization/lgbt-stats/?topic=LGBT&area=32#about-the-data.

UNLV. (n.d.-a). About UNLV. www.unlv.edu/about.

UNLV. (n.d.-b). Facts and stats. www.unlv.edu/about/facts-stats.

U.S. Census Bureau. (2015). Detailed languages spoken at home and ability to speak English for the population 5 years and over: 2009–2013. www.census.gov/data/tables/2013/demo/2009-2013-lang-tables.html.

Vetter, M. A., & Sarraf, K. S. (2019). Assessing the art + feminism edit-a-thon for Wikipedia literacy, learning outcomes, and critical thinking. *Interactive Learning Environments*. https://doi.org/10.1080/10494820.2020.1805772.

Wikipedia contributors. (2020, September 22). Wikipedia: Translation. *Wikipedia, The Free Encyclopedia*. Retrieved September 24, 2020, from https://en.wikipedia.org/w/index.php?title=Wikipedia:Translation&oldid=979764156.

CHAPTER 10

CROWDSOURCING AND COLLABORATION: ACADEMIC LIBRARIES AS PARTNERS IN NNLM'S #CITENLM WIKIPEDIA EDIT-A-THONS

Kelsey Cowles,[1] Ann Glusker,[2] Aimee Gogan,[3] Alicia Lillich,[4] Margie Sheppard,[5] Elaina Vitale,[6] Liz Waltman,[7] Tess Wilson,[8] and Amanda J. Wilson[9]

[1] NNLM Middle Atlantic Region, [2] University of California, Berkley, [3] National Library of Medicine, [4] National Institutes of Health Library, [5] NNLM MidContinental Region, [6] Dartmouth College, [7] NNLM Southeastern/Atlantic Region, [8] NNLM Middle Atlantic Region, [9] National Library of Medicine

Author Note

Funding details: This work was supported by the National Library of Medicine (NLM), National Institutes of Health (NIH) under cooperative agreement numbers UG4LM012342 with the University of Pittsburgh, Health Sciences Library System; UG4LM012340 with the University of Maryland, Baltimore; and UG4LM012344 with the University of Utah Spencer S. Eccles Health Sciences Library. The content is solely the responsibility of the authors and does not necessarily represent the official views of the National Institutes of Health.

DOI: https://doi.org/10.3998/mpub.11778416.ch10.en

Abstract

Although academic skepticism of Wikipedia's value as an information resource is widespread, the collaboratively created online encyclopedia is in fact one of the most frequently used health information resources in the world, including among students and professionals. As a result, the U.S.-based Network of the National Library of Medicine (NNLM) has, since 2018, organized biannual "#CiteNLM" edit-a-thons aimed at strengthening Wikipedia's health pages by adding content and citations to trusted sources of information.

The first #CiteNLM edit-a-thon was a one-day virtual event in April 2018; since then NNLM's edit-a-thons have evolved into month-long campaigns engaging primarily academic libraries with in-person edit-a-thons as well as virtual events. Hundreds of students, faculty, and library staff across the country (many of whom were new to Wikipedia editing) have collaborated in NNLM's efforts to support universal access to high-quality health information. To date, over 600 health articles have been edited by over 400 editors. The current #CiteNLM campaign structure makes it easy for either individuals or groups to contribute or host affiliated events, which can include classroom exercises, citizen science projects, or library engagement efforts.

Introduction

Despite widespread skepticism of the value of Wikipedia as an information resource both within and outside academia, the collaboratively created online encyclopedia is one of the most frequently used health information resources in the world (Heilman & West, 2015). This includes students and professionals and also holds true in the medical field, with over 90 percent of medical students (Heilman & West, 2015; Metcalfe & Powell, 2011) and 50–70 percent of physicians (Heilman et al., 2011) using Wikipedia to find health information. Wikipedia's health articles receive over 6.5 billion page views annually and are written in over 255 languages (Heilman & West, 2015).

As a means of improving this popular and accessible health information resource, the Network of the National Library of Medicine (NNLM) has, since 2018, organized biannual "#CiteNLM" edit-a-thons focused on using trusted sources of health information to add citations and content. The National Library of Medicine (NLM), which is part of the U.S. National Institutes of Health (NIH), is the world's largest biomedical library and repository of digital and print health information resources. NNLM serves as an outreach arm of NLM focused on consistent and innovative engagement with both individuals and organizations, delivery of specialized trainings, and facilitation of health-focused events.

NNLM's #CiteNLM campaigns dovetail nicely with two goals of NNLM and NLM. First, part of NNLM's mission is to improve the public's access to information to enable them to make informed decisions about their health (NNLM, Mission and Goals, para 1, n.d.-b). Although NLM is known for its digital resources (e.g., PubMed and MedlinePlus), a huge proportion of Internet users seek health information on websites like Wikipedia, making it an important resource for libraries providing health information to be aware of and familiar with. Much of NNLM's work aims to promote health equity and informed decision-making by increasing digital health literacy. Improving the reliability of Wikipedia's health pages is one way to meet Internet users where they are already comfortable looking for health information online for themselves and their families. NNLM believes that if it applies its human resources to enhancing Wikipedia articles, new partners will engage with NNLM's work and more of the public will be reached by the broad spectrum of NLM's health information resources.

Second, NNLM and NLM also have a formal commitment to promoting and supporting citizen science and crowdsourcing activities (NNLM, Crowdsourcing, para 1, n.d.-a). NNLM works to encourage community participation in the entire scientific research process via training for information professionals and collaboration with organizations working in this field. While these activities have reached a wide variety of audiences, academic libraries have been particularly strong partners, especially in #CiteNLM campaigns. Wikipedia editing is a form of crowdsourcing and an avenue for public participation in the dissemination of high-quality research and health information. As of December 2020, over 400 individuals across the country have participated in #CiteNLM by editing over 600 health articles. Seven academic libraries have also contributed by hosting affiliated events.

Campaign History and Evolution

Background

The initial idea for implementing a series of online edit-a-thons began at NLM in a conversation with Wikipedian Ashleigh Coren during fall 2017, at a time when NNLM leadership was seeking innovative methods of engagement to expand beyond one-way communications like email newsletters. Edit-a-thon campaigns presented a creative opportunity to engage members through health topics of broad interest. After a call for interested parties in January 2018, a project planning team, the Wikipedia Working Group (WWG), was formed of librarians from NNLM's regional and national offices. The WWG held a series of conversations with the Wikipedia medical community about their needs. Notably, trailblazer Dr. James Heilman, the founder of WikiProject:Medicine, consulted and later provided training. Due to its adaptability and simplicity, Wikipedia Library's already established and widely recognized #1Lib1Ref campaign, which encourages librarians to improve Wikipedia by adding citations, served as a model ("The Wikipedia," 2020).

2018 Campaigns

The topic chosen for the inaugural NNLM edit-a-thon in spring 2018, a one-day virtual event, was rare diseases. The WWG, which at the time included just one experienced Wikipedia editor, quickly learned the basics of editing biomedical articles in order to teach others. The WWG also created a project page in Wikipedia and a Wikimedia Labs Programs & Events Dashboard (NNLM Edit-a-thon, 2018), so participants could easily locate suggested articles and other information about the project and the WWG could quantitatively track event participation.

Once issues like time zone differences and platform choices had been ironed out, the next major challenge was to communicate plans for a virtual edit-a-thon to potential participants who were likely either unfamiliar with Wikipedia editing or accustomed to in-person editing events. Fortunately, since NNLM is an outreach-focused organization, various channels for project promotion already existed and creation of the #CiteNLM hashtag allowed participants to 'gather' on social media, both synchronously and asynchronously, to follow the work of their fellow editors across the country.

Ahead of the one-day edit-a-thon, Dr. James Heilman presented a well-attended customized training on behalf of the WWG which subsequently formed the basis for all future #CiteNLM trainings. Although the inaugural #CiteNLM event lasted only one day, it ran for twelve hours to give participants across the country ample time to join. WWG members took two-hour shifts staffing a virtual meeting room that participants could visit at any time to edit, ask questions, and connect with fellow participants and campaign organizers.

To evaluate the first campaign, the WWG gathered quantitative data from the Event Dashboard (NNLM Edit-a-thon, 2018), from Wikipedia itself, and from NNLM social media accounts. At least thirty-two editors edited at least 111 articles. Notably, Dashboard statistics likely underestimated true participation because the importance of Dashboard registration was not heavily emphasized during training and promotion for the first event. Participants came predominantly from the library community, which reflected the audiences reached most effectively by existing NNLM communication channels. Although overall engagement was lower than the WWG had hoped given the number of attendees at the training session, and it became evident that quantitatively measuring the impact of edit-a-thons can be complicated, this campaign proved that #CiteNLM could be a creative and successful way to engage member organizations and individuals.

Ready to test an improved campaign structure and grow #CiteNLM, the WWG soon began planning the Fall 2018 campaign focused on women's health. The broader topic of the second campaign raised a new question: with so many women's health-related topics, how should an editor choose an in-scope article to edit? A simple way is to focus on articles that, according to Wikipedia's quality scale, rank lower:

C-class, Start-class, and Stub-class articles typically have lots of room for improvement, while B-class and above articles are already fairly complete ("Wikipedia Assessment," 2020). Lower-ranked articles were selected for recommendation to participants as editing targets.

The WWG planned wider promotional activities and more robust training. Three training sessions, each hosted by two NNLM staff, included an overview of Wikipedia, editing basics, and NLM resources for improving articles. Lasting around thirty minutes, these were intentionally brief to ensure ease of repeatability and minimize the time commitment needed from participants, were offered well in advance of the one-day edit-a-thon, and were recorded for asynchronous viewing. The virtual editing event utilized the same all-day drop-in structure as the spring 2018 event.

The second campaign, as expected, went more smoothly than the first. Dashboard numbers were more robust, owing partly to greater participation and partly to an increased proportion of participants registering so that their contributions could be tracked: at least fifty editors edited at least 204 articles. Following the now-repeated success of #CiteNLM, WWG members began to give presentations and poster sessions about the campaigns at a variety of conferences around the country. Presentations remain an important component of #CiteNLM outreach and have led to new professional connections and more detailed self-reflection. The WWG also remained committed to continual improvement and internally evaluated each aspect of the fall 2018 campaign by assessing content and processes from multiple perspectives to identify potential modifications for the next campaign.

2019 Campaigns

As an example of the WWG's willingness to try new approaches, the WWG chose to hold its spring 2019 event at the 2019 Medical Library Association (MLA) annual meeting. This in-person session, sponsored by the MLA Health Disparities Special Interest Group, focused on the topic of health equity. Because the event occurred at the MLA conference, promotion was primarily aimed at health sciences librarians through channels like NNLM regional blogs and social media, MLA chapter email lists, and the MLA newsletter. Though the WWG had successfully held virtual events in the past, it was gratifying to work with fifty-four volunteer editors in person to improve content related to health disparities. The collaborative atmosphere and success of this event inspired the WWG to explore ways to incorporate in-person events for future campaigns, leading to significant structural innovations for the fall 2019 campaign.

In advance of the fall 2019 campaign, the WWG focused on enhancing the #CiteNLM experience with a more user-friendly web presence and a longer campaign period—two full months—coupled with support for institutions to host affiliated local events at any time during this period. This campaign did not offer a dedicated one-day virtual edit-a-thon; the WWG instead invited individual participants to attend a kickoff training session and then edit independently throughout October and November. The WWG built a new web page (https://nnlm.gov/national/guides/ccs/wikipedia-edit-thon) with everything needed to host affiliated events or participate as an individual. A new #CiteNLM Guide for Organizers, adapted from #1Lib1Ref, laid out the steps for hosting independent events in a straightforward PDF format. This campaign was the WWG's most successful yet, with at least 108 editors and 9 affiliated events, several of which are detailed below.

2020 Campaigns

The WWG planned for spring 2020 largely by looking to build on the successes of fall 2019; the only major change was a reduction in the campaign period from two months to one to reduce the amount of staff time required. Unfortunately, April 2020 proved to be an extremely difficult time for libraries to offer programming as institutions scrambled to shift operations from in-person to virtual in the midst of a global pandemic. It is also likely that individual participation was reduced by the dramatically altered circumstances as potential participants focused on core job responsibilities and adapting to the rapidly evolving situation. As a result, overall participation was fairly low: forty-nine editors participated and only two institutions held affiliated editing events. The WWG viewed the challenges of the spring 2020

#CiteNLM campaign not as failures but as informative setbacks that provided motivation to make #CiteNLM more flexible and better able to meet the ongoing need for virtual programming opportunities.

Acknowledging the altered working conditions due to the COVID-19 pandemic, the WWG approached the fall 2020 campaign with renewed energy and developed a new hybrid campaign structure combining a month-long campaign period for affiliated events with a scheduled two-hour live collaborative edit-a-thon for individuals. The campaign training webinar featured strategies and resources for institutions to host their own virtual #CiteNLM edit-a-thon any time during the month of October. At the live event, participants received a brief training and then joined breakout sessions to edit articles related to the campaign topic of maternal and child health, chat and ask questions about Wikipedia, and connect with the #CiteNLM community. Over thirty editors participated in this virtual event and many have expressed excitement about making their first Wikipedia edit during the session.

Leading up to the fall 2020 event, a new outreach campaign was launched aimed at reaching library and information science (LIS) students. This group is an intended audience for NNLM outreach and LIS students are well-situated to be excellent Wikipedia contributors due to their likely interest in information literacy, research, and reference. The WWG invited students to join the two-hour live editing event, pitching it as an opportunity to meet practicing information professionals and network with other LIS students from around the country while also learning about Wikipedia editing and Wikipedia's health information. Messaging was sent to MLIS programs promoting the #CiteNLM edit-a-thon as an opportunity to build reference skills, health information literacy, familiarity with trustworthy health information resources, and an understanding of how to utilize Wikipedia responsibly. As a result of this simple campaign, LIS students from at least six different programs across the country joined the virtual editing event. The WWG hopes that these new editors will continue to contribute to Wikipedia and pass information about the importance and ease of doing so along to their colleagues as they finish their degrees and enter the field.

To reach a broader audience, training opportunities were expanded to include a four-week asynchronous online course entitled *Wikipedia + Libraries: NNLM* (https://nnlm.gov/wikipedia-libraries-nnlm), which ran concurrently with the campaign and was taught by members of the WWG. Tailored to a librarian audience, the course introduced over thirty participants to the importance of Wikipedia's health and medical information, the basics of Wikipedia editing, and suggestions for incorporating Wikipedia into their library's programming and instruction. In total, between the virtual event, *Wikipedia + Libraries* students, and other participants, eighty-six editors edited seventy-seven Wikipedia articles for the fall 2020 campaign.

Academic Libraries as Partners

Through the six #CiteNLM campaigns to date, academic librarians and libraries have been vital partners in NNLM's work to improve health information on Wikipedia. Academic libraries are well-situated to do this work since they tend to have existing information or health literacy programming that #CiteNLM can be used alongside; experience with instruction; topical expertise; and a connection with academic infrastructure that places value on dissemination of high-quality health information and research. Examining academic libraries' motivations for participating in #CiteNLM and their experiences hosting campaign-affiliated editing events provides valuable insight into the campaigns' successes and challenges. These events are also informative case studies for incorporation of Wikipedia editing into academic library programming and instruction. Through the spring 2020 #CiteNLM campaign, seven academic libraries hosted affiliated editing events, and four of these responded to a survey about their experiences. The host libraries were Indiana University Ruth Lilly Medical Library, Massachusetts College of Liberal Arts Freel Library, Radford University McConnell Library, University of California, Los Angeles Biomedical Library (UCLA), University of Maryland, Baltimore Health Sciences and Human Services Library (UMB), University of Massachusetts Lamar Soutter Library (UMass), and University of Pennsylvania Biomedical Library (UPenn).

Choosing to Host

The Wikipedia Working Group employed a suite of engagement tools to reach academic partners and raise awareness of #CiteNLM. Several libraries became involved with #CiteNLM through their established connection with NNLM as hosts of NNLM Regional Medical Libraries (UCLA, UMass, UMB). UPenn, which does not host a Regional Medical Library, learned of #CiteNLM through individual librarians' participation in the 2019 MLA immersion session. The remaining partner libraries learned of #CiteNLM via online trainings and promotional messages distributed via social media and email.

Regardless of how they learned about #CiteNLM, academic library partners ultimately chose to host #CiteNLM events for several reasons. UMB noted that holding an in-person #CiteNLM event simply allowed for a fun, collaborative library program to engage faculty and students from across campus without much staff time needed for development. Several institutions cited the high number of residents and medical students utilizing Wikipedia on a daily basis as a driving factor. Participating in a #CiteNLM event allows medical students to learn more about this information resource and have a hand in directly improving health information widely utilized by providers and patients. In alignment with the core mission of the #CiteNLM campaigns, the desire to make Wikipedia a more credible and reliable information resource was also an important factor in why libraries decided to host #CiteNLM events. As UMass noted, engaging knowledgeable people to edit Wikipedia allows subject matter experts to share their expertise on a topic and provides the public with a more credible source of health information.

Implementation and Collaboration

UCLA and UPenn collaborated creatively with other university departments to position #CiteNLM alongside Health Literacy Month and Open Access Week. UCLA also hosted their event in conjunction with

UCLA's Centennial Initiative, pulling in faculty and audiences from on campus and from the wider University of California system. Others libraries opted to hold stand-alone events that better suited their programming needs. Some partner libraries hosted multiple sessions (e.g., a training preceding the actual edit-a-thon or several scheduled editing events to allow varied audiences to participate), while others held one event combining training and editing. The range of ways in which academic library partners have tailored #CiteNLM to fit their programming needs demonstrates the campaign's adaptability to various contexts even within the academic library.

To facilitate connections between planned library programming and #CiteNLM, academic library partners effectively utilized both NLM's wide array of digital health information resources (e.g., MedlinePlus) and NNLM Wikipedia editing resources (e.g., the Organizers' Guide and online trainings). All of the WWG's academic library host partners stated that they utilized the Organizers' Guide to help plan their event and then adapted NNLM's materials in various ways to fit their local needs. For example, UPenn created training materials based on NNLM's but with additional information about their locally available databases. UMB used NNLM's trainings as a basis for the training offered at their in-person event and utilized linked resources from the #CiteNLM web page to identify articles in need of editing. UMass relied on NNLM's promotional materials to publicize their event and on NNLM's recorded trainings to introduce remote editors to Wikipedia editing. Partnering with NNLM's Pacific Southwest Regional office, librarians from the UCLA Biomedical Library created training materials specific to the campus. They promoted directly to the UCLA MLIS program, recruiting students to participate in the campaign and even help with creating the event Dashboard. The team also heavily promoted the event through the OpenUCLA Centennial Initiative, which was open to the entire campus as well as the public. Finally, many institutions diverged from the topic of the current #CiteNLM campaign, choosing instead to adapt the materials to a topic of greater interest to their local audience.

Evaluation

Each partner library learned valuable lessons and identified opportunities for improvement of future #CiteNLM events. Most partners identified a desire for a greater number of participants at their events and plan to address this issue in several ways. Since upcoming events will most likely be virtual for the foreseeable future, some institutions are exploring the possibility of holding edit-a-thons as asynchronous events similar to the main #CiteNLM month-long campaigns to enable more students, staff, and faculty to participate as their schedules allow. Partner libraries also mentioned plans to expand promotion to wider audiences (e.g., through posted advertisements in spaces frequented by students and hospital staff), advertise earlier, and collaborate with university health sciences departments to draw in more editors by emphasizing the educational potential of edit-a-thon participation.

In some cases, event location may have contributed to low participation. Due to space restrictions, UMB held their event in library classrooms located in the basement away from the usual library traffic. They hypothesized that moving future in-person events to a central location on campus or in the library may pique the curiosity of passers-by and lead to increased attendance. UMass experienced difficulties tracking participation because not all participants joined the event dashboard, so their edits were not captured. In spite of reported lower-than-desired attendance in some cases, all responding partner libraries agreed that taking part in #CiteNLM helped transform Wikipedia users into contributors by changing their perceptions of Wikipedia. Participants and hosts both learned that they could make an impactful contribution to Wikipedia by becoming editors and improving the encyclopedia's health information.

The NNLM WWG is extremely appreciative of the work their academic library partners have done to bolster the success of #CiteNLM and hopes that these collaborations will grow even stronger for future editing campaigns. Partner feedback has consistently proved essential for shaping the future direction of #CiteNLM and academic libraries will continue to be a core audience for the WWG's efforts to improve health information on Wikipedia, even as the WWG continues to think about ways to effectively tailor the campaigns for new audiences.

Looking Forward

Looking to the future, the WWG has identified several avenues to expand the reach and impact of #CiteNLM campaigns. Given the success of the fall 2020 virtual edit-a-thon, this format will be repeated in spring 2021. The *Wikipedia + Libraries* course will also be offered again alongside the spring 2021 campaign. The WWG plans to continue and expand its outreach to LIS students and programs by repeating fall 2020's outreach campaign and pilot testing a program-in-a-box designed to make it easy for LIS faculty to teach about evaluating and contributing to Wikipedia's health information in any class where it would be relevant. Finally, the WWG hopes to partner more closely with health sciences students and faculty for future campaigns, as their topical expertise is a largely untapped but promising resource.

The WWG continually takes qualitative and quantitative feedback into account in improving each successive campaign in order to better reach and serve its audiences (see Cowles et al., 2020 for greater detail). It is their hope that as a result, #CiteNLM will continue to engage new editors and empower them to contribute further to the important and ongoing work of improving the reliability of Wikipedia's health information.

References

Cowles K., Sheppard M., Waltman E., & Wilson T. K. (2020). Crowdsourcing and collaboration from coast to coast: NNLM's #CiteNLM Wikipedia edit-a-thons. *Journal of Electronic Resources Librarianship*, 32(4), 267–75. https://doi.org/10.1080/1941126X.2020.1821991

Heilman, J. M., Kemmann, E., Bonert, M., Chatterjee, A., Ragar, B., Beards, G. M., Iberri, D. J., Harvey, M., Thomas, B., Stomp, W., Martone, M. F., Lodge, D. J., Vondracek, A., de Wolff, J. F., Liber, C., Grover, S. C., Vickers, T. J., Meskó, B., & Laurent, M. R. (2011). Wikipedia: A key tool for global public health promotion. *Journal of Medical Internet Research, 13*(1), e14. https:// doi.org/10.2196/jmir.1589

Heilman J. M., & West A. G. (2015). Wikipedia and medicine: Quantifying readership, editors, and the significance of natural language. *Journal of Medical Internet Research, 17*(3): e62. https://doi.org/10.2196/jmir.4069.

Metcalfe, D., & Powell, J. (2011). Should doctors spurn Wikipedia? *Journal of the Royal Society of Medicine, 104*(12), 488–89. https://doi.org/10.1258/ Jrsm.2011.110227.

Network of the National Library of Medicine. (n.d.-a). Crowdsourcing and citizen science. https://nnlm.gov/national/guides/ccs.

Network of the National Library of Medicine. (n.d.-b). Mission and goals. https://nnlm.gov/mar/about/mission.

NNLM Edit-a-thon. (2018, April 30). In Wikipedia Outreach Dashboard. https://outreachdashboard.wmflabs.org/courses/National_Network_ of_Libraries_of_Medicine/NNLM_Edit-a-thon_-_spring_2018/home.

The Wikipedia Library/1Lib1Ref. (2020, December 10). In Wikipedia. https:// meta.wikimedia.org/wiki/The_Wikipedia_Library/1Lib1Ref.

CHAPTER 11

BIBLIOWIKIS: THE VOLUNTEER-DRIVEN, CATALAN CASE STUDY OF LIBRARIES AS HOTSPOTS FOR NEW WIKIPEDIANS AND HIGH-QUALITY SOURCES

Francesc Xavier Dengra i Grau,[1] Carme Fenoll i Clarabuch,[2] Vicenç Allué Blanch,[3] Francesc Fort i Silvestre,[4] Francesc García Grimau,[5] and Amparo Pons Cortell[6]

[1] KU Leuven and Amical Wikimedia, [2] Universitat Politècnica de Catalunya, [3] Autonomous University of Barcelona and Amical Wikimedia, [4] Amical Wikimedia, [5] Universitat de Barcelona, [6] Museu Valencià d'Etnologia and Amical Wikimedia

Abstract

The Catalan Wikipedia (Viquipèdia) is a successful free-knowledge platform with a strong community of editors that has significantly contributed to the normalization of this minoritized language on the Internet. In 2012, the NGO Amical Wikimedia and the Public Library Service of the Catalan Ministry of Culture launched #Bibliowikis, an initiative that has involved several hundreds of librarians and public libraries in the improvement of this version of the online encyclopedia. This unique, successful model was presented to the United Nations Educational,

DOI: https://doi.org/10.3998/mpub.11778416.ch11.en

Scientific, and Cultural Organization (UNESCO) and has been highlighted as a case study by the International Federation of Library Associations and Institutions (IFLA). The project involves the so-called *Amical-way*, in which scaffolded training, long-term self-management, and the geographically available Wikipedian volunteers constitute the three fundamental working pillars. #Bibliowikis' success has experienced different levels of applicability and regularity over the Catalan-speaking territories, especially in the Land of Valencia and Andorra, and may be endangered by global online dynamics, loss of the volunteering principles, and prioritization of economic resources in the fast-changing Wikimedia environment. However, #Bibliowikis' characteristics are fully aligned with those of Open Access, thus it is easily combined with academia and the public knowledge transfer at universities. Its robust ethical discourse on social contribution, negligible infrastructure, and linguistic heritage protection has allowed #Bibliowikis to be feasible and easily implemented in the increasing context of teleworking and the need for social digitization of bibliographic repositories.

Keywords

Catalan, Wikipedia, Viquipèdia, Libraries, Open Access, Volunteering, GLAM, Digitization.

Introduction: Catalan Language, Wikipedia, Geography, and Public Libraries

The Catalan language is a Western Romance language spoken by approximately 10 million people (Plataforma per la llengua, 2020). Its natural linguistic domain comprises four European states, but it is not a dominant language in most of the regions where it is naturally spoken: Spain (autonomous communities of Catalonia, Land of Valencia, Balearic Islands, Aragón, and Murcia), France (department of *Pyrénées-Orientales*, known as Northern Catalonia), Andorra, and Italy (in the Sardinian city of Alghero). Catalan shares its original territory with strong, state-supported languages such as Spanish, French, and Italian. The territorial fragmentation of Catalan has resulted in different denominations, levels of protection, and officiality depending on the region (Hawkey, 2018; Miller & Miller, 1996). In addition, the use of Catalan has been forbidden several times throughout history—most recently in Spain during the Franco dictatorship (Vallverdú, 1984). Catalan is a threatened language that needs active promotions in order to keep its usage alive and foster generational transmission.

In this linguistic context, *Viquipèdia* (Catalan Wikipedia, 2020), the Catalan-language edition of Wikipedia, was the second Wikipedia edition in a language other than English (Hinojo, 2016). It was the third to be created, in March 2001—just after the German edition. By 2020, it was ranked as the twentieth language by number of articles and had an active community of about 1,500 monthly editors. Since it was launched, both Wikipedia and the rest of Wikimedia projects have been proven as a major tool to foster Catalan normalization on the Internet and for a proper digital arrangement of ascertainable knowledge in this language (Dengra i Grau, 2018; Rius, 2019).

Amical Wikimedia is the nonprofit organization that promotes freely accessible Catalan culture and knowledge through the values and engagement of individuals and organizations in *Viquipèdia* (Amical Wikimedia, 2020; Amical Wikimedia, Qui som, 2020). It has conducted several projects to achieve Wikipedia's mission, including the #Bibliowikis project. Since 2012 Amical Wikimedia has been involved with nearly 500 public, academic, and special libraries located within the Catalan-speaking areas (Proffitt, 2018).

This chapter aims to further explain the origin, ethical conception, linguistic and territorial context, strengths, and weaknesses of the #Bibliowikis case study that has been an initiative to bring librarians into Catalan Wikipedia editing and online free knowledge participation in this language. In addition, this chapter provides applicable examples, some strategies that allow it to bond with academia, and discusses future possibilities, threats, and fate in a quickly changing digital and socioeconomic world.

The Start of #Bibliowikis in Catalonia's Public Libraries

In 2011, the relationship between Catalan Wikipedia and the librarianship ecosystem (also applicable to the educational sphere) was fraught with distrust. Professional librarians, who had been trained to thoroughly search

Figure 1 Sticker motif implemented during the first years after #Bibliowikis was launched. It served as a cohesive symbol among the participating libraries and engaged the interest of the public libraries' users in Catalan Wikipedia-related activities. (From left to right: Amical Wikimedia-Servei de Biblioteques de Catalunya, CC-BY-SA 3.0; Francesc Fort, CC-BY-SA 4.0; Àlex Hinojo, CC-BY 3.0).

traditional reference tools and other proven sources of information, did not see Wikipedia as an ally but rather as an intruder not to be trusted. That's why the first big step in 2011, and the real trigger toward a better relationship, was the scaffolded training designed by Amical Wikimedia along with the Public Library Service of the Catalan Ministry of Culture (Proffitt, 2018), led at that time by Carme Fenoll i Clarabuch.

The first step of this project made it possible for the vast majority of librarians in the Catalan network of public libraries to learn, in detail, about the values of Catalan Wikipedia—its editing criteria and the existing GLAM (Galleries, Libraries, Archives, and Museums) projects. This educational partnership, between Amical Wikipedia and public libraries in Catalonia, took place mainly between 2012 and 2013. Afterward, follow-up training was conducted with more engaged and experienced librarians (Proffitt, 2018). Later on, an annual motif was created to bring together the actions of the nearly 400 public libraries involved and the international annual campaign, #1Lib1Ref (in Catalan, #1Bib1Ref), was also folded into the #Bibliowikis activities with great success.

Wikipedia's Benefits and Opportunities for Catalan Librarians

What does an eighteen-year-old, computer-savvy Wikipedian working from home have in common with a local librarian? The passion to share information and help citizens. When this symbiosis was recognized by Catalan Wikipedians and librarians, the initial mistrust started to fall. Librarians learned about a cohesive, online meritocracy of volunteer work that complemented the librarian ethos. On the flipside, Wikipedians learned about the commitment and dedication of librarians, the scope of bibliographic collections pending digitization, and the different timelines, needs, and characteristics of public institutions. Moreover, the issue of gender bias in Wikipedia acquired more significance. In the Catalan-language context, 80 percent of librarians are women while approximately 85 percent of Wikipedians are men (Roqueta, 2014). Reducing gender bias in Wikipedia became one of the biggest challenges of this case study.

What is more, as a minoritized language (Hawkey, 2018; May, 2013), editing the Catalan Wikipedia allows librarians to reinforce their role of promoting language diversity, especially in the case of Libraries specializing in local or heritage collections. It becomes an opportunity to normalize and digitalize the content of knowledge compendiums in this language, as well as to make visible and add value in the network on resources that can be found in their libraries. In areas with low usage of Catalan, #Bibliowikis can serve librarians as a tool to linguistically engage their users and provide them with sources that would not be consulted in other circumstances.

The Catalan Model of Librarians' Involvement: A Volunteer-Driven Philosophy

Amical Wikimedia, as a nonprofit organization of about 120 volunteers, counts some of the most active Catalan Wikipedians among its members (Amical Wikimedia, 2020). Hence, the dual role of Amical Wikipedia's volunteers, both *in-wiki* and *off-wiki*, becomes the best asset for the outreach of the organization and the free encyclopedia. Volunteers connect and engage with institutions (i.e., libraries for this topic) by introducing them to the values of Wikipedia. In addition, they transfer knowledge by mentoring

beginners, providing technical support, and giving general guidance for the development of events. Finally, these volunteers (as
experienced Wikipedians) are already part of the day-to-day mechanisms and community debates within the Wikimedia projects.
Therefore, the integration of new users, data, and subprojects on the
local levels is seen as natural and tiered growth, and not as external
meddling outside of an already existing community (Meta-Wiki,
2014; Wikimedia Outreach, 2017).

From 2012 to mid-2020, the structure and functional core of the
organization, the so-called *Amical-way*, relied on a collaboration
between a project director and its more than 100 volunteers. This single employee was selected from the Catalan Wikipedian community,
based on their past participation as an Amical volunteer. A small commission of the most involved volunteers ensured a professional and
rigorous follow-up and direction of the employee's tasks. This way, a
horizontal bond was ensured between the employee, external Wikipedia editors, internal Amical members, external institutions, and
individual librarians (Meta-Wiki, 2014). Nonetheless, the philosophy
of the organization has always been to promote an endpoint of self-
sustainability and scaffolded training among its members and institutions. In the beginning of a project, volunteers and institutions are
provided with guidelines and a regionally available volunteer who
serves as a truly human support; then there is a progressive decrease
in support until the beginners have become competent, and eventually
trainers are released to focus on other projects (Fenoll, 2016; Meta-
Wiki, 2014; Proffitt, 2018; Wikimedia Outreach, 2017).

Scaling the Project: Deployment of the #Bibliowikis to Other Catalan-Speaking Areas

Amical Wikimedia has been able, with partial success, to expand the
#Bibliowikis impact outside of Catalonia and implement it in other
Catalan-speaking territories. The most significant deployment has
been in the Land of Valencia and Andorra. Also, there has been sporadic activity in Northern Catalonia and the Balearic Islands. The

leading figure for those initial expansions was Àlex Hinojo Sánchez, who was Amical Wikimedia's project director from 2012 to 2018, with the support of local volunteers and the development of targeted and integrated events like the annual gathering of participant libraries, *Trobada de Bibliowikis*, which was held in 2016 (Núvol, 2016).

The start of #Bibliowikis in the Land of Valencia started with a relationship between Amical Wikimedia and Valencian Museum of Ethnology in 2016 (Pons et al., 2019). Later that year, the first Wikipedian-in-residence (WiR) began to volunteer in the library of the Valencian Museum of Ethnology (Pons et al., 2019). Here, the #Bibliowikis program was adapted to integrate it into GLAM outcomes. In this case, the library acted as a gateway to the museum. During this stable collaboration, documents and multimedia were uploaded to Wikimedia projects and several editing contests and edit-a-thons were held, such as the *Wiki Loves Falles* contest to upload popular, cultural content to Wikimedia Commons (Pons et al., 2019). In this case, the #Bibliowikis approach favored the adoption of the same discourse and engagement by another Wikimedia affiliate, Wikimedia España, which boosted the trust of the already involved librarians and increased the linguistic outreach of the ongoing activities.

Although Valencian public libraries have never hosted a consolidated #Bibliowikis project like the one in Catalonia, this hybrid GLAM-library partnership with Amical has resulted in other specific and individual activities hosted in various locations, with only one regular annual edit-a-thon in the library of L'Eliana (Gascó Comeche, 2017, 2020), but this particular event has evolved toward a self-sustained activity (Gascó Comeche, 2020). To revert the standstill and increase the number of involved libraries, the Official College of Librarians and Documentalists of the Land of Valencia (COBDCV) signed formal agreements in late 2019 with Amical Wikimedia and Wikimedia España that aim to collaborate, train, and raise the awareness of Valencian chartered professionals toward Wikimedia projects and activities such as #1Lib1Ref.

Similarly, the implementation of #Bibliowikis in the micro-country of Andorra has been irregular, although mostly successful. Two events were pivotal to the Andorran librarians' confidence in the project. First, the first-ever Catalan and non-English Wikipedia article, "Àbac," was created in Andorra (Fernández, 2019; Hinojo, 2016). Second, Andorra became the first country in the world to have all of its heritage monuments photographed and uploaded to Wikipedia thanks to Amical Wikimedia volunteers' tenacity within the *Wiki Loves Monuments* global initiative (Govern d'Andorra, 2011; Hinojo, 2016). As #Bibliowikis grew in importance in Catalonia, the National Library of Andorra took the lead in 2013 when they had the Public Library of the Government of Andorra contribute by adding articles and organizing their first edit-a-thon (Hinojo, 2016). Although Andorra libraries have seen successful with wikiprojects, other governmental GLAM and university wikiprojects hosted in the country did not fully incorporate librarians in subsequent years. However, in early 2019, the National Library significantly increased its activity once again and provided bibliographic sources and editing mentorship to high school students (Diari d'Andorra, 2019). Differently from Catalonia and the Land of Valencia, though, and given the circumstance of unknown or insufficiently active Catalan editors in the country, the help for this new kick-off was initially provided on-site by an Amical volunteer from Catalonia, but progressively switched to online support. Despite their lower activity, as compared to other #Bibliowikis and the impediments derived from the Andorran Copyright Law (no "Freedom of Panorama"), they keep regular and self-managed additions and activities (e.g. #1Lib1Ref) to promote new content and draw in new Wikipedians (Blasco, 2020; Fernández, 2019; Hinojo, 2016).

Strengths, Weaknesses, Threats, and Uncertainties
of the Catalan Model
In one decade, the #Bibliowikis project has demonstrated its ability to become a tool of reference and introduction to open knowledge to the public. Library involvement has also boosted this format and the librarian-Wikipedian tandem has come to stay. Its discourse, ease, cost (free), and applicability have allowed the project to become an international case of study. It has been endorsed by Europeana

Foundation as an opportunity to further engage GLAM and heritage initiatives (Hinojo, 2013), by the International Federation of Library Associations and Institutions (IFLA) for public libraries (Fenoll, 2016), and was presented at the United Nations Educational, Scientific, and Cultural Organization (UNESCO) (Parreño Mont, 2017). Additionally, #Bibliowikis' impact and recognition was a crucial push for the final recognition from the Wikimedia Foundation of Amical Wikimedia as the first, worldwide official affiliate that was not framed in the boundaries of a state but rather in the defense of a language (Ara, 2013). One year after, Amical received the National Prize of Culture 2014 by the Catalan Government (Gran Enciclopèdia Catalana, 2015).

The proper visualization of a volunteer workforce joined with public entities, such as libraries, allowed #Bibliowikis to scale up. Even in the case of less institutional support and volunteering impact, good results, such as QR codes for two-dimensional items uploaded to Wikimedia Commons, were shared by the Valencian #Bibliowikis in national conferences hosted by the Spanish Federation of Societies of Archivist, Librarians, Documentalist, and Museology (FESABID) (Pons et al., 2019)—proving the social and academic influence of different asymmetric, but valid scalings. In all cases, Wikipedia edits and multimedia uploads contributed to facilitate the understanding and development of Open Access public policies and, therefore, allowed them to be the seed of change.

However, the *Amical-way* has some weaknesses and uncertainties in relation to libraries. Unlike other Amical Wikimedia initiatives, #Bibliowikis has no financial cost, except for the travel or basic expenses of its volunteers (Meta-Wiki, 2014). Thus, its weaknesses do not depend on the monetary basis but on the volunteering commitment and discursive self-development, as well as on librarians and their regulatory bodies to maintain a self-sustained scaffolded training and engagement. A loss of the top-down institutional support and outreach, which happened in Catalonia in 2017 with the sudden change of the Head of Public Libraries (Martínez, 2017), can result in a mid- or a long-term impact decrease of the project. In fact, a loss of volunteering activity has consequently decreased follow-up meetings, libraries involved, and a break of the "librarians train librarians" institutionally agreed-upon activities in the Catalan #Bibliowikis in the latest stages.

#Bibliowikis' robustness currently relies on the adoption of a discourse by the active volunteers, librarians, and the gained recognition. However, there is much uncertainty about its future linked to the transmission of these values by all stakeholders. Organizational priorities and tasks managed by Amical volunteers have been limited due to the community size and a small, internal core of very active members who assume most of the workload (Meta-Wiki, 2014). In future crisis environments, librarians may increase their workload and diminish their availability for activism. In this way, #Bibliowikis' life may be endangered despite its prestige. Finally, the future success of these and other projects is constrained by two factors. One of them is the lack of generational renewal of new Wikipedians with the same sharing principles and volunteering enthusiasm that has been observed in the Catalan community (Hinojo, 2020). Some of its members have become inactive without conducting prior experience transfer to newcomers, while some of the latter have not shown enough interest to keep up with successful initiatives. The second one is the sum of wrong global tendencies affecting the Wikimedia Foundation and some Wikimedia affiliates. Staff members and economical resources are becoming the key limiting factors of their goals instead of Wikipedia's natural ecosystem: volunteers (Hinojo, 2020). This drifting influence has strongly affected some Wikimedia affiliates including Amical, therefore triggering profound ethical and governance disagreements that endanger its continuity. In other territories, external agents without close bonds to the Wikipedian communities are opening the gate to contractual librarian projects (Bañares, 2018; Martinsen, 2019). Profitability might become the trend and eventually displace charitable ideas such as the ones represented by #Bibliowikis.

The Nexus between #Bibliowikis and Academic Libraries

Catalan university libraries have become a nexus of both #Bibliowikis and #Eduwiki (educational) programs. University repositories play a key role within Wikipedia: they provide access to sources and can assess the impact of Creative Commons licensing in public knowledge transfer from higher educational institutions to the general public (Universitat Autònoma de Barcelona. Comissió d'Accés Obert, 2020). Academic libraries possess deep expertise in Open Access research and education. Hence, they incorporate their skills on best practices on how to promote open knowledge values and its transfer to classrooms, research groups, and administrative communities, and consequently in academic outreach. As a result of this commitment, some Catalan universities, such as the Universitat Autònoma de Barcelona (UAB), have updated their institutional policies to enrich horizontal transmission of knowledge with licensing conditions suitable for Wikipedia (Universitat Autònoma de Barcelona, 2012).

As previously mentioned, the figure of a university librarian who is engaged with the Wikimedia values (and, in general, with the free knowledge movement) is of great value as it normalizes the still reluctant bond with the academic community. In the Catalan context, small- and large-scale projects have been developed, and are intended to promote Wikipedia's academic impact. Examples of these combined systems, in which University libraries take the lead, are the creation of the *Honoris Causa* biographies; online librarian trainings during the COVID-19 pandemic; release of archive images to Commons; and ORCID links to Wikidata of admissible personnel at the Autonomous University of Barcelona's (UAB) (Allué & Casaldàliga, 2018); and the *Viquidones* permanent space edition at the Pompeu Fabra University (UPF) (Dengra i Grau, 2020; Martija, 2019). Other activities have involved edit-a-thons and scoring wikiprojects for students jointly promoted by librarians and professors at the Catalonia College of Music (ESMUC) (Catalunya Ràdio, 2020) or the above-mentioned support and mentoring to high schools by the National Library of Andorra (Diari d'Andorra, 2019).

In the same regard, librarians have contributed to official, long-term agreements between Amical Wikimedia and UAB or with the Open University of Catalonia (UOC) in order to promote workshops, training, conferences, open-access engagement, and #eduwiki projects

with students and professors led by volunteers. Some social researchers aligned with the *Amical-way* have integrated acquired knowledge
in Catalan #Eduwiki and #Bibliowikis projects by preparing help
manuals and ethical guides on editing Wikipedia in bachelor's theses
(Castells, 2020), highly skilled academic research, or regular teaching
(Aibar, 2016; Lerga Felip & Aibar Puentes, 2015).

Different educational initiatives promoted by academic libraries
have been carried out that link open teaching and Wikipedia. University libraries have lines of work related to supporting the development
of open, online teaching materials. For this reason, some events related
to open education have been carried out, such as the *Open Education
Weeks* (Solé, 2020). Under the title "Open Educational Resources: Sharing to Educate," UAB hosted a working day dedicated to deal with open
educational initiatives in the framework of Wikimedia programs with
participation of librarians, teaching staff, and Wikipedians (Universitat Autònoma de Barcelona. Servei de Biblioteques, 2020). University
librarians are an example of transition toward a prioritization of digital
environments. In this context and amid the experience of COVID-19,
initiatives with added value and reduced face-to-face public services,
such as #Bibliowikis, can play a big role in the pursuit of common goals
with little physical interaction. In all educational levels, a reformulation
of didactic approaches is proposed with the addition of new enjoyable
distance learning environments and embedding technologies for new
generations (Rapanta et al., 2020).

Conclusion

The main difficulty faced by librarians editing Wikipedia has been the
lack of time and the impossibility of naturally integrating editing into
their daily routine—librarians necessarily prioritize ordering and face-
to-face reference service at the counter. The successful philosophy of
#Bibliowikis has relied on the values of volunteering, overturn, and
scaffolded training, which are evolving asymmetrically among both
librarians and Wikipedians in a changing sociodigital and Wikimedia environment. Despite this, #Bibliowikis has shown its success by

playing a big role in responding to an awakening community pride to work on similar information projects regardless of age, academic knowledge, gender, location, and even social distancing. In addition, it has united librarians across different library types. #Bibliowikis, given its free, pliable, and volunteer-driven structure, can be a model for library systems outside of Catalan-speaking areas. Librarians should consider it a priority to include open education and free knowledge goals, which are fostered by projects such as #Bibliowikis.

References

Aibar Puentes, Eduard. (2016). Guia de recomanacions i bones pràctiques per a editar el contingut científic de Viquipèdia. http://hdl.handle.net/10609/57384 (in Catalan).

Allué, Vicenç, & Casaldàliga, Núria. (2018). Viquipèdia i UAB, una relació amb perspectives de futur. *Biblioteca Informacions.* https://blogs.uab.cat/bibli otecainformacions/2018/12/19/viquipedia-i-uab-una-relacio-amb-per spectives-de-futur-allue-vicenc-casaldaliga-nuria/ (in Catalan).

Amical Wikimedia. (2020). In *Wikimedia.* https://meta.wikimedia.org/wiki/Amical_Wikimedia.

Amical Wikimedia, Bylaws. (2020), In *Wikimedia.* https://meta.wikimedia.org/wiki/Amical_Wikimedia/Bylaws.

Amical Wikimedia, Qui som. (2020). In *Wikimedia.* www.wikimedia.cat/pre sentacio/ (in Catalan).

Bañares, Ilya. (2018). U of T Libraries hires first Wikipedian in residence. *Toronto Star.* www.thestar.com/news/gta/2018/11/01/u-of-t-libraries-hires-first-wikipedian-in-residence.html.

Blasco, Joan Josep. (2020). Les biblioteques enriqueixen la xarxa. *El Periòdic d'Andorra.* www.elperiodic.ad/noticia/77532/les-biblioteques-enriqueix en-la-xarxa (in Catalan).

Castells, Eva. (2020). Treball de Fi de Grau d'edició de la Viquipèdia. Manual d'ajuda. https://ddd.uab.cat/record/218016 (in Catalan).

Catalan Wikipedia. (2020). In *Wikipedia.* https://en.wikipedia.org/wiki/Catalan_Wikipedia.

Catalunya Ràdio. (2020). Amb la Viquimarató, el treball que es fa a l'Escola no queda a l'aula, sinó que arriba a la societat. *Corporació Catalana de Mitjans Audiovisuals.* www.ccma.cat/catradio/alacarta/assaig-general/amb-la-viquimarato-el-treball-que-es-fa-a-lescola-no-queda-a-laula-sino-que-ar riba-a-la-societat/audio/959201/ (in Catalan).

Dengra i Grau, F. Xavier. (2018). És cert allò fiable? Els mecanismes de rigor de la Viquipèdia. *Terminàlia, 18,* 50–52. www.doi.org/10.2436/20.2503.01.126 (in Catalan).

Dengra i Grau, F. Xavier. (2020). Viquiprojecte:UAB. Espai de formació docent. https://ca.wikipedia.org/wiki/Viquiprojecte:UAB/Formaci%C3%B3_docent (in Catalan).

Diari Ara. (2013). L'associació Amical Wikimedia rep el reconeixement internacional després de cinc anys de lluita per aconseguir-ho. *Diari Ara.* www. ara.cat/tecnologia/Lassociacio-Amical-Wikimedia-reconeixement-inter nacional_0_933506826.html (in Catalan).

Diari d'Andorra. (2019). Sandy ja té qui n'escrigui. *Diari d'Andorra.* www. diariandorra.ad/noticies/cultura/2019/05/14/sandy_qui_escrigui_ 145786_1127.html (in Catalan).

Fenoll, Carme. (2016). Opportunities for public libraries and Wikipedia. *International Federation of Library Associations and Institutions.* www.ifla.org/ files/assets/hq/topics/info-society/iflawikipediaandpubliclibraries.pdf.

Fernández, Júlia. (2019). Tot un "viqui-univers" al teu servei. *Diari Bondia Andorra.* www.bondia.ad/opinio/tot-un-viqui-univers-al-teu-servei (in Catalan).

Gascó Comeche, Barbara. (2020). Viquiprojecte l'Eliana: Història Local a Viquipèdia. *Bastida, 2,* 25 (in Catalan).

Gascó Comeche, Barbara. (2017). Viquiprojecte l'Eliana: Història local a la Viquipèdia. *Símile, 37* (in Catalan).

Generalitat Valenciana (2018). Mapa de Biblioteques de la Comunitat Valenciana. http://webapp.cult.gva.es/hdfi/ESLAB-BIBLIO/bibliotecas_cpru.jsp (in Spanish).

Govern d'Andorra. (2011). La imatge de Sant Joan de Caselles, guanyadora de l'edició Wiki Loves Monuments 2011 d'Andorra. www.govern.ad/cultura/ item/3370-la-imatge-de-sant-joan-de-caselles-guanyadora-de-l'edició-wiki-loves-monuments-2011-andorra (in Catalan).

Gran Enciclopèdia Catalana. (2015). Wikipedia. www.enciclopedia.cat/ ec-gec-0283878.xml (in Catalan).

Hawkey, James. (2018). *Language attitudes and minority rights: The case of Catalan in France.* Palgrave Macmillan. https://doi.org/10.1007/978-3-319-74597-8.

Hinojo, Àlex. (2013). How Europeana helps Wikipedia editor and GLAM ambassador. *Europeana Foundation.* https://pro.europeana.eu/post/ how-europeana-helps-wikipedia-editor-and-glam-ambassador.

Hinojo, Àlex. (2016). Viquipèdia i Andorra. *Ex-libris Casa Bauró, 19.* www. cultura.ad/images/stories/Accio_Cultural/Publicacions/ex-libris/2016/ Ex-Libris_19-2016.pdf (in Catalan).

Hinojo, Àlex. (2020). Somien els viquipedistes en enciclopèdies elèctriques? Present i futur de la Viquipèdia i el rol de la comunitat catalanoparlant. *Revista de Llengua i Dret, Journal of Language and Law*, 73, 133–45. https:// doi.org/10.2436/ rld.i73.2020.3424 (in Catalan).

Lerga Felip, Maura, & Aibar Puentes, Eduard. (2015). *Best practice guide to use Wikipedia in university education.* http://hdl.handle.net/10609 /41662

Martija, Patricia. (2019). Las editoras que feminizan Wikipedia. *Metrópoli Abierta.* www.metropoliabierta.com/quien-hace-barcelona/entidades/edi toras-feminizan-wikipedia_14269_102.html (in Spanish).

Martínez, Dídac. (2017). El cas Carme Fenoll. *Núvol.* www.nuvol.com/llibres/ el-cas-carme-fenoll-43208 (in Catalan).

Martinsen, Jorid. (2019). Oslo Metropolitan University hires "Wikipedia-assistants". *Wikimedia Outreach.* https://outreach.wikimedia.org/wiki/ Education/News/February_2019/Oslo_Metropolitan_University_hires_% E2%80%9CWikipedia-assistants%E2%80%9D.

May, Stephen. (2013). *Language and minority rights: Ethnicity, nationalism and the politics of language.* Routledge. ISBN 9781136837067.

Meta-Wiki. (2014). Organizational effectiveness/case studies/Amical Wiki-media. https://meta.wikimedia.org/wiki/Organizational_effectiveness/ Case_studies/Amical_Wikimedia.

Miller, H., & Miller, K. (1996). Language policy and identity: The case of Cata-lonia. *International Studies in Sociology of Education*, 6(1), 113–28.

Núvol. (2016). Bibliowikis, un model a seguir. *Núvol.* https://www.nuvol.com/ llibres/bibliowikis-un-model-a-seguir-41450

Parreño Mont, David. (2017). Amical Wikimedia presenta a la UNESCO la col·laboració amb les biblioteques. *Amical Wikimedia.* www.wikimedia. cat/2017/02/21/amical-wikimedia-presenta-la-collaboracio-amb-les-bib lioteques-a-la-unesco/ (in Catalan).

Plataforma per la llengua. (2020). InformeCat 2020: 50 dades sobre la llen-gua. www.plataforma-llengua.cat/media/upload/pdf/informecat-2020_ 267_11_2406.pdf (in Catalan).

Pons Cortell, A., Fort Silvestre, F. J., et al. (2019). Un wikipedista en la Biblio-teca del Museu Valencià d'Etnologia. *Cuartas Jornadas sobre bibliotecas de museos: Estrategias sostenibles y alianzas en bibliotecas de museos. Actas de las IV Jornadas BIMUS*, 121–36. https://dialnet.unirioja.es/servlet/articu lo?codigo=7246951 (in Spanish).

Proffitt, Merrilee. *Leveraging Wikipedia: Connecting communities of knowl-edge.* American Library Association. ISBN 9780838916322.

Rapanta, C., Botturi, L., Goodyear, P., et al. (2020). Online university teaching during and after the Covid-19 crisis: Refocusing teacher presence and learning activity. *Postdigit Sci Educ*, *2*, 923–45. https://doi.org/10.1007/s42438-020-00155-y.

Rius, Clàudia. (2019). Internet, els influencers i la normalització del català. *Núvol*. www.nuvol.com/llengua/internet-els-influencers-i-la-normalitzacio-del-catala-62248 (in Catalan).

Roqueta, Marta. (2014). Com és que no hi som? *Revista Digital Dones*. www.donesdigital.cat/noticia/981/com-es-que-no-hi-som/ (in Catalan).

Solé, Esther. (2020). La Viquipèdia segueix consolidant-se com l'eina acadèmica lliure a l'Open Education Week de la UAB. *Biblioteca Informacions*. https://blogs.uab.cat/bibliotecainformacions/2020/04/15/la-viquipedia-segueix-consolidant-se-com-leina-academica-lliure-a-lopen-education-week-de-la-uab-sole-i-marti-esther/ (in Catalan).

Universitat Autònoma de Barcelona. Comissió d'Accés Obert. (2020). Creative Commons licenses recommended in the UAB. https://ddd.uab.cat/record/129205.

Universitat Autònoma de Barcelona. Consell de Govern (2012). Open access institutional policy. https://ddd.uab.cat/record/89641.

Universitat Autònoma de Barcelona. Servei de Biblioteques (2020). Recursos educatius en obert: comparteix per educar: Jornada sobre iniciatives docents en el marc de la viquipèdia. Open Education Week Initiative by UAB Library Service Video collection and presentations of each participants available: https://ddd.uab.cat/search?f=publication&p=Open%20Education%20Week&ln=ca (in Catalan).

Vallverdú, F. (1984). A sociolinguistic history of Catalan. *International Journal of the Sociology of Language*, *47*. https://doi.org/10.1515/ijsl.1984.47.13.

Wikimedia Outreach. (2017). GLAM/case studies/Catalonia's network of public libraries. https://outreach.wikimedia.org/wiki/GLAM/Case_studies/Catalonia%27s_Network_of_Public_Libraries.

SECTION 3
WIKIPEDIANS-IN-RESIDENCE

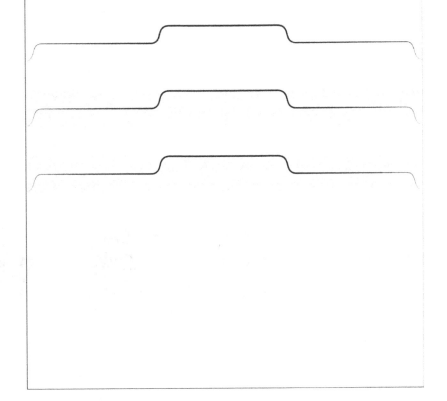

CHAPTER 12

BEYOND THE WIKIPEDIAN-IN-RESIDENCE, OR HOW TO KEEP THE FLAME BURNING

Silvia E. Gutiérrez De la Torre[1]

[1] El Colegio de México

Abstract

In 2017, the Biblioteca Daniel Cosío Villegas, an academic (and public) library in Mexico City, drafted the first grant-funded project in the region for training academic librarians in the Wikimedia universe. Drawing on my experience coordinating this project, this case study outlines suggestions for ensuring the continuity of Wikipedia and other Wikimedia endeavors in libraries. Before going in detail, I offer background data on Wikipedians-in-Residence (WIR) experiences around the globe, followed by the specific characteristics this position has had in different libraries. I then present a brief timeline of our project, an overview of our first "flame" (the #1Bib1Ref campaign), the ways we kept the "Wiki-flame" burning: leveraging our team's strengths and collaborating, and some ideas on how to build your own "fireplace" through a minimal viable product approach, documentation, and feedback (where I share some thoughts on why Wikipedia may not even be the fireplace you were looking for, and that's ok).

Keywords

Wikipedians-in-Residence, Open GLAM, Academic libraries.

DOI: https://doi.org/10.3998/mpub.11778416.ch12.en

Introduction

Spanish is the second most spoken mother tongue in the world with around 500 million Spanish speakers worldwide (González, 2020, p. 47; Instituto Cervantes, 2019, p. 6). Although a multilingual country, Mexico has the greatest number of native Spanish speakers, and it ranks among the top fifteen countries with the greatest number of Internet users (Instituto Cervantes, 2019, p. 50; Navarro, 2020). Yet, between 2009 and 2013, Spanish represented less than 7 percent of the global share of Wikipedia edits, and edits from Mexico represented only around one-tenth of the Spanish contributions (Zachte, 2013). This missing perspective in the world's largest encyclopedia was one of the main drivers of our project—and who better to fill an information gap than librarians.

WIRs in Libraries: A Very Brief History of Previous Fires

The figures now available on the amount of Galleries, Libraries, Archives, and Museums (GLAM) that have collaborated to Wikimedia projects (Wikipedia, Wikidata, Wikimedia Commons, etc.,) seem to confirm that this partnership has been suitable for at least 100 libraries around the world (Gill, 2020). Moreover, there have been around forty Wikipedians-in-Residence (WIR) working in libraries, but who are they and what are they doing in our institutions?

A WIR oversees the integration of an open knowledge strategy that leverages the usage of Wikimedia projects into the workflows and practice of a library or other cultural institutions. This type of collaboration was first developed and tested in 2010 at the British Museum (BM). The experienced Australian Wikipedia editor Liam Wyatt (User:Wittylama) held the residency as a volunteer for five weeks and ran interesting initiatives like the £100 giftshop voucher prize for new featured article or the "one-on-one collaborations" in which Wikipedians got to work with BM curators on a particular topic, which also caught the eye of the media (see Cohen, 2010). Unfortunately, the story following this mythical genesis is not so easy to track. There is no official data on WIR positions. However, there are two sources that can help us reconstruct a timeline: a Wikidata query (WQ)[1] and a scrubbed version of the "Mapping GLAM-Wiki collaborations" (MGW) collaborative spreadsheet (Gutiérrez De la Torre, 2020a).[2]

According to MGW, the earliest Wikimedia-library liaison was in 2011, ten years after Wikipedia was first launched (Shin, 2017). This liaison consisted in a Wikimedia Commons project conducted by the State Library of Queensland in Australia. The main objective was the donation of 50,000 public domain images and their metadata (ACULibrary, 2011). Months later, in December, Daniel Tsvi Framowitz became the first WIR in a library.[3] This position was held at the National Library of Israel, and the focus was directed toward improving Wikimedia's coverage of the library's collection. In addition to several national libraries that hired WIRs in Chile, North Macedonia, Scotland, Switzerland, Wales, and so on, university libraries also became a part of this collaborative endeavor starting from 2014 (see figure 1). Following WQ's results, Rob Velella became the first WIR in an academic

Number of WIRs employed by Libraries and other Institutions

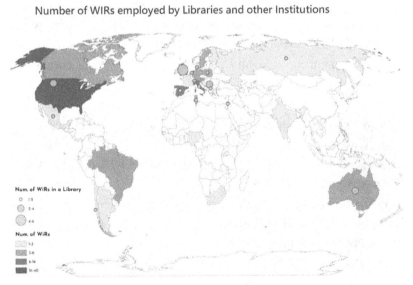

Figure 1 A map of WIRs in libraries (2011–2020) according to the WQ data (see interactive version at Gutiérrez De la Torre, 2020c).

library, when he joined Harvard University's Houghton Library from May until December of 2014 (Garber, 2014; Velella, 2014). The Scientific Library of Lomonosov Moscow State University followed suit that September. Russian historian and publisher Mikhail Melnichenko became a resident in cooperation with the "Oral History Foundation" to load pictures, audio, and video materials about outstanding Soviet and Russian scientists (*Число Российских Вики-Резидентов Удвоилось*, 2014).

Library-based residencies' activities could be summarized with the following five main activities:

1. Writing pieces about their collections or improving Wikipedia citations utilizing the library's collections (British Library Project Page, 2013; Harold B. Lee Library, 2020; Wikipedia Collaboration at the University of Alberta, 2020).
2. Digitizing, uploading, and open-licensing of their media (Basel University Library, 2018; Wikiprojekt Biblioteki Narodowej, 2019; Универзитетска библиотека 2014, 2019).
3. Improving their discoverability or metadata through Wikidata (*National Wikimedian at the National Library of Wales*, 2019).
4. Creating training and event planning strategies and practices (*The National Library of Scotland GLAM Project*, 2020; 'Wikipedia 101' Series, 2020).
5. Documenting successful cases and guides for their communities (Вики Библиотекар/2019, 2020).

However successful these initiatives have been, they seem less common. If we take a look at a WIR timeline (see figure 2), depending on the source, one can see a peak around 2015 or 2016 and a steady decrease from 2017 onward.

While this could be due to a data capture problem, after parsing the mentions of WIRs in "This Month in GLAM" newsletter, a similar decline is observed after 2017 (see figure 3).

This decline could be a permanent trend or a normal fluctuation of the hype that will eventually grow back again. However scarce these

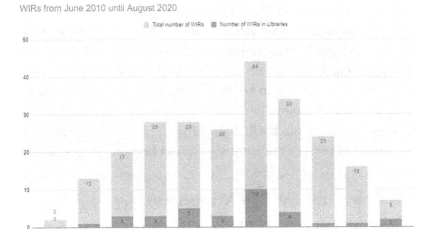

Figure 2 Approximate number of WIR mentions in libraries according to MGW and WQ.

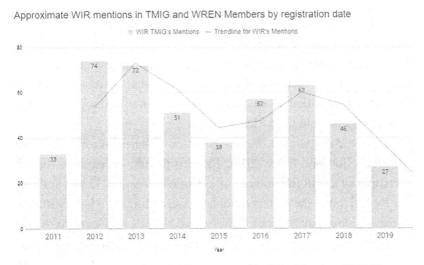

Figure 3 Approximate number of WIR mentions in the "This Month in GLAM" newsletter. Bar plot showing the Wikipedian-in-Residence mentions in a GLAM newsletter.

collaborations may be in the future, if the purpose of these collaborations is to leverage an organizations' capacity to improve their strategy
for open and public engagement (Stinson & Evans, 2018, p. 43), we
should be thinking about an important face of sustainability: continuity. If WIRs continue to be short residencies, how can we keep
these "little fires" burning? In the next section, I hope to show how we
addressed this matter in the Biblioteca Daniel Cosío Villegas (BDCV),
and thus share some of the many ways we can keep our "flames" alight.

The BDCV Experience

In March 2017, when the BDCV's dean Micaela Chávez and I decided
to apply for a Wikimedia grant to hire a WIR we knew there had been
no other residencies in Spanish-speaking academic libraries, and
we wanted to build a plan not to be the last.[4] The BDCV is the academic library of El Colegio de México in Mexico City, an institution
of higher learning specializing in the humanities and social sciences.
In March 2016 and August 2017, prior to the WIR experience, we had
given Wikipedia workshops (*Education/Countries/México . . .*, 2019)
and organized one edit-a-thon (Quiroa, 2017). These initiatives had
started to catch the eye of other institutions (especially other libraries) and they wanted us to give workshops and share documentation.
Unfortunately, our daily tasks left us almost no time to do anything
else, and that is when the idea came to us: what if we applied for a
Wikimedia grant that could help us bring together the tools we needed
to help others build their own "fireplace"?

In June 2017, we got one of the seven Offline Outreach Wikimedia grants (Johnson & Jue, 2017). The next month, we launched the call
searching for a WIR (Biblioteca Daniel Cosío Villegas, 2017), and by October we had found the perfect candidate: Aidee Murrieta, a library student
at the National Autonomous University of Mexico, who came to the job
interview with handouts for everyone and a clear timeline for the project.

One year later, we were writing in our project's final report about
the more than 100 articles that were written in our events, the 600
plus references our team added, the more than 300 elements created
in Wikidata, the 13 workshops we conducted, the 4 edit-a-thons we

organized, and the 4 classes that integrated Wikipedia in their assignments (Gutiérrez De la Torre, 2017). In this section, I will try to dissect
the actions that led us to get those little fires burning, but moreover, the
steps to build our own hearth.

Starting the Fire: Our First Spark #1Bib1Ref
The first step was to ensure that the Wiki project resonated with the
BDCV librarians' views and values. Murrieta and I decided to start
with #1Bib1Ref, an Ibero-American initiative that seeks to motivate
librarians to add references to Wikipedia and thus enhance the quality
of one of the most visited websites in the world. We decided to make
this our first task for two main reasons: it did not require much technical knowledge, and it offered the BDCV the opportunity to interact
with a community that is close both linguistically and culturally. The
aftermath of this event seemed to indicate this was the right starting
point: it lay the foundations of our first library-to-library liaison (with
the University of Guadalajara's Library Network), the tutorials that
Aidee Murrieta prepared for the campaign were featured in one of the
most famous librarian blogs in our region (infotecarios.com), our "call
for action" is one of the most viewed #1Bib1Ref videos in YouTube
(*¿Cómo Participar En La Campaña #1BIB1REF?*, 2018), and our workshop was viewed more than 340 times.

Moreover, it was exciting to see how our own team made this project
their own in a proactive and creative manner. For example, reference
librarian Máximo Domínguez devised a strategy for our social networks using the 1Bib1Ref logo. In one month, Domínguez's strategy
got 139 likes and 72 retweets (Twitter Search, 2018). Another reference
librarian, Tomás Bocanegra, printed out of his own pocket stickers for
the team and volunteered to run a Facebook group to answer questions
from other librarians who wanted to join the movement. This group
has, to date (November 2020), sixty-two members (#1Bib1Ref, n.d.).

To sum up, there were three factors that helped us light this first fire:
our library dean's support by integrating this activity into the library's
annual plan; having someone in charge of planning, documenting, and
creating liaisons (in this case it was Aidee Murrieta and myself, but

other libraries could contact their local chapter or select people in their organization that could lead this initiative); and the right environment to let librarians creatively do what they do best: share.

Keeping the Fire Going: Leveraging Strengths and Collaborating
From what we have seen, many edit-a-thons are initiated by institutional perspectives, which can be powerful if the institution holds a collection many are passionate about, or a community that usually engages with these types of events. Since our main purpose was to engage our own library community and ensure the continuity of the project, we thought of a different strategy: find a sweet spot between the strengths of our collection, the research areas at our university, and the expertise of our librarians. Following WIR Kelly Doyle's idea, that Wikipedia can be an attractive outlet for research-based activism (Doyle, 2017), we came up with three edit-a-thon subjects: *Haciendo y deshaciendo el género* [gender issues], *La lucha por la memoria* [social movements], and *De voz en voz* [indigenous languages]. Each of them, led by librarians who built partnerships within El Colegio de México's academic programs and other institutions. But more importantly, each one of them leveraged our teams' strengths: Reference librarian, Camelia Romero—who is an expert in gender thesaurus (Romero Millán, 2017) and has cocreated a digital collection for the history of gender in Mexico (Cano & Romero Millán, 2020)—was in charge of the gender edit-a-thon. Among her activities, she was in charge of engaging the Gender Studies Program at El Colegio de México (COLMEX) and curating a selection of books and documents for the to-be-created articles.

Furthermore, this edit-a-thon would not have been possible without our collaborators: the Librosb4tipos Collective, which is devoted to disseminate the writings of woman authors; the Colegio de Etnólogos y Antropólogos Sociales A.C. (CEAS, College of Ethnologists and Social Anthropologists), which has a special task force devoted to feminist anthropology; and the Institute of Ecology of the National Autonomous University of Mexico, which has a science outreach program devoted to sharing the research of women scientists. Librosb4tipos's donated Jane Austen books that were offered as a prize for participants (Librosb4tipos, 2019), and together with CEAS and the Institute of Ecology, we co-organized a rich round table with scientists, anthropologists, and sociologists to discuss gender, catholic feminism, feminist anthropology, and other fascinating subjects (see *Mesa Redonda—Haciendo y Deshaciendo El Género*, 2018).

In like manner, the indigenous languages edit-a-thon was organized by our university's Center for Linguistics studies' reference librarian Israel Escobar, whose doctoral research explored variations on contemporary Nahuatl writing (Escobar Farfán, 2019). Among other things, he was in charge of reactivating our institutional connections with the Summer Institute of Linguistics, the Nanginá Research and Intercultural Services Cabinet, and Mexico's Wikimedia Chapter (see figure 4, left). Like in the previous example, this edit-a-thon would not have been the same without the community support provided by Mixtec activist Verónica Aguilar who partnered with the craft binder

Figure 4 Official poster for the indigenous languages at the BDCV (left) and press-printed poster by Ombligo del Libro. One poster with a digital image and information event; the other with press-printed letters.

and printer *Ombligo del Libro* and donated a wonderful design and press-printed poster featuring the word "voice" translated into several indigenous languages (see figure 4, right).

The same can be said for the social movements edit-a-thon, for which reference librarian Máximo R. Domínguez created a collaboration with the Colegio Nacional de Bibliotecarios [National College of Librarians] and the Library Services Unit of the University of Guadalajara, in order to both organize a book and poster exhibition of the Mexican Movement of 1968 and print commemorative stickers and T-shirts for participants and reproductions of the aforementioned posters that were offered as gifts for contributors (Biblioteca Colmex, 2018). I would like to underline that strengths can also mean passions. For instance, every year since 2017, my colleague Tomás Bocanegra writes reviews about Queer culture books in our library's blog *Amontonamos las palabras* (Bocanegra Esqueda, 2017). This year, in 2021, he will organize an edit-a-thon with different NGOs in Mexico City around this subject.

Building Fireplaces

Keep your Fireplace Simple: The MVP Approach

A minimum viable product (MVP) can be defined as "that version of a new product which allows a team to collect the maximum amount of validated learning about customers with the least effort" (Ries, 2011). The MVP is not a prototype but rather a functionable yet simple product that allows a development team to collect information about its creation using the least amount of time, money, and effort possible, in order to later have those resources to iterate new and better versions based on experience and not just hypotheses. In my department at the BDCV, Coordinación de Innovación Digital, one of our regular tasks is to provide innovative solutions. Innovation is risky. It is hard to know if a new idea will have the impact one hopes, especially since many factors tend to be at play (budget, community acceptance, technical difficulties, etc.). The MVP approach has been extremely useful in this framework, and the BDCV's Wikimedia engagement's continuity plan was no exception. Thus, for 2019 we integrated only two Wiki activities to our annual plan: participating in the #1Bib1Ref campaign and organizing one edit-a-thon. We wanted to test three aspects: evaluate the fitness of our human and material resources to fulfill these tasks without Murrieta's assistance, the aptness of the documentation we had created with our WIR's help, and get feedback from both our colleagues and the community for our next iteration.

Regarding the first aspect, we learned that not only our resources were sufficient but also that the liaisons forged during our WIR's residency continued to enrich our assets. Additionally, we found out that if our goals were kept simple but also creative, we could achieve more with less. For instance, in the 2019 and 2020 iteration of #1Bib1Ref we set an "MVP" goal for our campaign (i.e. adding five citations per librarian) but also updated a collaborative spreadsheet of contributions with our weekly contributions. This was a great way of both ensuring an achievable goal and promoting a healthy competition. The result was that in 2020, two years after our first #1Bib1Ref training, BDCV librarians contributed one-quarter (n = 309) of the references of that year's campaign (Gutiérrez De la Torre, 2020b). Since the second and the third aspect (documentation and feedback) are not directly related to the MVP approach, I will treat them in the following two sections.

GETTING YOUR BRIQUETTES READY: DOCUMENTATION

In all of our events, Murrieta was key in documenting three types of records: editable files for our recurrent events (publicity or bureaucratic procedures); checklists for crucial actions; and "how-to" tutorials (for instance, how to insert a manual reference in a Wikipedia article). As for the editable files, they can be summarized as follows:

1. A folder in our institution's shared storing space (SharePoint Teams) with all the materials we need. We established different subfolders for each campaign, so, for instance, in the #1Bib1Ref folder we have the collaborative spreadsheet in which we register our #1Bib1Ref contributions.
2. E-mail templates for the reminders we send every year before the campaign starts.

3. A list of tools that the #1Bib1Ref coordinator can use to identify Wikipedia articles that are susceptible of improvement (PetScan, CitationHunt).

4. Tutorials with the most important steps to find articles that need citations and how to add them.

5. Poster and social media image templates with the campaign's logo.

6. A curated Zotero collection in which we have a list of useful material in our collection that can be used as source for the edit-a-thons. This list is especially useful since it includes each materials' call number and it makes them easier to retrieve (see figure 5).

This checklist was created after our first edit-a-thon, and it has been fine-tuned after each edit-a-thon (Murrieta et al., 2018). This tool, together with our manuals collection, has proven extremely useful in minimizing time needed for planning and assessing, and enabling the continuity of these type of events. The checklist contains every aspect of the event from how to book the snack room (which we use in our edit-a-thon breaks) to how to ask for dedicated Wi-Fi (which one may need if too many people attend your Wikipedia editing event).

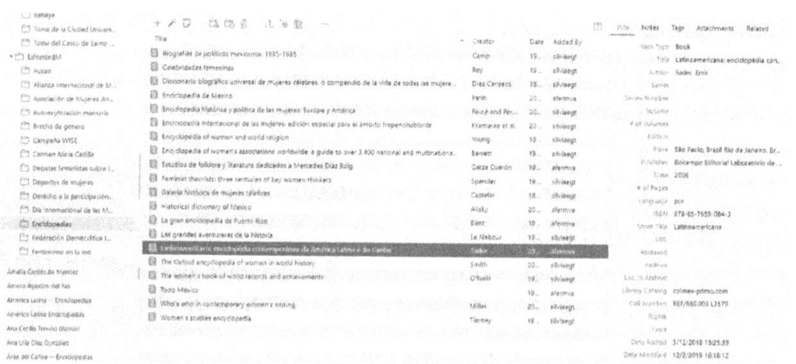

Figure 5 Screenshot showing the Zotero curated list of bibliographic material for the gender edit-a-thon.

Finally, a few remarks about our "how-to" tutorials. Murrieta and I created these based on recurrent questions we received during our workshops such as: how to start an account, how to add a reference, how to upload an image. Many of these skills were already available in video form (Wikimedia Argentina, 2017); however, during our edit-a-thons, some of our older participants expressed the need to have those instructions printed out or as a still image so that they could come back to them in a format they felt more comfortable with. Initially, in our grant's plan proposal, we had thought about creating an offline publishing booklet with these materials (Gutiérrez De la Torre, 2017). However, given the richness of formats (webinars, slides, video tutorials, manuals, etc.) that had been created by the Spanish-speaking Wikimedia community, we thought about another strategy. Why not curate these resources (which had been shared with Creative Commons licenses) in an online digital collection? With a metadata librarian mindset and powered by an open-source content management system (Omeka), we launched *Wikipedia y Bibliotecas* (https://wiki-bibliotecas.colmex.mx/). Apart from the traditional metadata search options, developer Jaime Cisneros and I created several entry points for the collection: Keyword tag clouds, subject indexes, and collections organized by format (slide presentations, cheat sheets, webinars, or video tutorials). We also included a map of Wikibrarians. As the name suggests, this section includes an interactive map with the names and contact forms of librarians from Latin America who are already collaborating within the Wikimedia universe so that they can be reached by potential collaborators.

A FIREPLACE GUARD: FEEDBACK

In May 2020, I conducted two in-depth, follow-up interviews with volunteer BDCV colleagues about the residency. In her interview, Claudia Escobar discussed her motives in joining the Wiki movement: one of these incentives was the fact that in our country there aren't enough librarians[5] and participating in Wikipedia is a way of amplifying our work by sharing what we do (whether it is curated information as bibliographies, Wikipedia workshops to teach critical information literacy, or participating in #1Bib1Ref initiatives in order to make articles more reliable). Camelia Romero, however, raised some interesting issues regarding the lack of information about how Wikipedia readers actually read the information we create.[6] She also questioned the lack of a consistent criterion behind protected pages (Protection Policy, 2020) and pointed out a troubling pattern for accepted and rejected edits in gender-related articles: many gender-related articles are "protected pages" that cannot be edited. Romero suggested that we should analyze which type of edits are accepted and which ones are rejected to better guide edit-a-thon participants.

Finally, event participants raised interesting questions that provided a humbling perspective on Wikipedia as an open-access, public-knowledge project. Mixe activist Tajëëw B. Díaz Roble expressed that for some indigenous people who are dealing with invasive resource extraction companies and forced displacement of their communities, editing Wikipedia is not always a priority. As a librarian, we often wish to use our privilege as a platform to write about these subjects. However, the "nothing about us without us" slogan has also made me rethink how Wikipedia, despite being a powerful tool to communicate to a part of the world—that part that has Internet access, technological devices, electricity, written knowledge culture, and proficiency in one of the Wikipedia Languages—well, it is just a *part* of the world. Moreover, even if people who belong to that part of the world *can* use Wikipedia, they may not necessarily *want* or *need* to communicate that way. In other words, to unlearn the unquestioned urgency (and illusion) of global impact. In November 2019, for example, the BDCV created a series of workshops for public libraries in Mexico City. One of them was about Wikipedia, and Claudia Escobar and I were in charge of it. We created a round of presentations where we asked participants to talk about their responsibilities in their library expecting to use those answers as a bridge between their activities and the Wikimedia Foundation's mission: "to empower and engage people around the world to collect and develop educational content under a free license" (Wikimedia Foundation, 2018). But then the answers came: painting furniture and fixing the light were not uncommon activities. Later, in what became almost a cathartic session, we learned how some of the participants have to close their library earlier in the day during the winter months because they have no electricity—let alone computers or Internet. Yet, without electricity, computers, or Internet, these librarians "collect and develop educational content" and they are in their own right a "fireplace" around which so many children have found not only knowledge but also warmth. In sum, feedback sessions, both with colleagues and with participants, can help to create better events (i.e., adjusting workshops with gender-specific Wikipedia issues) and to identify strategies and tools relevant to the communities they will bring light to.

Final Remarks

As a student attending a state university in a country where all major bureaucratic, productive, and cultural units are around the capital city, Wikipedia changed the opportunities I had to access knowledge. For this reason, I have tried to give back to this amazing project and share the power I have had the privilege to cultivate. Working in an academic library, I have been able to fulfill this sense of purpose, thanks to the open hearts and minds of my university's authorities and my colleagues who have supported and broadened the Wikipedia initiative in our library. More importantly, I have had the privilege to encounter others who fulfill this mission in other ways, and who have allowed me to understand the multiplicity of platforms from which we can reach the goal of open knowledge. I would like to finish this chapter with a photograph that illustrates these final thoughts (see figure 6). This photograph was uploaded to Wikimedia Commons during the *Movimientos Sociales* edit-a-thon. In it one can see people of different ages burning paper to illuminate the night of the 1968 protests in Mexico. I imagine some of them were using newspapers, others an old magazine. But that does not matter, because their faces are all lit. In a similar way, I believe it is less important which tools we choose to light up our "fires." What matters is that if we understand librarianship as an opportunity to share the privilege of knowledge some of us have,

Figure 6 Students holding hands and burning a newspaper during the demonstrations of the Student Movement in Mexico City, October 1968. Image donated by photographer Héctor Gallardo (CC-BY-4.0) during the Social Movements Edit-a-thon. A 1968 picture of people in a protest in Mexico City, some holding hands, some holding burning pieces of paper.

as an opportunity to create safe spaces for conversations and facilitate access and discovery, we must build our "hearth." We need it, because, as many have shouted with hope, "if we don't burn together, who will light this darkness?"

Notes

1 The Wikidata Query can be retrieved here: https://tinyurl.com/y3a68vmo.

2 For more information on how the data was cleaned as well as a complete file with the changes, please go to the released data in Zenodo (Gutiérrez De la Torre, 2020a).

3 This information can be found both in WQ and MGW.

4 Bear in mind that there have been other collaborations with libraries that have not been officially named as WIRs (i.e., Wikimedia Argentina, 2020) but have been declared as a WIR elsewhere (see Horvat, 2019).

5 According to a 1995 study, from 1990 until 1992 only twenty-five librarians nationwide had defended their bachelor's thesis (Brito et al., 2013, p. 154)

6 Until 2014, there was no literature focused on the readers of Wikipedia and other aspects of its readership (Okoli et al., 2014), although some studies have followed there has not been any studying the Mexican case.

References

#1Bib1Ref. (n.d.). Grupos de Facebook; Grupos de Facebook. Retrieved December 19, 2020, from www.facebook.com/groups/242309702983405/.

ACULibrary. (2011, January 7). State Library of Queensland donates. . . *Library News.* https://web.archive.org/web/20111108093954/https://blogs.acu.edu.au/library/2011/01/07/state-library-of-queensland-donates/.

Basel University Library. (2018, April 23). Wikimedia Commons. https://commons.wikimedia.org/wiki/User:Basel_University_Library.

Biblioteca Colmex. (2018, October 1). Nuestra primer wikipedista con la playera oficial patrocinada por @USB_REBIUdeG #WikiDBCV #M68 #WikiM68. . . ¡participa y ven por la tuya! Https://t.co/TJ6RKl-VOxw [Tweet]. *@BiblioColmex.* https://twitter.com/BiblioColmex/status/1046836659768238080.

Biblioteca Daniel Cosío Villegas. (2017, August 1). Wikipedista en residencia. *Biblioteca Daniel Cosío Villegas.* https://web.archive.org/web/20171001120850/https://biblioteca.colmex.mx/index.php/noticias/276-wiki.

Bocanegra Esqueda, T. (2017, June 1). Las bibliotecas con el Orgullo: Tres libros sobre cultura gay [Billet]. *Amontonamos las palabras: Blog de la Biblioteca de El Colegio de México.* https://bdcv.hypotheses.org/428.

British Library Project Page. (2013, May 7). Wikipedia, the Free Encyclopedia. https://en.wikipedia.org/w/index.php?title=Wikipedia:GLAM/British_Library/Articles&oldid=553933758.

Brito, E. B., Rivero, E. G. S., García, M. J., & Alvarez, F. F. (2013). Bibliografía comentada de los egresados de las escuelas de bibliotecología de México. *Boletín del Instituto de Investigaciones Bibliográficas, 0*(7), Article 7. http://publicaciones.iib.unam.mx/index.php/boletin/article/view/546.

Cano, G., & Romero Millán, C. (2020). *Estudios de Género. Fuentes para su historia.* https://historiageneromexico.colmex.mx/.

Cohen, N. (2010, June 4). Venerable British Museum Enlists in the Wikipedia Revolution. *The New York Times.* www.nytimes.com/2010/06/05/arts/design/05wiki.html.

¿Cómo participar en la campaña #1BIB1REF? (2018, May 7). El Colegio de México A.C. www.youtube.com/watch?v=_KQN2S-m_bs&t=5s.

Doyle, K. (2017, June 1). Creating A Model for Helping Women Thrive in Wikipedia—Women's Media Center. *WMC Speech Project.* https://womensmediacenter.com/speech-project/creating-a-model-for-helping-women-thrive-in-wikipedia.

Education/Countries/México/El Colegio de México. (2019, February 13). Wikimedia Outreach. https://outreach.wikimedia.org/wiki/Education/Countries/M%C3%A9xico/El_Colegio_de_M%C3%A9xico.

Escobar Farfán, J. I. (2019). Nahuatl contemporary writing: Studying convergence in the absence of a written norm [PhD Thesis]. University of Sheffield.

Garber, M. (2014, March 12). Harvard's Looking for a 'Wikipedian in Residence'. *The Atlantic.* www.theatlantic.com/technology/archive/2014/03/harvards-looking-for-a-wikipedian-in-residence/284373/.

Gill, S. (2020, March). Mapping GLAM-Wiki collaborations. *This Month in GLAM, X*(III). https://outreach.wikimedia.org/wiki/GLAM/Newsletter/March_2020/Contents/WMF_GLAM_report.

González, A. (2020). La lengua española y las culturas hispánicas. *Versants. Revista suiza de literaturas románicas, 3*(67), Article 67. https://doi.org/10.22015/V.RSLR/67.3.4.

Gutiérrez De la Torre, S. E. (2017, March). First Wikipedian in (Academic) Residence in Latin America. *Wikimedia Meta-Wiki.* https://meta.wikimedia.org/wiki/Grants:Project/ColMex/First_Wikipedian_in_(Academic)_Residence_in_Latin_America.

Gutiérrez De la Torre, S. E. (2020a). Scrubbed data on Wikipedians in Residence in Libraries based on the Mapping GLAM-Wiki collaborations [Data set]. *Zenodo.* https://doi.org/10.5281/zenodo.4367626.

Gutiérrez De la Torre, S. E. (2020b). Datos finales de la campaña #1Bib1Ref 2020 [Data set]. *Zenodo.* https://doi.org/10.5281/zenodo.4367343.

Gutiérrez De la Torre, S. E. (2020c). WiRs in Libraries [Map]. *CARTO.* https://silviaegt.carto.com/builder/9754d64c-600e-4d52-bec5-60a9e9f5ecf2.

Harold B. Lee Library. (2020, April 15). Wikipedia, the Free Encyclopedia. https://en.wikipedia.org/w/index.php?title=Wikipedia:GLAM/Harold_B._Lee_Library&oldid=951126474.

Horvat, A. (2019, November 4). Quién es y qué hace el joven argentino que está detrás de Wikipedia. *La Nación.* www.lanacion.com.ar/sociedad/quien-es-que-hace-joven-argentino-esta-nid2302912.

Instituto Cervantes. (2019). El español una lengua viva (p. 95). *Departamento de Comunicación Digital del Instituto Cervantes.* www.cervantes.es/imagenes/File/espanol_lengua_viva_2019.pdf.

Johnson, M., & Jue, M. (2017, June 9). Ten community-led projects awarded Project Grants. *Wikimedia Foundation.* https://wikimediafoundation.org/news/2017/06/09/project-grants-round-one-2017/.

Librosb4tipos. (2019, March 15). Terminamos una sesión más del Editatón junto con @Wikimedia_mx, creamos y mejoramos entradas en Wikipedia sobre acoso sexual. Muchas gracias a quienes nos acompañaron y felicidades a las ganadoras del los ejemplares que nos dio @Langosta_Lit 1. https://t.co/S6l0S6ClaB [Tweet]. @Librosb4Tipos. https://twitter.com/Librosb4Tipos/status/1106352906960363520.

Mesa Redonda—Haciendo y deshaciendo el género. (2018, March 5). www.youtube.com/watch?v=GyTUtfaBFCo.

Murrieta, A., Gutiérrez De la Torre, S., & Chávez, M. (2018). Lista de Control para organizar un editatón. https://doi.org/10.5281/zenodo.1249696.

National Wikimedian at the National Library of Wales. (2019, June 17). Wikipedia, the Free Encyclopedia. https://en.wikipedia.org/w/index.php?title=User:Jason.nlw/National_Wikimedian_at_the_National_Library_of_Wales/Data&oldid=902204436.

Navarro, J. G. (2020, April 7). Number of internet users in Mexico from 2001 to 2019 [Statista]. *Statista.* www.statista.com/statistics/731290/number-of-internet-users-mexico/.

Okoli, C., Mehdi, M., Mesgari, M., Nielsen, F. Å., & Lanamäki, A. (2014). Wikipedia in the eyes of its beholders: A systematic review of scholarly research on Wikipedia readers and readership. *Journal of the Association for Information Science and Technology, 65*(12), 2381–403. https://doi.org/10.1002/asi.23162.

Protection policy. (2020, December 15). Wikipedia, the Free Encyclopedia. https://en.wikipedia.org/w/index.php?title=Wikipedia:Protection_policy&oldid=994355906.

Quiroa, L. (2017, July 5). Wikipedia: Editatón Louis Pouzin en la Biblioteca Daniel Cosío Villegas [Billet]. *Amontonamos las palabras: Blog de la Biblioteca de El Colegio de México.* https://bdcv.hypotheses.org/485.

Ries, E. (2011). *The lean startup.* Crown Business.

Romero Millán, C. (2017). Modelo terminológico para representar documentos sobre género en México [PhD thesis]. Universidad Nacional Autónoma de México.

Shin, A. (2017, January 5). Wikipedia was born in 2001. And the world got a bit truthier. *Washington* Post. www.washingtonpost.com/lifestyle/magazine/wikipedia-was-born-in-2001-and-the-world-got-a-bit-truthier/2017/01/04/1d082742-bb0f-11e6-ac85-094a21c44abc_story.html.

Stinson, A., & Evans, J. (2018). Bringing Wiki(p/m)edians into the Conversation at Libraries. In M. Proffitt (Ed.), *Leveraging Wikipedia: Connecting Communities of Knowledge* (pp. 31–54). ALA Editions.

The National Library of Scotland GLAM Project. (2020, July 7). Wikipedia, the Free Encyclopedia. https://en.wikipedia.org/w/index.php?title=Wikipedia:GLAM/NLS/Events&oldid=966520053.

TwitterSearch(#1Bib1Ref)(from:BiblioColmex)until:2018–05–30since:2018–04–26. (2018, May 30). Twitter. https://twitter.com/search?q=%28%231bib1ref%29+%28from%3abibliocolmex%29+until%3a2018-05-30+since%3a2018-04-26.

Velella, R. (2014, August 5). User:Rob at Houghton. *Wikimedia Commons.* https://commons.wikimedia.org/wiki/User:Rob_at_Houghton.

Wikimedia Argentina. (2017, February 13). Tutoriales. www.youtube.com/watch?v=a-yzdxe_PaY&list=PLFKNtUouDusw4y4yZQmLpEAQ_LziFKKhm.

Wikimedia Argentina. (2020, October 30). Proyecto de digitalización. *Wikimedia Meta-Wiki.* https://meta.wikimedia.org/wiki/Wikimedia_Argentina/GLAM/Proyecto_de_digitalizaci%C3%B3n.

Wikimedia Foundation. (2018, May 31). Wikimedia Foundation mission. *Wikimedia Foundation.* https://wikimediafoundation.org/about/mission/.

'Wikipedia 101' series. (2020, August 21). Wikipedia, the Free Encyclopedia. https://en.wikipedia.org/w/index.php?title=Wikipedia:GLAM/UAlberta Library/WikiWeds&oldid=974179876.

Wikipedia Collaboration at the University of Alberta. (2020, August 21). Wikipedia, the Free Encyclopedia. https://en.wikipedia.org/w/index.php?title=Wikipedia:GLAM/UAlbertaLibrary/WIR&oldid=974180648.

Wikiprojekt Biblioteki Narodowej. (2019, April 12). Wikipedia. https://pl.wikipedia.org/w/index.php?title=Wikiprojekt:GLAM/Biblioteka_Narodowa&oldid=56429709.

Zachte, E. (2013, September 30). Page Edits Per Wikipedia Language. *Wikimedia Traffic Analysis Report.* https://stats.wikimedia.org/wikimedia/squids/SquidReportPageEditsPerLanguageBreakdown.htm.

Вики библиотекар/2019. (2020, January 8). Википедију, Слободну Енциклопедију. https://tinyurl.com/y2dxl44o.

Универзитетска библиотека 2014. (2019, March 11). Википедију, слободну енциклопедију. https://tinyurl.com/yxn7aj54.

Число российских вики-резидентов удвоилось. (2014, October 10). Викиновости. https://tinyurl.com/y57hthpx.

CHAPTER 13

CHANGING THE WAY STORIES ARE TOLD: ENGAGING STAFF AND STUDENTS IN IMPROVING WIKIPEDIA CONTENT ABOUT WOMEN IN SCOTLAND

Ewan McAndrew[1]

[1] University of Edinburgh

Abstract

The University of Edinburgh was the first UK university to employ a Wikimedian-in-Residence (WiR) to support students and staff across the whole university. Over the last five years, the project aimed to develop information literacy and digital research skills and to address the gender disparity of editors and participants in the community. The project has demonstrated the University of Edinburgh's commitment to foster staff and student engagement as active digital citizens of the world and was awarded the 2019 Herald Higher Education Award for "Innovative Use of Technology in the Curriculum."

The residency also focuses on addressing the content on gender gaps and improving coverage of women in science, technology, engineering, and mathematics (STEM). Our first Wikipedia edit-a-thon in 2015 was based on "the Edinburgh Seven"—the first women to study medicine at the University. The WiR collaborated with the University archives team to develop an exhibit celebrating

Scotland's Suffragettes and facilitated a student internship that was awarded the Digital Humanities Award for Best Data Visualization 2019 for the Wikidata Map of Accused Witches in Scotland.

This chapter will showcase stories of student engagement and collaboration inside and outside the curriculum, providing exemplars of how students have engaged with, and been intrinsically motivated by, researching and publishing their scholarship online in a real-world application of their learning. This chapter will also outline why employing a Wikimedian-in-Residence, alongside other learning technologists and digital skills trainers, is a worthwhile return of investment for universities.

Keywords

University of Edinburgh, Wikimedian-in-Residence, Gender gap, Digital skills, Information literacy.

So [in Wikipedia] we've created the greatest creation of the 21st century and we talk about open, we talk about open a lot. And yet, we've created a place where a group of people, who are *not* a minority . . . Hands up anyone who has met a woman? Any in their families? . . . Wikipedia seemed such an amazing opportunity to democratise information and for everyone to participate but we're already at a place where we've created a place where women are choosing not to spend time or contribute . . . We need to be doing more. (Highton, 2015)

Introduction

Founded in 1582, the University of Edinburgh is one of Scotland's ancient universities and the sixth oldest in the English-speaking world. Its mission is the creation, dissemination and curation of knowledge and it aims to make a "significant, sustainable and socially responsible contribution to Scotland, the UK and the world" (Vision and Mission, 2016)

In 2014, a national debate was taking place in Scotland about how to make a fairer, better, more inclusive society in the run up to the referendum on Scottish independence (Libby Brooks, 2014). This was also the year that the students' association encouraged the University's senior managers to explore how learning materials could be made open, not only for students within the university but across Scotland and the wider world. Student engagement and co-creation have been fundamental aspects of open education resources (OERs) work at the University of Edinburgh ever since.

Open Edinburgh

The University's OER vision, championed by Assistant Principal for Online Learning, Dr. Melissa Highton, sought to meet the modern-day challenges the university faced in terms of scale, sustainability, and reuse. This vision was backed by an OER policy (approved by the Senate Learning and Teaching Committee in 2015) which articulates that the creation of open knowledge and open educational resources is fully in keeping with the institutional vision, purpose and values—"to discover knowledge and make the world a better place, while ensuring that our teaching and research is diverse, inclusive, accessible to all and relevant to society" (About - Open.Ed, 2016). To implement the OER policy, a new OER Service was created to help advise and support academic colleagues, along with the role of Wikimedian-in-Residence, to further embed open practice at the university.

"You Can't Afford Not To"

The value proposition for the new OER policy had to be something that senior managers could say "yes" to. One of the most compelling reasons for investing in open educational resources at the institutional level is the concept of "copyright debt" (Highton, 2015). This concept looked at creating and using OERs as an important way to ensure longevity of access to course materials, which can benefit staff, students and the university itself. The reason being that if you don't get the licensing right first-time round, it will cost more to fix it further down the line. And the cost and reputational risk to the university could be significant if copyright is breached.

Senior managers also have budget lines earmarked to support key institutional commitments, so the Wikimedian-in-Residence role was closely aligned with these. Employing a Wikimedian therefore represented value for money for the University as there would be a manifest return of investment. The reason being that the kind of activities Wikimedians support are ones which evidence institutional commitment to a multitude of the key priorities currently challenging the UK higher education sector. Namely, supporting the information literacy and digital skills needs of staff and students and meeting strategic commitments to open knowledge, open science and gender equality (Gender Equality, 2020).

Promoting Knowledge Equity and Twenty-First-Century Skills

Hosting a Wikimedian at the university is a vehicle to deliver on these commitments and to promote knowledge equity, through sharing "histories and perspectives that may have been excluded by structures of power and privilege" (Wikimedia, Promoting Knowledge Equity, 2020).

In 2014, biographies about women on English Wikipedia, the largest OER in human history, stood at a mere 15.53 percent (Mathewson, 2020). Surveys have indicated that only 15–20 percent of editors are female with one particular 2011 survey suggesting that around 91.5 percent of editors were male (Balch, 2019; Wikimedia, 2011). The residency was a way to inspire women through celebrating women role models and making them visible on Wikipedia, the most public of digital platforms, and to recruit a *diversity* of Wikipedia editors to help address content that was skewed or less than fulsome. A way to "do more." Particularly where Edinburgh had a rich story to tell.

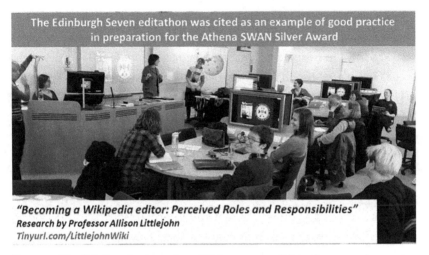

The Edinburgh Seven editathon was cited as an example of good practice in preparation for the Athena SWAN Silver Award

"Becoming a Wikipedia editor: Perceived Roles and Responsibilities"
Research by Professor Allison Littlejohn
Tinyurl.com/LittlejohnWiki

Figure 1 The Edinburgh edit-a-thon, February 2015. (McAndrew, 2019).

The Edinburgh Seven

The very first University of Edinburgh Wikipedia editing event, or edit-a-thon, took place in February 2015, with the aim of increasing female involvement in Wikipedia editing. Melissa Highton was interested to see how colleagues would take to these editing events, what their impact could be, and whether they could support teaching and learning.

The theme was "Women in Science and Scottish History" (Women, Science and Scottish History editathon series, 2015), and the event ran over four days, with visiting Wikimedian-in-Residence, Dr. Ally Crockford from the National Library of Scotland and Dr. Sara Thomas from Museums and Galleries Scotland. They facilitated the training of new editors to create Wikipedia pages about "the Edinburgh Seven." Led by Sophia Jex-Blake, the Edinburgh Seven were the first group of matriculated undergraduate female students at any British university when they began studying medicine in 1869. This theme was apposite in that it allowed participants to consider both the culture of the University, then and now, and the culture of Wikipedia—in terms of women "breaking into an area where they weren't welcome" (Highton, 2015). Beyond this, participants had to consider how to tell this story for a global audience; how best to honor the struggle of the Edinburgh

Seven and their refusal to accept the stories *they* were told—that university education was not for women. And how to communicate their legacy and the positive strides made since; where female undergraduates now form the majority enrolled at the University of Edinburgh (University factsheet, 2020).

Participants came together at the university's Appleton Tower and were guided each day to create, improve, and illustrate pages on Wikipedia with a focus on people and places relating to Edinburgh's role in the history of medicine. Professor Allison Littlejohn helped evaluate what was happening during the Edinburgh edit-a-thon and her published research revealed there was formal and informal learning occurring at these editing events, contributing to the formation of networks of practice and social capital (Rehm et al., 2018). Participants considered the edit-a-thon an important part of their professional development and workplace learning of digital skills. A second paper examined the process of becoming a Wikipedia editor through quasi-ethnographic interviews with edit-a-thon participants (Hood & Littlejohn, 2018). Bringing these stories to light was seen by participants as a form of knowledge activism. Particularly, in addressing areas of underrepresentation, as there was a realization among participants that when learning becomes personal it triggers forms of agency (Littlejohn, 2019).

Balance for Better—The Edinburgh Residency

If you put your Wikimedian alongside your digital skill trainers and learning technologists, their impact can be significant.

—Melissa Highton, February 2017.

Professor Littlejohn's research evidence from the Edinburgh Seven edit-a-thon helped cement the business case for hosting a Wikimedian-in-Residence to support staff and students across the institution as part of the university's digital skills agenda. The residency commenced in January 2016 and was immediately positioned as a centrally available resource within the Information Services Group (ISG), a converged library and information technology service, which acts to support the work of the University's three teaching colleges.

The resident, Ewan McAndrew, worked with course teams to quickly generate real examples of technology-enhanced learning activities appropriate to the curriculum. As a result, students in a variety of disciplines benefit from learning new digital and information literacy skills appropriate for the modern graduate. The published outputs of their learning have an immediate public impact in addressing the diversity of editors and diversity of content shared online. For example, World Christianity postgraduate students wrote new pages about women in religion and on topics such as Asian Feminist Theology, and Reproductive Biology undergraduate students, where each year ~90 percent of the cohort are female, worked collaboratively to create missing articles related to reproductive health.

Many of the training workshops facilitated by the residency focused on addressing underrepresentation of topics on Wikipedia and encouraging more women to become editors. Student societies have been motivated to initiate collaborations with the residency and have designed and lead edit-a-thon events focused on such topics as Women in Science, Technology, Engineering and Maths (STEM), LGBT+ History Month, Black History Month, Mental Health Week, and Edinburgh's global alumni.

Between 2016 and 2020, the residency has worked with over a dozen course programs, facilitated over 200 training workshops along with 100 edit-a-thon events celebrating: International Women's Day; Ada Lovelace Day; Gothic Writers; Feminist Writers; Women Architects; Contemporary Scottish Artists, Scottish women authors; Women in Anthropology, Women in Chemistry, Women in Law and Global Health; Women in Engineering; and Women in Espionage. A thousand students and 500 staff have now been trained to edit Wikipedia, with an estimated 3,500 articles created and improved. Stories that may not have been shared otherwise are now discoverable and being read, added to and improved, as OERs shared with the world for the benefit of all.

Women in Red Workshops

Wikipedia has a gender problem. In considering the diversity of editors and content, "the "overwhelming majority of contributors are male" and the vast majority of biographies (81 percent on English

Wikipedia) are about men (Ford & Wajcman, 2017). This means there is *clear* gender bias in terms of the stories being disseminated online, the choices being made in their creation and curation and who is writing these stories (Allen, 2020).

Yet, 69 percent of participating editors at the University of Edinburgh have been women, demonstrating that Wikipedia editing does not *have* to be the preserve of "white, college-educated males" (Wikimedia, 2011). Addressing systemic bias and underrepresentation online has consistently been a key motivator for staff and students at the University—working toward building a fairer, more inclusive Internet and society.

The residency has facilitated monthly "Wiki Women in Red" workshops for the last four years and created a supportive setting where students and staff can come together to learn a new digital skill. Attendees research a notable woman not yet represented with a page on Wikipedia (a red hyperlinked article title on Wikipedia indicates people or topics without a Wikipedia page . . . yet), then apply their new skills by turning this red link "blue" through writing and publishing a brand-new page as a blue clickable link as a tangible outcome they can be proud of. As a result of the success of this approach, Wikipedia Women in Red edit-a-thons are now included in the University's Athena Scientific Women's Academic Network (SWAN) charter plan to highlight female achievement in science, technology, engineering, and mathematics (STEM) to encourage and inspire new STEM careers.

The Map of Accused Witches in Scotland

The Data Visualization Internship was organized through Equate Scotland Careerwise—an initiative that arranges paid placements in industry for women working in STEM subjects. Geography undergraduate Emma Carroll spent three months working with the residency, learning new digital and data literacy skills, in order to add coordinate positions for all the locations cataloged in the landmark Survey of Scottish Witchcraft database to Wikidata (The University of Edinburgh, 2003).

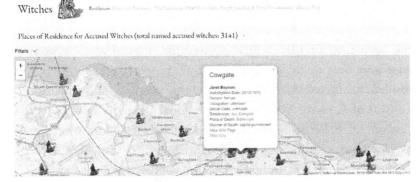

Figure 2 Screengrab of the Wikidata-driven map of accused witches in Scotland. University of Edinburgh, CC-BY-SA Available at: witches.is.ed.ac.uk.

At project completion, the places of residence for 3,141 men and women accused of witchcraft in Scotland (85 percent of them women) were geolocated on a Wikidata-driven map website so that anyone in Scotland can find out about the accusations of witchcraft that happened near them. The map succeeds in highlighting the sheer scale and intensity of the Scottish witch hunts to a modern audience, as well as in localizing and humanizing the individual stories of the women who were persecuted. Additionally, "Women in Red" editors at the University created pages for over twenty notable women accused of witchcraft in Scotland. One of which includes Lilias Adie, the only accused witch in Scotland for whom we can put a face to, thanks to forensic artists at the University of Dundee digitally reconstructing her face and then sharing this image to her newly created Wikipedia page (Younger, 2017).

Since the map website launched in September 2019, this project has gained worldwide media coverage, stimulating interest in these stories and Emma has since presented on her work at the second "Remembering Scotland's Accused Witches Conference" in November 2020. The conference is part of growing grassroots movement to memorialize what happened to these women and the Wikidata map is viewed as an important resource in furthering this aim and for uncovering more of these women's stories.

Scotland's Suffragettes

In recognition of the centennial celebration of the Representation of the People Act of 1918, which ensured the right to vote for women who were over thirty and met minimum property qualifications, the resident facilitated three Wikipedia editing events for the university's Festival of Creative Learning, International Women's Day, and Processions 2018. Participants researched, published, and illustrated new Wikipedia articles about Scotland's suffragettes. These newly published open educational resources are an act of solidarity and celebration so that the stories of these extraordinary women's contributions to women's suffrage will be read, added to, and remembered.

In total, staff and student volunteer editors surfaced 34 new biography articles on Wikipedia about Scotland's suffragettes and improved 220 more articles so that people could discover all about the important contributions these women made in the fight for women's suffrage, individually and collectively. Images of these women help make their stories more impactful, more real, and more human. Editors identified images and contacted libraries, archives, and museums to ask if they would consider sharing these images openly as a gift to the cultural commons. Many were only too happy to help illustrate these new pages, and, by extension, help bring these stories to a modern audience through the creation of a new interactive timeline of women's suffrage in Scotland.

An Interactive Timeline of Women's Suffrage

A hybrid exhibition, showcasing both digital and physical artifacts, was created by the residency in collaboration with the Library and University Collections team in November 2018. The exhibition unveiled a bespoke Histropedia digital timeline of women's suffrage in Scotland (Vote 100— Histropedia Timelines, 2018) allowing the newly created Wikipedia pages on Scotland's suffragettes to be explored collectively via an interactive website, accessible online and on a smart table in the library foyer.

The physical artifacts illustrated how some of the University of Edinburgh's first female graduates advocated for equal

Figure 3 Screengrab of the women's suffrage in Scotland Navbox, specially created to add at the foot of each of the Scottish suffragette's Wikipedia pages. CC-BY-SA.

enfranchisement in the United Kingdom and focused on the three students who demonstrated at the House of Lords in November of 1908: Chrystal MacMillan, Margaret Nairn, and Frances Simson (University of Edinburgh's suffragettes fight for the right to vote, 2018). The exhibition was praised by Students Association vice president for education, Diva Mukherji, who connected this historical event to the present moment when speaking about how inspiring the women were for students today, showing that students had fought for their rights and for equality.

New navigation templates (figure 3) have also been created to pull all these women's stories together so that when reading about one of Scotland's suffragettes, it is also possible to navigate easily to other related stories, through hyperlinks grouped and organized in a box at the foot of the page. So that all these stories can be more easily discovered, navigation boxes were also created and added to each of the Edinburgh Seven's pages, every page about an accused witch in Scotland and all nineteen of the extraordinary women chemists who petitioned the Chemical Society for Fellowship in 1904.

Conclusion

Representation matters. Learning about these stories matters. Gaps in our shared knowledge excludes the vitally important contributions of many within our community. Universities can help remove barriers and kick open more doors. They have access to knowledge and information and, with that, an ethical responsibility to share that knowledge for the greater good. These edit-a-thons, or 'diversithons', are one way to start nudging the door open.

Diversity matters because gender inequality in science and technology is all too real (Women in STEM | Percentages of Women in STEM Statistics, 2021). Increasing the visibility and diversity of topics and inspirational role models online can not only encourage more into STEM careers but also help inform and shape our physical environments to be more inclusive spaces.

> Meanings are projected not just by the buildings themselves, but by how they are furnished and decorated. And where almost every image—portrait, photograph, statue—of academic achievement and leadership is masculine (and nearly always white middle-aged), the meaning is clear: to be a successful leader, gender and ethnicity matter. (Spiller & Moffat, 2017)

The Edinburgh Seven have now finally been awarded their degrees posthumously at a special ceremony (Edinburgh gives female medical students their degrees—150 years late, 2019). A blue plaque was erected, marking the Seven's rightful place in history. It's impossible to know exactly how many people have walked past it, or stopped to read it. But we know their Wikipedia pages are being found, with over 78,000 page views for Sophia Jex-Blake's page and 52,000 page views for the Edinburgh Seven page.

While there is no known image of all seven women together, a new portrait by photographer Laurence Winram (figure 4) has been commissioned by the University of Edinburgh's Medical School, which now hangs in its Sophia Jex-Blake common room, to commemorate them. The new portrait draws inspiration also from the present-day students featured in the portrait, who collected the posthumous

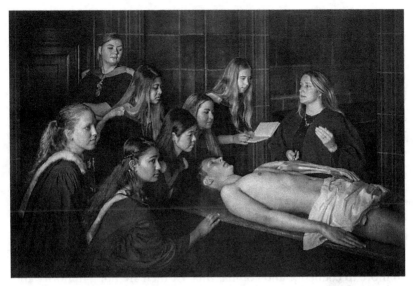

Figure 4 The Edinburgh Seven. A reimagining of a Rembrandt painting from 1632 called "The Anatomy Lesson of Nicolaes Tulp." Those featured are the students who collected the posthumous degrees on the Seven's behalf: Simran Piya, Megan Cameron, Ella Crowther, Caitlyn Taylor, Izzie Dighero, Mei Yen Liew, Sorna Paramananthan, Liam Parkinson—cadaver, and Alethea Kelsey—teacher. Photographer Laurence Winram. Copyright University of Edinburgh.

degrees on the Seven's behalf and who are now forging their own careers in medicine.

> Their acts opened up a door to a university education which remains open
> for thousands of students today. (Kelly, 2019)

There is something very "real and tangibly useful" in doing this work and surfacing these women's stories, something that remains after the publishing of a page (Seery, 2017). There's a lasting sense of pride, satisfaction, and achievement that these stories are out there in the world. And that others will discover them, learn from them, be provoked by them. These pages will have a life of their own as OERs released into the world and will grow, change, and spark ideas. They may very well even outlive us.

The lives and contributions of extraordinary women are recorded in various sources. It's about choosing to write their stories on Wikipedia. There is a labor to this work, undoubtedly. But it's worthwhile work. And while the size of the challenge is massive, we have the numbers to rise to it—Wikipedia is a website that anyone can edit after all—but only if we choose to undertake and *value* this work. And only if we acknowledge that committing to equality and diversity is a collective responsibility we all should shoulder. It isn't only for women to write about the women who came before them. And we shouldn't have to wait 150 years to remember extraordinary women either. There are brilliant women doing brilliant work today. Extraordinary stories to be told and learn from today.

So many are entirely absent from our search results and we could do more to challenge and combat this. Women are not a minority and we can't accept the paucity of stories and role models currently available online that try to tell us that message. We can change the way stories are told and make different, better choices. We can empower new content creators, create new heroes, and inspire readers all around the world. Gender equality should be a key institutional commitment and a Wikimedian placed alongside your digital skills trainers and learning technologists is a tangible and impactful way of demonstrating this commitment.

Universities have privileged access to knowledge and can play a pivotal role in choosing to value this work. It is a choice after all. Work that could and should be prioritized, funded, and facilitated. These stories of pioneering women are too important to remain hidden. Search is the way we now live (Hillis, Petit and Jarrett, 2012) and what is right or wrong or missing on Wikipedia affects the entire internet (Wadewitz, 2014). Given Wikipedia's undoubted reach and influence, the importance of encouraging a diversity of editors to engage with Wikipedia editing is crucial in terms of increasing the visibility of female role models online to, in turn, encourage, inspire and empower the next generation of dangerous women who can continue to kick doors open and shape our world for the better.

References

Allen, R. (2020, April 11). Wikipedia is a world built by and for men. Rosie Stephenson-Goodknight is changing that. *The Lily*. www.thelily.com/wiki pedia-is-a-world-built-by-and-for-men-rosie-stephenson-goodnight-is-changing-that/?.

Balch, O. (2019, November 28). Making the edit: Why we need more women in Wikipedia. *The Guardian*. www.theguardian.com/careers/2019/nov/28/making-the-edit-why-we-need-more-women-in-wikipedia.

Brooks, L. (2014, September 9). Scottish independence: Everything you need to know about the vote. *The Guardian*. www.theguardian.com/politics/2014/sep/09/-sp-scottish-independence-everything-you-need-to-know-vote.

Edinburgh gives female medical students their degrees—150 years late. (2019, July 6). *The Guardian*. www.theguardian.com/uk-news/2019/jul/06/edinburgh-gives-female-medical-students-their-degrees-150-years-late.

Ford, H. and Wajcman, J., 2017. 'Anyone can edit', not everyone does: Wikipedia's infrastructure and the gender gap - Heather Ford, Judy Wajcman, 2017. [online] SAGE Journals. Available at: <https://journals.sagepub.com/doi/full/10.1177/0306312717692172> [Accessed 24 March 2021].

Gender Equality. (2020, October 2). *Equality, Diversity and Inclusion at the University of Edinburgh*. www.ed.ac.uk/equality-diversity/inclusion/gender-equality.

Highton, M. (2015). Changing the way stories are told. *Wikipedia Science Conference*. Wikimedia UK.

Highton, M. (2015, April 24). Technical debt for OER. *Thinking.is.ed.ac.uk*. https://thinking.is.ed.ac.uk/melissa/2015/04/24/technical-debt/.

Hillis, K., Petit, M. and Jarrett, K., 2012. Google and the culture of search. Routledge, p.5.

Hood, N., & Littlejohn, A. (2018, March). Becoming an online editor: Perceived roles and responsibilities of Wikipedia editors. *Information Research, 23*(1). Retrieved from www.informationr.net/ir/23-1/paper784.html.

Kelly, N. (2019, July 5). A fair field and no favour: A history of the Edinburgh Seven. *The Edinburgh Seven*. https://blogs.ed.ac.uk/edinburgh7/2019/07/05/a-fair-field-and-no-favour-a-history-of-the-edinburgh-seven/.

Littlejohn, A. (2019). [Un]intended consequences of educational change: The need to focus on literacy development. *LILAC Information Literacy conference—keynote speech*. Nottingham.

McAndrew, E. (2019). *Embedding Wikimedia in the curriculum.* https://www.slideshare.net/infolit_group/embedding-wikimedia-in-the-curriculum-mcandrew.

Mathewson, J. (2020, October 14). *10 years of helping close Wikipedia's gender gap. Wiki Edu.* https://wikiedu.org/blog/2020/10/14/10-years-of-helping-close-wikipedias-gender-gap/.

Open.ed.ac.uk. 2016. About – *Open Ed—Open Educational Resources.* University of Edinburgh [online].https://open.ed.ac.uk/about.

Processions. (2018). www.processions.co.uk/.

Rehm, M., Littlejohn, A., & Rienties, B. (2018). Does a formal wiki event contribute to the formation of a network of practice? A social capital perspective on the potential for informal learning. *Interactive Learning Environments, 26,* 308–19. doi:10.1080/10494820.2017.1324495.

Seery, M. (2017, May 17). Wikipedia and writing. *michaelseery.com.* http://michaelseery.com/wikipedia-and-writing/

Spiller, J., & Moffat, S. (2017). You can't be what you can't see. In J. Robertson, A. Williams, D. Jones, L. Isbel, & D. Loads (Eds.), *EqualBITE: Gender equality in higher education* (pp. 209–11). Sense Publishers.

Stemwomen.co.uk. 2021. Women in STEM | Percentages of Women in STEM Statistics. [online] https://www.stemwomen.co.uk/blog/2021/01/women-in-stem-percentages-of-women-in-stem-statistics.

The University of Edinburgh. (2003). History of the project. *The Survey of Scottish Witchcraft.* www.shca.ed.ac.uk/Research/witches/history.html.

University factsheet. (2020, September 23). *University of Edinburgh.* www.ed.ac.uk/governance-strategic-planning/facts-and-figures/university-factsheet.

University of Edinburgh's suffragettes fight for the right to vote. (2018, November 29). *The University of Edinburgh—Information Services.* www.ed.ac.uk/information-services/vote-100/the-university-of-edinburghs-suffragettes.

Vision and Mission. (2016, April 7). *The University of Edinburgh.* www.ed.ac.uk/governance-strategic-planning/content-to-be-reused/vision-and-mission#:~:text=Our%20Mission,against%20the%20highest%20international%20standards.

Vote 100—Histropedia Timelines. (2018, November 29). *University of Edinburgh—Information Services.* www.ed.ac.uk/information-services/vote-100/histropedia-timelines.

Wadewitz, A., 2014. 04. Teaching with Wikipedia: the Why, What, and How. [online] HASTAC. Available at: https://www.hastac.org/blogs/wadewitz/2014/02/21/04-teaching-wikipedia-why-what-and-how.

Wikimedia. (2011, April). Wikipedia editors study. *Wikimedia Commons.* https://upload.wikimedia.org/wikipedia/commons/7/76/Editor_Survey_Report_-_April_2011.pdf.

Wikimedia. (2020). Promoting knowledge equity. *The Wikimedia Foundation*. https://wikimediafoundation.org/our-work/education/promoting-knowledge-equity/.

Women, Science and Scottish History editathon series. (2015, February). *Wikimedia UK*. https://wikimedia.org.uk/wiki/Women,_Science_and_Scottish_History_editathon_series.

Younger, D. (2017, October 31). Face of 313-year old witch reconstructed. *University of Dundee University News*. www.dundee.ac.uk/news/2017/face-of-313-year-old-witch-reconstructed.php.

CHAPTER 14

NOTES FROM THE FIELD: THREE WIKIMEDIAN-IN-RESIDENCE CASE STUDIES

Erin O'Neil[1] and Sarah Severson[1]

[1] University of Alberta

Abstract

When the University of Alberta Library hired its first Wikimedian-in-Residence (WIR) in 2019, the team had difficulty finding detailed information about how to plan for a WIR and set up the role for success. This chapter details two Wikipedia residencies that served as a guide for the Alberta team in building their WIR project. Case studies of the University of Toronto and Concordia University in Montréal are presented alongside a case study of the University of Alberta. Each study includes details about how the role was approved and funded, how hiring decisions were made, how the WIR focused their efforts, and the impact at their institution. Together, these three examples demonstrate the variety of options for funding and hiring a WIR role and for the focus of the WIR's work in their term. The chapter poses concrete questions for librarians considering implementing a WIR role at their institution and offers recommendations from each WIR experience as guidance in answering those questions.

Keywords

Wikimedian-in-Residence, Outreach.

DOI: https://doi.org/10.3998/mpub.11778416.ch14.en

Introduction

A Wikimedian used to be an easy shorthand for the community of editors who created and expanded the online encyclopedia, Wikipedia. Today we've seen the Wiki "universe" expand to encompass a variety of interrelated projects and a growing understanding that a Wikimedian is anyone who engages with the encyclopedia in a critical self-reflexive frame, which includes a much wider community than before. As academic readers and users we must take ownership of our role and relationship to Wikipedia to see that we are all members of this online community and equally complicit in its construction.

Creating a Wikimedian-in-Residence (WIR) program is one way a library can engage with this online community but is far from a one-size-fits-all experience. What the resident will do and how the program is set up depend on many factors including institutional priorities, funding options, community expectations, and existing programming.

To better understand the role of a WIR in an academic library and to look at the institutional factors that shaped the residencies, we interviewed colleagues at two different Canadian academic libraries with recent WIR programs and used our experiences to complete three descriptive case studies.

In this chapter, we cover each residency, including its achievements and the factors that shaped it. From these three experiences, we pulled out some of the common questions that should be considered when thinking about how to engage in a successful WIR program. The goal is to act as an introduction to the topic of WIR and illustrate what these positions can look like at different academic libraries, with the hope that this will guide others to create their own successful WIR programs.

What Is a WIR

Over the past ten years, WIR positions have become a popular way to establish collaborative working relationships with the larger Wikimedia community in an effort to increase the quality and quantity of content across Wikimedia projects. Some WIRs focus on content creation using library resources, which could be editing Wikipedia articles or uploading digitized public domain content to Wikicommons. Other activities

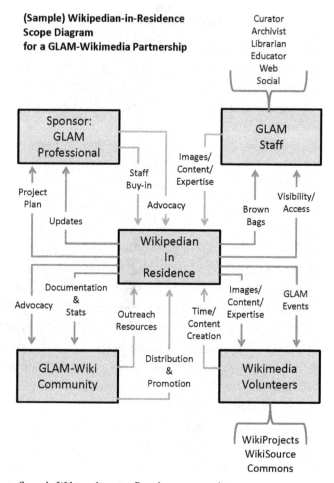

Figure 1 Sample Wikimedian-in-Residence scope diagram.

could include organizing events and training sessions to help facilitate contributions. These training sessions might cover Wikipedia editing generally or explore how information in Wikimedia projects is created, contested, and disseminated online. Having a Wikimedian who is familiar with the Wikipedia editorial processes can provide a range of opportunities on who to engage within the Wikimedia community.

With more than 175 self-reported residencies on the WIR Wikimedia Meta page, there are no shortage of examples for what a position could look like. Some positions are paid, as in our example case studies, while others are volunteer positions, tied to earning class credit or

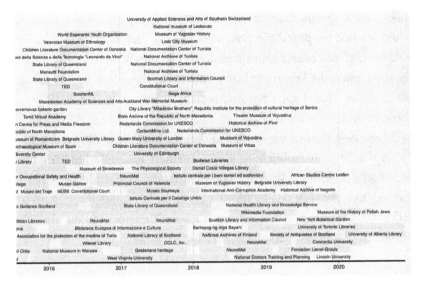

Figure 2 Screenshot of an interactive timeline of Wikimedian-in-Residence positions to illustrate the breadth of positions.

incorporated into existing position duties. The interactive timeline of all WIRs listed in Wikidata featured on figure 2 is an excellent visual tool to illustrate the diversity of WIR positions worldwide.

Resources

A variety of community guides already exist to help institutions create a WIR position. There is an excellent starting page on the Wikimedia Meta-Wiki titled "Creating a Wikimedian in Residence position" (2020), which outlines everything from the variety of roles a WIR can take on to the steps in getting started. Once a WIR has been established, the "Wikimedians in Residence Exchange Network" (2020) " can provide peer-to-peer support for organizations and individuals engaged in sharing open knowledge in the Wikimedia platform.

Three Case Studies

Given the myriad of WIR examples, those new to the Wikimedia community can find it difficult to understand which one might be the best model for a specific institution. At the University of Alberta Library, when we first proposed the position, we were fortunate enough to be able to reach out to our colleagues at the University of Toronto Libraries and Concordia Library to learn from them about how best to set up the position. This chapter represents an extension and formalization of those early conversations.

These case studies are similar in that they are situated in a specific cultural context of publicly funded Canadian academic libraries, but each had a different approach. To compile these case studies, we interviewed both the supervising librarian and the WIR and asked them to reflect on how the position got started, what they focused on, and the impact they felt both personally and institutionally.

University of Toronto Libraries

The University of Toronto Libraries is one of the largest academic library systems in Canada with more than forty libraries spread over three campuses (About | University of Toronto, n.d) and is located in Canada's largest city. There were existing pockets of Wikipedia work already happening in the library around campaigns like #1lib1ref. This precedent gave Jesse Carliner, communications librarian in the Chief Librarian's Office, an opportunity to approach the chief librarian about creating the WIR position. Carliner positioned the residency as part of the conversation around promoting special collections, arguing, "Students are going to Wikipedia articles to find resources, so that's where we need to be!" (personal communication, August 17, 2020). Because of the library's unionized environment, the role was created as a student library assistant position and advertised in the regular hiring channels, like the Library Website and listservs. In September 2018, the University of Toronto Libraries posted a position to "improve the discoverability of University of Toronto Libraries resources and collections in Wikipedia" (personal communication, August 17, 2020) and hired graduate student, Ji Yun Alex Jung, for a one-year, part-time contract. Jung brought some Wikipedia editing experience, and his work in Toronto's Civic Tech community prepared him for the independent work and the task of communicating sometimes complex information to a general audience.

Residency Focus
Of our three case studies, University of Toronto focused the most on article creation and editing work. At Toronto, Jung's writing work focused on adding information from the library's unique digital collections to Wikipedia. He contributed work related to the discovery and early development of insulin, including new articles for "Connaught Laboratories" (2020), an institute at the University of Toronto that manufactured insulin, and "Rodney Bobiwash" (2020), an Anishinaabe activist and scholar who helped expand First Nations student support in Canadian education systems.

Jung created a comprehensive GLAM page at "Wikipedia:GLAM/ University of Toronto" (2020) Libraries for reporting on and tracking Wikipedia editing activity at the university and encouraging collaboration in the community. He also created a Wikidata aware "Template for archival records" (2020), so they could be linked to a Wikipedia page later in residency. While events and community engagement were not a focus for Jung's residency, he did support edit-a-thons and other events when approached.

Residency Impact
As part of his editing work at University of Toronto libraries, Jung tracked the traffic from Wikipedia back to the university's digital collections and found a significant increase in referral traffic. This gave the Library quantifiable data to show that Carliner's goal of "being where the researchers were" was working (personal communication, August 17, 2020). This data helped them move Jung into a new Open Technology Specialist position that is covered in another chapter of this book. Statistics are not the only way to show WIR impact, but Jung's tracking clearly shows how the library collection was being accessed and used by Wikipedia users.

In terms of the impact on the individual, Jung said the WIR helped him develop his research and writing skills and honed "writing for the sake of documenting rather than in support of an argument" (personal communication, August 10, 2020). Looking back at the experience, he was pleased at how his understanding of library services and collections expanded and how he had a new appreciation for the volume and scope of the collections.

Concordia University Library

Concordia University is a public comprehensive research university and one of four major academic institutions located in the bilingual city of Montreal, Quebec. Lorie Kloda, Associate University Librarian of Planning & Community Relations, had heard about successful WIR initiatives and felt it aligned well with "Concordia digital strategy" (n.d) and what Kloda called the library's "experimental mindset" (personal communication, August 20, 2020). Concordia Library funded the position with unrestricted donor funds, so they had an open hiring process and advertised the position both at the university and in the community at large with a posted salary of $10,000 CAD plus benefits. There are many active local Wikimedians in Montreal; the city is the geographical home of Wikimedia Foundation Canadian Chapter and there is a history of Wikipedia engagement at other GLAM institutions in the city. Concordia Library hired Amber Berson, a Montreal-based writer, curator, and Wikimedian as WIR from June 2019 to May 2020. Amber worked part-time, one full day per week. She brought extensive experience as both a Wikipedia editor and instructor from her ongoing role with Art + Feminism.

Residency Focus

At Concordia, teaching and outreach were the main components of the WIR, with minimal article creation or editing work. Berson used most of her limited time to develop and deliver training to library staff and the broader Montreal community. Guided by her philosophy that Wikipedia is about mentorship, sharing, and giving, she delivered more than thirty training workshops in the community. Workshop topics included Wikipedia 101, Wikidata, and topic discussions such as bias on Wikipedia. The workshops were typically smaller, and Berson found them invaluable teaching experiences, noting that low attendance doesn't detract from the experience of those who attend and in fact allows more instruction for each person. She also set up a framework for library staff to teach information literacy with Wikipedia. Kloda noted that decentralizing information literacy work from the WIR to library staff positively influenced the receptiveness to Wikipedia training and ongoing editing work at the institution (personal communication, August 20, 2020).

During her WIR term, Berson also took a creative approach, organizing an exhibition about the history of Wikipedia as part of a research-creation project mounted at Concordia to explore the impact of going digital on Concordians' lives and work. This was helpful to get the community thinking about Wikipedia but also provided something Berson could reference back to when talking about the importance of understanding Wikipedia in our modern context. Berson had plans for two projects that are not yet completed: creating resources about sourcing and citation for journalism students and developing a peer-edited feminist best-practice manual for Wikipedia. The WIR program wound down when COVID-19 lockdowns began in the last two months of Berson's contract, and she hopes to return to the unfinished work at a later date.

Residency Impact
At Concordia, the desired outcome for their first WIR was an increase in information literacy and informed engagement with Wikipedia. Kloda felt strongly that Berson achieved that. Another one of the outcomes Berson anecdotally observed was a shift in how the community perceived Wikipedia, from thinking about it as a secondary source to a tertiary source of information. In workshops, guest lectures, and one-on-one consultations, she found a good reception for conversations about the history of Wikipedia, open-source culture, and anti-capitalist struggle. This gave her an opportunity to speak with a lot of students who now have a better understanding of how and why to critically appraise information on Wikipedia and to contribute to the site.

University of Alberta Library

The University of Alberta is a public research intensive university located in Edmonton, Alberta, and the library has a long history of supporting open movement projects. When a call went out to the library looking for short-term projects to be funded with donor money, Digital Projects librarian Sarah Severson pitched a WIR project. In February 2020, the University of Alberta Library hired Erin O'Neil, a digital humanities graduate student, to work part-time until August 2020, which was later extended to December 2020. The project had a $14,000 CAD budget and O'Neil's hours fluctuated to accommodate her student schedule; she worked almost full-time in summer 2020 and up to 10 hours per week during winter and fall semesters. She brought some Wikipedia editing experience to the role as well as experience in community facilitation. O'Neil and Severson worked closely together throughout the residency as Severson had Wikipedia experience.

Residency Focus

One of the residency goals at Alberta was to engage the wider community to better learn how Wikipedia could help improve users' access to our collections. In the first month of the residency, O'Neil participated in a #1lib1ref edit-a-thon organized at the library by Severson and helped facilitate a larger collaborative Art + Feminism edit-a-thon on March 5, 2020. When the COVID-19 lockdowns became a reality in Albert in mid-March of 2020, we moved all our programming plans online. O'Neil and Severson designed an online Wikipedia 101 course to give any interested library staff more in-depth training. The six-week course was delivered in March and April, and again in June and July. We also tried a few efforts to run virtual office hours and collaborative editing sessions but these didn't find the same uptake. In an attempt to open up conversations beyond learning "how" to edit on the site and tackle the "why," O'Neil and Severson ran an online, public speaker series in fall to dive deeper into three issues: public accountability, Indigenizing Wikipedia, and information activism.

Like Jung at University of Toronto, O'Neil created a GLAM page at "Wikipedia:GLAM/UAlbertaLibrary" (2020) to collect all the Wikipedia work she was doing at the University of Alberta. The page contains archives of the Wikipedia 101 course, ongoing editing tracking, and resources about using Wikipedia as a pedagogical tool. During her WIR term, O'Neil supported several classes with Wikipedia assignments and noticed increased interest in Wikipedia as university instructors planned for online delivery of classes during COVID-19 restrictions.

At University of Alberta, writing Wikipedia articles was a core component of WIR activity. Early on in the WIR term, we collaborated on a list of articles and themes that were either featured in the library's collection or of interest locally, and this list is posted on the GLAM page. Two examples of article creation are "Miriam Green Ellis" (2020), whose archives are housed in the Bruce Peel Special Collections at the University of Alberta Library, and the "Indigenous Art Park" (2020) recently created in Edmonton in a neighborhood adjacent to the university.

Residency Impact

When the COVID-19 pandemic hit and we had to change many of our original plans for the residency, we were not sure how to measure impact resulting from the residency. We very consciously did not tie any specific quantifiable outcomes, like number of participants for the speaker series or number of edits to Wikipedia, to any of the activities. What we did observe was there was considerable community enthusiasm for Wikimedia, both in the library and at the university, and we learned a lot through the conversations and questions. O'Neil used the GLAM page as a place to bring together what she learned and curate resources for the campus community.

In terms of the impact on the individual, O'Neil said the WIR term was an excellent experience for building community at the university and stoking a passion for open knowledge, and being a WIR gave her graduate student life a stimulating new dimension. As a result, she will be continuing to engage in Wikipedia work at the university and in Edmonton after her WIR term concludes.

Recommendations and Questions to Consider

After our interviews and conversations, we found that there were a few themes that emerged when the WIR positions were set up. We reframed these as questions to pose when thinking about how to engage in a successful WIR program at a library and offer recommendations.

What's Happening at the Institution Already?

Coming into the residency, each of our case studies had varying levels of institutional Wikipedia engagement. We each knew anecdotally of some pockets of activity either in the university where professors are engaging library resources for a Wikipedia article writing assignment, library space being used for edit-a-thons, or library staff regularly editing as a part of their job, but there was no centralized activity on any of the campuses. None of us felt it necessary to have regular Wikimedia contribution activity on campus in order to justify the WIR, but the University of Toronto Libraries used the existing vibrancy of programming as a part of their pitch. At the University of Alberta Library, Severson was new to her role and used the WIR as a means of learning more about what was happening on campus and how the library could better support those activities with existing services.

Who Should Be Hired into the Role?

When writing a WIR position description, it's good to think about the ideal candidate for the specific institution. For example, some institutions are looking to hire someone who can bring Wikimedia expertise. At Concordia, Kloda was not a Wikipedia editor and wanted to hire someone with experience in the Wikimedia ecosystem, so they could direct the position projects. Their library already had a successful Researcher-in-Residence program, so a residency model with someone from outside coming in was familiar to the library.

An alternative is to hire someone with more institutional experience and less Wikimedia experience and include a learning component in the position. Both Toronto and Alberta situated the WIR as a student role and were ready to invest in more time for training. Internationally, there is a lot of support available from local Wikimedia chapters and the Wikimedia community is full of resources on how to edit, so learning and then teaching about Wikipedia is very doable. Jung spoke about how spending the first part of his residency exploring and learning about the Wikimedia ecosystem helped him feel confident in the role. At the University of Alberta Library, we felt that by hiring a student we could gain an important perspective from outside the library on our collections and resources.

Will the Position Be Paid?

In the tradition of Wikipedia editors, many of the early WIR positions were filled on a volunteer basis. In all three of our case studies, the role was a paid one. Whether or not there are funds to pay an editor, and how much, will impact how the role is shaped. Another consideration is where to find the funding for the role. In all three of our case studies the WIR positions were funded internally through either discretionary or donor funds, which meant the positions were treated more as a special project rather than ongoing roles. This gave the libraries flexibility on who they could hire but also meant that they had a finite life span. Other options for funding a position could include project grants from the Wikipedia Foundation or partnering with a local Wikipedia chapter.

If the decision is made to create a paid WIR role, it is best practice for them to be clear about any affiliations and to be aware of Wikipedia's conflict of interest policy. While the community considers WIR editing acceptable, they are expected to identify their WIR status on their user page and on talk pages related to their organization when they post there. One recurring debate is if WIR should be required to go through the Article for Creation (AFC) process, which means that any new pages must be submitted as drafts and then reviewed by experienced editors. While in theory this process is sound, those who oppose argue on the "Wikipedia talk:Conflict of interest" (2020) page that it is an overreach of the AFC original scope and intent and in the process assumes bad faith that discourages editors even if they are not WIR. Others are concerned that placing the constraint of the AFC could cause "significant collateral damage to the partnerships, collaboration and relationships with GLAM organisations and higher education institutions" (Joseph, 2020).

How Will Institutional Priorities Translate into Residency Goals?

Before even writing the WIR position description, it's helpful to reflect on the priorities of the institution hiring them. Does the library have unique and special collections that could be added to Wikicommons and/or used to enhance Wikipedia and that could be made more discoverable like the University of Toronto? Maybe the library values experimentation and administration is comfortable leaving the residency with very broad goals? For example, the UAL included the goal to improve UAL's understanding of the role large collaborative platforms like Wikipedia can play in improving users' access to our collections.

In all of our interviews, both WIRs and librarians cited one of the biggest advantages of working with the Wikimedia ecosystem was that there were so many project possibilities. This was reflected in the goals of each of the position's descriptions. Each of the librarians talked about wanting to leave the position as open as possible, so the residency could be shaped based on the WIR's research interests and skills and the unique library collections. In some respects, this was a real advantage. The candidates who applied for these WIR roles were from a wide variety of backgrounds, so waiting until the WIR was selected before considering specific project work allowed for a greater flexibility to empower and benefit from the specific skills and interests of each WIR. Hiring candidates who demonstrated creativity and a range of experiences both with open knowledge and in digital media made this flexibility in the role work best. In each of our case studies, the first part of the residency process was combining knowledge about WIR programs with institutional goals and proposing a project plan from there.

However, it does take time to decide on projects to tackle, and giving a WIR flexibility to choose their projects should not mean that the WIR is left alone to navigate the library or Wikipedia ecosystems on their own. At Toronto and Alberta, where the WIRs were graduate students and not veteran Wikimedians, there was a learning curve to understand the kind of language and information appropriate for Wikipedia articles. The other unanticipated learning curve was understanding some of the libraries' more unique archival or special collections, which were cataloged in sometimes complicated ways. This challenge had not been anticipated, so it taught us a lot about how we present our collections, which was invaluable.

How Will Engagement Be Generated?
The news of a WIR hire can be very exciting for an institution. It is a good news story that often aligns with institutional goals around digital and community engagement. Reaching out to institutional communications teams and news services is also important to achieve almost every other task as a WIR: when people know about the work, they are more likely to reply to emails or attend a workshop. Both Berson and Jung began their roles with outreach, earning both internal institutional attention and mainstream media coverage (local papers and local TV news). To announce the WIR role at Alberta, O'Neil did several interviews with campus media. Media coverage is especially useful to explain why a library needs a WIR or would engage with Wikipedia at all, as there are still many misconceptions about the site on campuses. Kloda and Carliner both noted that using the good news story angle also brought positive attention to their libraries, universities, and Wikipedia work in their cities.

Future Directions
Everyone we talked to said they would do a residency again if they could. When asked about future plans, Concordia said they would be interested in doing another WIR but imagined it would be completely different in terms of projects or perspectives. At Toronto, Carliner hopes that future Wikipedia work will shift to a balance between

Wikidata projects and Wikipedia article creation and editing. Here at Alberta, we'd like to try the Toronto model where article creation and editing work is focused on a precise area of the library's collections.

The Wikimedia ecosystem goes far beyond Wikipedia articles, and there is great potential for WIR roles focused on Wikidata in particular. While Wikipedia is an excellent pedagogical tool for exploring information literacy, reliable sources, and notability, Wikidata offers students the chance to engage with issues of data completeness, data processing, data analysis, and data ethics.

Conclusion

In the end, each WIR is as unique as the institution that hosts them, but it can be difficult to know how to set up the role for success if it is the first WIR at the institution. This chapter illustrated some of the commonalities and differences between three Canadian university library WIRs and how factors such as institutional priorities, funding options, and community expectations shaped these positions. We hope that by framing the common themes we noticed in our WIR experience, we have offered helpful guidance for colleagues who are building a case for a WIR at their institution. WIRs are critical to building meaningful connections on campuses for expanding Wikipedia and engaging with its complex issues of bias, representation, notability, and editor alienation. The WIR trend is growing, and we hope that this chapter will be one helpful piece in an ongoing conversation about how to make WIRs work well for institutions and Wikipedia alike.

References

About | University of Toronto. (n.d.). https://onesearch.library.utoronto.ca/about

Connaught Laboratories. (2020, October 4). In Wikipedia. https://en.wikipedia.org/w/index.php?title=Connaught_Laboratories&oldid=981869046.

Creating a Wikimedian in Residence position. (2020, October 3). https://meta.wikimedia.org/w/index.php?title=Wikimedian_in_residence/Creating_a_Wikimedian_in_Residence_position&oldid=20703329.

Concordia Digital Strategy | Office of the Provost and Vice-President, Academic. (n.d.). www.concordia.ca/provost/about/areas/digital-strategy.html.

Indigenous Art Park. (2020, 21 September). In Wikipedia. https://en.wikipedia.org/w/index.php?title=Indigenous_Art_Park&oldid=979606589.

Joseph, Mylee. (2020, September 2). Comment on the post "This proposal would see Wikimedians in Residence, and any staff they train, required to use the 'Articles for Creation' process, as paid editors, rather than simply creating new articles, on en.wikipedia.". In the Wikimedia + Libraries group. Facebook. www.facebook.com/groups/WikiLibrary/permalink/1735597089934602/?comment_id=1735670106593967.

Miriam Green Ellis. (2020, August 21). In Wikipedia. https://en.wikipedia.org/w/index.php?title=Miriam_Green_Ellis&oldid=974210924.

Rodney Bobiwash (2020, May 12). In Wikipedia. https://en.wikipedia.org/w/index.php?title=Rodney_Bobiwash&oldid=956287586.

Template:Archival records. (2020, August 25). https://en.wikipedia.org/w/index.php?title=Template:Archival_records&oldid=974893117.

Wikimedians in Residence Exchange Network. (2020, September 30). https://meta.wikimedia.org/w/index.php?title=Wikimedians_in_Residence_Exchange_Network&oldid=20596684.

Wikipedia:GLAM/University of Toronto Libraries. (2020, September 10). In Wikipedia. https://en.wikipedia.org/w/index.php?title=Wikipedia:GLAM/University_of_Toronto_Libraries&oldid=977741411.

Wikipedia:GLAM/UAlbertaLibrary. (2020, August 26). In Wikipedia. https://en.wikipedia.org/w/index.php?title=Wikipedia:GLAM/UAlbertaLibrary&oldid=975073085.

Wikipedia talk:Conflict of interest. (2020, September 2). In Wikipedia. https://en.wikipedia.org/w/index.php?title=Wikipedia_talk:Conflict_of_interest&oldid=976352513.

CHAPTER 15

THE OPEN TECHNOLOGY SPECIALIST AT THE UNIVERSITY OF TORONTO LIBRARIES: A COMPREHENSIVE APPROACH TO WIKIMEDIA PROJECTS IN THE ACADEMIC LIBRARY

Jesse Carliner[1] and Ji Yun Alex Jung[1]

[1] University of Toronto

Abstract

Wikipedian-in-Residence (WIR) programs are becoming more common in academic libraries. Although they hold a great deal of promise, they are often limited in scope given their frequently short-term and sometimes part-time nature. After a successful one-year, part-time WIR pilot, the University of Toronto Libraries (UTL) has piloted a one-year, full-time Open Technology Specialist (OTS) role to build upon the WIR's accomplishments and allow for a more comprehensive approach to Wikimedia activities in the library. Through extensive research, outreach, and relationship-building, the OTS has considerably expanded the scope of WIR's activities to advance a wide range of institutional strategic priorities for the long term. In line with UTL's commitment to barrier-free access to all of the right information, the OTS incorporates Wikimedia activities into existing workflows across the library system in ways that prioritize support for historically excluded communities and collections while being sensitive to issues of access

DOI: https://doi.org/10.3998/mpub.11778416.ch15.en

and description. In its pilot year, the OTS has created a network out of previously isolated Wikimedia engagement across the library system, trained staff, and volunteers across and beyond UTL, and helped launch formal projects that deepen institutional engagement. The OTS has also continued to contribute to Wikipedia, expanding their editing scope to the appropriate use of archival sources and the development of tools, which help bridge the gap between Wikipedia and Wikidata. Through the OTS, UTL has systematically deepened its contributions to the open Web. The UTL OTS pilot experience has demonstrated that positions dedicated to engagement in Wikimedia or other open technologies hold a great deal of potential and are worthy of further consideration for ongoing investment of staff and budget resources by academic libraries.

Keywords

Open Technology, Wikimedia, Academic Libraries.

Introduction

The University of Toronto Libraries (UTL) established an instance of a GLAM-Wiki (Galleries, Libraries, Archives, and Museum) with the launch of a Wikipedian-in-Residence (WIR) program in 2018. Initially launched with the explicit goal of facilitating Wikipedia-based access to UTL's special collections, the GLAM-Wiki project evolved to include a range of Wikimedia activities such as events, development of toolkits, and editing and article creation. UTL expanded the project in December 2019 into a full-time pilot position dubbed the Open Technology Specialist (OTS). The OTS has enabled UTL to considerably expand activities beyond the WIR, in order to advance a wide range of institutional strategic priorities. The OTS has further expanded training for staff members through editing events and consultations, made accessible documentation available to current and future staff, and incorporated Wikimedia activities into existing workflows across the library system.

In this chapter, we will describe the history of Wikimedia activities at UTL within the context of the institution's support for linked and open-access infrastructure. We will describe how the WIR position evolved into the OTS, and how the OTS enables a sustainable and comprehensive approach to Wikimedia activities in the academic library. Finally, we will discuss how Wikimedia activities have been incorporated into existing workflows and reflect on the impact of these activities.

Background

Located in Toronto, Ontario, Canada, the University of Toronto (U of T) is a public, research intensive university with three campuses in the greater Toronto area. From 2018 to 2019, the university had a total enrollment of 93,081 students and 21,556 faculty and staff (University of Toronto, n.d.). The UTL system is the largest academic library in Canada and is consistently ranked among the largest of its peer institutions in North America according to the Association of Research Libraries Investment Index (Morris & Roebuck, 2019). The system consists of forty-two libraries, with around 500 librarians and paraprofessional staff members and supports the teaching and research requirements of the University of Toronto's more than 980 programs of study (University of Toronto, n.d.). Eighteen central libraries directly report to the UTL chief librarian, while the remaining libraries report to their college, campus, and departmental administration. In addition to more than 15 million volumes in 341 languages, the library system currently provides access to millions of electronic resources in various forms and over 31,000 linear meters of archival material.

Open Access and Open Digital Collections at UTL
UTL has for many years engaged in open-access initiatives, leading to the creation of the UTL Scholarly Communications and Copyright Office (SCCO) in 2013. The UTL SCCO helps researchers make their research available through open access, thereby improving the impact of their research and supporting researchers around the world who may not otherwise have access to this scholarship. UTL also operates TSpace, an open-access repository. Research deposited

into TSpace is freely available via Google Scholar and other search engines, but findable only to a limited extent without the help of Wikipedia's reference.

In addition to supporting open-access publication of university-produced research, UTL has created numerous digitized special collections that are freely available online. A great deal of staff resources and infrastructure go into creating and maintaining these digital collections, but they are not easily discoverable on the Web unless made to be so. Notable examples include *The Discovery and Early Development of Insulin Collection* and the *Wenceslaus Hollar Digital Collection*. Initially, discovery and use of UTL's digital collections had primarily relied on search-based traffic or traditional library marketing strategies like social media and website news items. Some of the resources had also been promoted at library workshops and in relevant research guides. However, these strategies did not create sustained growth of collections use. Increases in traffic would usually only be temporary—perhaps indicating a sporadic influx of curious users who were not actively researching the topic.

By contrast, collection items linked to Wikimedia projects were found and used more readily by the average web user. Over the years, editors not affiliated with the library had linked or uploaded collection items to Wikipedia and Wikimedia Commons. These links have more effectively brought these collections within reach of the average web user, and in the appropriate information-seeking context. These edits, in combination with GLAM-Wiki familiarity on the part of pioneering staff, made for a basic proof of concept for a more organized effort to deepen UTL's Wikimedia contributions.

Wikipedia Initiatives at the UTL

Beyond some sporadic Wikimedia engagement by library and archives staff throughout the UTL system, the first systematic pilot of Wikimedia activities took place in the summer of 2018. A librarian and an intern in the information technology department carried out a pilot project to assess the impact of Wikipedia contributions on the use of digital collections. Selected items from the *Wenceslaus Hollar*, *Agnes Chamberlin*, and *Anatomia* collections were linked to the English and German Wikipedia through citations, external links, and images. Usage statistics showed that Wikipedia edits had significantly increased and sustained traffic to these collections, suggesting that Wikipedia edits had been more effective at improving collections access than the use of traditional library news items and social media. In particular, images uploaded from the *Anatomia* collection demonstrated the value of adding collections material as visual aids to highly visible Wikipedia articles.

Based on the successful summer pilot, the UTL chief librarian funded a year-long WIR pilot for the 2018–2019 academic year. The pilot was launched with the explicit goal of facilitating Wikipedia-based access to UTL's special collections but also to support editing events and create toolkits that others could repurpose for their own events. Due to UTL's labor environment, the WIR position was posted as a part-time graduate student library assistant (GSLA) position. All University of Toronto graduate students were eligible to apply to the posting, and of the thirty-five applicants, only two had prior Wikipedia editing experience.

During the year-long pilot, the WIR activities fell into three broad categories—creating a work plan and infrastructure around their activities, carrying out the activities, and then developing documentation for a successor to carry on the work of the pilot. The WIR initially developed their plan of work through an environmental scan of more than fifty institutional WIR positions, examining their best practices and activities. The environmental scan also reviewed the summer pilot and lessons learned, including approaches to editing, project documentation, collections of focus (e.g., Chamberlin, Hollar), discussion on sources and copyright (especially in relation to images), and resources for learning. Next, the WIR identified strengths of the UTL digital collections and collection themes, looking for collections that would be appropriate for citation in Wikipedia. Factors considered in selecting a digital collection to work with included status (is the collection still maintained?), location (where is the collection hosted?), ease of use, copyright, content sensitivity, notability, and overall "Wikipedia friendliness" of content. Some digital collections were judged more Wikipedia-friendly than others in the kinds of material they contained and in the availability of reliable secondary sources that provide a basis for interpretation.[1] In some cases, digital collections were reserved for future collaboration given their potential to perpetuate harm to user communities in the absence of adequate historical understanding and relational work.[2]

The Discovery and Early Development of Insulin Collection was chosen as the focus of the WIR pilot for three reasons: It was deemed to be "Wikipedia-friendly"; it was likely to be of broad public interest given the 100th anniversary of the discovery of insulin (2021–2022); and it was considered a premiere collection given its inscription into the UNESCO Memory of the World register (The Discovery of Insulin and Its Worldwide Impact | United Nations Educational, Scientific, and Cultural Organization, n.d.). Over the course of the pilot, the WIR verified Wikipedia's existing content on the topic, updating and adding citations as appropriate. They also added comprehensive articles and sections on notable but unwritten histories adjacent to the collection, including the history of diabetes and institutions such as the Connaught Laboratories and the Academy of Medicine of Toronto.[3] Some of these contributions have since played a crucial role in public discourse. In late November 2020, the Connaught Laboratories article came to public attention in the context of COVID-19 response shortcomings, "vaccine nationalism," and damage to Canadian vaccine production capacity suffered as the result of the Labs' privatization in the 1980s. Page views increased 500 to 1,000-fold as the Wikipedia article was shared widely.

In addition to edits based on the Discovery of Insulin collection, the WIR also provided community guidance on Wikipedia-related matters, facilitated events, and developed editing and event hosting toolkits for broader use.[4] Regular analytics assessments have demonstrated sustained increases in UTL's digital collection usage, as well as increasing correlation between Google search traffic and traffic to the Discovery of Insulin collection. At the time of writing (November 2020), UTL's digital collection usage has increased—in comparison to the average for the year-long period before Wikipedia contributions—by a multiplier of 4.87 in earlier months (with only external links) to 9.35 (after more research-intensive contributions) in linked

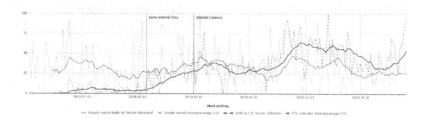

Figure 1 Changing correlation between Google search traffic and usage of the Discovery and Early Development of Insulin Collection by week, normalized to a range of [0, 100].

collections. Figure 1 reflects this increase in usage as well as increasing correlation between Google search traffic and usage of the Discovery of Insulin collection based on the keywords "insulin discovery." Collection usage began to increasingly reflect search traffic as external links (July 2018) and detailed citations (December 2018) were added. While there are multiple paths in a user's journey from search results to a UTL digital collection involving any number of Wikipedia articles and non-Wikipedia sites, this correlation speaks to the bidirectional impact of the WIR's contributions to in-Wikipedia collections discovery as well as increased library website visibility gained through the numerous inbound links generated by this work. It would be difficult to be more discoverable at any given moment than the levels of interest at that time as indicated by Google Trends, insofar as the average web user relies on search engines to find resources, and insofar as Google dominates the search engine market at 92.16 percent worldwide in November 2020 (Search Engine Market Share Worldwide | StatCounter Global Stats, n.d.).

The Open Technology Specialist

Based on the demonstrated potential of the part-time WIR position, UTL established a full-time pilot of the OTS in December 2019 at the direction of the chief librarian. The full-time OTS role would build on the work of the WIR with a more comprehensive scope of activities and objectives. Most importantly, the OTS position would support research and learning at the University of Toronto by improving discoverability of UTL resources and collections—primarily through Wikimedia projects during the pilot—and by building community capacity for participation in these initiatives. The job posting highlighted the potential for the OTS to enable a more comprehensive, coordinated, and systematic approach to engaging in Wikimedia activities. In addition to the WIR activities, the OTS would promote participation in new or existing WikiProjects related to UTL holdings; support the U of T staff and community in their use, participation in, and understanding of Wikimedia; and identify and engage in other collaborative open technology initiatives. Finally, the OTS job posting emphasized that, where possible, programming and initiatives should advance the UTL's commitment to equity, inclusion, and diversity.

Throughout the first ten months of the pilot, the OTS has further advanced the UTL strategic goals of "barrier-free access to all of the right information" to "build physical and digital infrastructure to make our library collections effortlessly accessible" (UTL Strategic Plan 2020–2025, 2020) by making it easier for UTL—as well as the broader Toronto and GLAM-Wiki community—to enrich the free Web.[5] The OTS role, in practice, grants capacity for UTL to holistically assess the uses and limits of Wikimedia projects as tools and to apply them strategically in ways that make sense to different library departments and functions. It functions as a translator between the broader movement toward open technologies, including GLAM-Wiki, and the library's existing constellation of people, relationships, and practices. If the UTL WIR's workflows were largely self-contained, with minimal engagement with other staff and units, the OTS has expanded this scope through a combination of research, communication, documentation, and internal and external relationship-building, in order to achieve sustained impact.

Deeper Resource Integration

Previous pilots at UTL had demonstrated the impact of linking library resources to Wikipedia, and of contributing narrative content on the basis of those links. Building on those accomplishments, the OTS has enabled deeper resource integration into Wikipedia in a number of ways.

First, the OTS has explored contribution using a greater breadth of sources from UTL. In particular, they have experimented extensively with the use of archival material and finding aids, to the extent that no interpretation is added by the editor. These sources are less understood in the context of Wikipedia yet invaluable for their potential to ground less visible topics that might otherwise go uncharted due to a lack of accessible citations. These efforts have yielded the contribution of Wikipedia biographies on important figures in the peripheries of popular knowledge—such as those of scholar-activists Rodney Bobiwash and Roxana Ng—for whom secondary source coverage had been sparse, particularly in digital format.

Second, UTL is moving beyond single-event contributions into maintenance of resource links on Wikipedia. Whereas Wikipedia has accumulated upward of 3,600 links to UTL through both third-party and library-initiated contributions, an estimated 40 percent of these links have expired over time and no longer direct users from Wikipedia to the intended pages. The OTS has begun to update these links, using persistent identifiers where possible in order to future-proof contributions.

Third, the OTS has begun to develop mechanisms for sustainable contribution to Wikipedia, which build on UTL's contributions to

Figure 2 Template:Archival records.

Wikidata. Among other uses, Wikidata has the function of simplifying data maintenance for library information on the Web.[6] One such mechanism is a Wikipedia template for use in the *External links* section (*Template:Archival records*), which syncs dynamically to Wikidata.[7] This "sync-piece" builds directly on Wikidata contributions from prior months by the Digital Initiatives librarian and her intern and has the effect of manifesting their infrastructural work to a more general audience. The template links to a Wikipedia help page (*Help:Archival materials*), also developed by the OTS, which is an introductory guide to archival sources and their use in research and in Wikipedia editing. The template has been similarly helpful to others in the GLAM-Wiki world also working with archival material, as indicated by the near-500 articles that link to the template at the time of writing.[8]

Library Capacity-Building

The OTS has built capacity for UTL staff participation based on the understanding that open, Web-based projects such as Wikipedia are foremost tools that allow library staff to better serve their respective communities by eliminating barriers to information access. Since the promise of linked open knowledge facilitated by Wikimedia platforms means different things to different libraries and functions, the OTS provides flexible support across departments, libraries, archives, and the university in ways that appropriately situate (and observe the limits of) Wikimedia platforms in each area according to their unique set of needs. For example, collaboration with subject liaisons demonstrates the potential of Wikimedia engagement as a core competency in information literacy or as a pedagogical tool. Support for IT and metadata infrastructure engages in Wikimedia projects that build upon past and ongoing efforts around linked data and custom ontologies. Meanwhile, community programming involving staff, students, and other volunteers across Toronto help balance histories and knowledge on Wikipedia by highlighting archival collections from historically excluded communities while being sensitive to issues of access and description.

The OTS has therefore helped interested parties determine their scope and method of engagement with Wikimedia projects with minimal hassle and maximal impact. For example, staff at the Music Library Archives were rapidly equipped (over the course of two meetings) to complete an initial set of contributions by adding collections information to Wikipedia biographies. Where possible, the OTS has delivered training and workshops, which demonstrate step-by-step workflows and situate those activities in the context of the Web and its discovery mechanisms. As of October 2020, more than fifty staff across all three U of T campuses had benefited from these workshops. Moreover, these trainings have themselves been opportunities for collaboration with other staff and interns, contributing to experiential learning at UTL in ways that integrate the Web into library production. Through these collaborations, the loose network of interested staff at UTL has rapidly come to cocreate clear descriptions and starting points for linked open knowledge projects.

The OTS has built bridges across campuses and departments to identify and connect interested staff for open technology engagement. The result is a loose network of staff who now share and receive updates through an open technologies email listserv and participate in various working groups, some of which span multiple library units. In general, the OTS capacity to bring together and logistically support interest groups has been key to developing momentum on multiunit collaborations, which might otherwise become deprioritized over time.

The impact of the move from WIR's relatively self-contained approach to the OTS's intentionally inclusive approach at UTL is fourfold. Most immediately, each resource thoughtfully contributed to Wikipedia becomes more useful to the web user, and in the appropriate context. The OTS actively works to increase the number of such contributors. Second, these contributions gain further significance where they also help balance inequities in knowledge representation. By pursuing work across the library system that enables fair and dignified knowledge production and discovery for all, the OTS builds another layer of consistency in the university's move toward equity. For example, the very first collaborative event (February 2020) with staff from University of Toronto Scarborough Library and Toronto Public Library contributed accessible coverage of Toronto's vastly underrepresented

Black history (Russell, 2020). The OTS now builds on this past initiative to bring multiple libraries together for a broader and more intentional effort to improve the coverage of local Black histories through February 2021. Third, through the OTS, the library has gained capacity to better assist the university in communicating its research to the broader public. This had been explored through a collaboration with the library's Scholarly Communications office and the Sophie Lucyk Virtual Library, a digital collection of research from the Factor-Inwentash Faculty for Social Work hosted on TSpace (The Sophie Lucyk Virtual Library | TSpace Repository, n.d.). And fourth, UTL's Wikimedia contributions to date have been doubly helpful to staff as accessible, comprehensive reference for special collections (Wikipedia) and as a hub for institutional data creation and maintenance across the large, decentralized library system (Wikidata).

Engagement beyond the Library and University
The broadly beneficial nature of the OTS approach allows the training, workshops, documentation, and consultation capacity generated by the role to enrich networks beyond the institution. This aligns with the University of Toronto's institutional goals and priorities to "leverage [the University's] urban location(s) more fully, for the mutual benefit of University and City" (Gertler, 2015). The OTS has therefore collaborated with staff from Toronto Public Library and the Ontario Science Centre, advised projects at the City of Toronto Archives, and trained volunteers at The ArQuives, Canada's LGBTQ2+ Archives located in Toronto, Ontario. Some collaborations have even extended beyond the Greater Toronto Area, as in the case of the Ontario Wikipedia Edit-a-thon during Ontario's Open Education Week (March 2–6, 2020) jointly led by staff at Fleming College and Mohawk College.[9]

The OTS also cofacilitates regular, cross-institutional programming through the LD4-Wikidata Affinity group. Through this network-building, the OTS has been able to bring more UTL staff into broader library community updates, including Program for Cooperative Cataloging (PCC)'s ongoing, one-year Wikidata pilot, by which no less than four projects across two U of T campuses are underway at the time of writing.

Conclusion

The impact of the OTS pilot so far demonstrates that a full-time position dedicated to Wikimedia and other open technology projects holds great potential to better link open-access library resources and archival and special collections to the Web. By enabling consistent support for Wikimedia activities, staff across UTL's large and decentralized system have been empowered to meet their users where they are and increase discovery and use of their collections with greater ease. This sustained staff development resulting in high-impact benefits to library and institutional priorities have come at a low cost, requiring only the flexible investment of staff time.

Beyond experimentation, open technology engagement requires extended support and maintenance in order to achieve lasting impact. WIR and OTS programs can be piloted to explore Wikimedia activities in the library and to introduce those activities to library staff when and where appropriate, laying the groundwork for additional investment of staffing resources and the incorporation of Wikimedia activities into existing workflows and job portfolios.

Notes

1 For example, many artifacts in the *Discovery and Early Development of Insulin* collection are published material (e.g., articles and newspaper clippings), which can be cited with minimal interpretation. This collection also benefits from readily available secondary sources that make sense of the collection and offer the reader an opportunity to cross-reference the published histories with the original sources.

2 For collections such as *The Barren Lands: J. B. Tyrrell's Expeditions for the Geological Survey of Canada, 1892–1894*, the WIR had found it necessary to cultivate capacity for edits informed by Indigenous perspectives, and to do so in collaboration with concerned communities.

3 See: History of diabetes (https://en.wikipedia.org/wiki/History_of_diabetes), Connaught Laboratories (https://en.wikipedia.org/wiki/Connaught_Laboratories), and Academy of Medicine of Toronto (https://en.wikipedia.org/wiki/Academy_of_Medicine_of_Toronto).

4 Toolkits and documentation are available on: https://en.wikipedia.org/wiki/Wikipedia:GLAM/University_of_Toronto_Libraries/Resources

5 As a general statement, Wikipedia is an unparalleled general information source for the everyday Web user in magnitude and use. More concretely in university settings, studies have consistently demonstrated students' heavy reliance on Web search engines and on Wikipedia. See Weber et al. (2018) for a relatively recent German study containing a literature review and Bury (2011) for a study from York University.

6 Data maintenance—of links to material and corresponding descriptions—is imperative to keeping information accessible and up-to-date in the long run. Wikidata, an open and collaboratively edited database "of all things" by the Wikimedia Foundation, is interesting in this light since it provides an easy and open interface for persistent description, which can serve as a single access point for data maintenance.

7 The template and documentation are available on: https://en.wikipedia. org/wiki/Template:Archival_records

8 An up-to-date list of articles linking to *Template:Archival records* can be viewed on: https://en.wikipedia.org/w/index.php?title=Special:What LinksHere/Template:Archival_records&namespace=0.

9 Formal edit-a-thon collaborations in 2020 include: International Day of Women and Girls in Science edit-a-thon at the Ontario Science Centre (https://rascto.ca/content/ontario-science-centre-international-day-women-and-girls-science) and Ontario Wikipedia edit-a-thon for Open Education Week (www.openeducationweek.org/events/ontario-wikipedia-edit-a-thon).

References

Bury, S. (2011). Faculty attitudes, perceptions and experiences of information literacy: A study across multiple disciplines at York University, Canada. *Journal of Information Literacy*, 5(1), 45–64. https://doi. org/10.11645/5.1.1513.

Gertler, M. (2015). *Three priorities: A discussion paper*. https://threepriori ties.utoronto.ca/wp-content/uploads/2015/10/Three-Priorities-Discus sion-Paper.pdf.

Morris, S., & Roebuck, G. (2019). ARL Statistics 2016–2017. https://publica tions.arl.org/ARL-Statistics-2016-2017/.

Russell, R. (2020, February 10). Wikipedia "edit-a-thon" helps fill information gaps about Black history in Canada. *University of Toronto Scarborough News*. Retrieved October 16, 2020, from https://utsc.utoronto.ca/news-events/our-community/wikipedia-edit-thon-helps-fill-information-gaps-about-black-history-canada.

Search Engine Market Share Worldwide | StatCounter Global Stats. (n.d.). Retrieved December 18, 2020, from https://gs.statcounter.com/search-engine-market-share.

The Discovery of Insulin and its Worldwide Impact | United Nations Educational, Scientific, and Cultural Organization. (n.d.). Retrieved December 18, 2020, from www.unesco.org/new/en/communication-and-information/memory-of-the-world/register/full-list-of-registered-heritage/registered-heritage-page-8/the-discovery-of-insulin-and-its-worldwide-impact/.

The Sophie Lucyk Virtual Library | TSpace Repository. (n.d.). Retrieved September 29, 2020, from https://tspace.library.utoronto.ca/handle/1807/70607.

University of Toronto. (n.d.). Facts & Figure 2019. *University of Toronto.* https://data.utoronto.ca/wp-content/uploads/2020/06/Finalized-Factbook-2019.pdf.

UTL Strategic Plan 2020–2025. (2020). Retrieved November, 30, 2020, from https://onesearch.library.utoronto.ca/strategic-plan/strategic-plan-2020-2025.

Weber, H., Becker, D., & Hillmert, S. (2018). Information-seeking behaviour and academic success in higher education: Which search strategies matter for grade differences among university students and how does this relevance differ by field of study? *Higher Education, 77*(4), 657–78. https://doi.org/10.1007/s10734-018-0296-4.

SECTION 4
WIKIPEDIA SISTER
PROJECTS

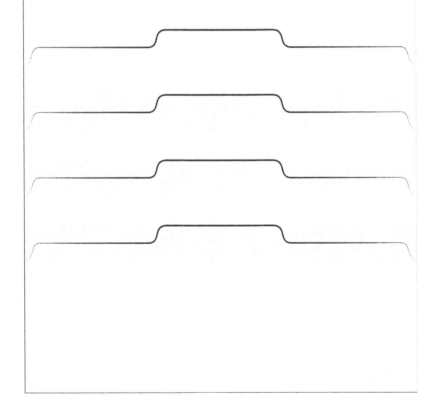

CHAPTER 16

HONG KONG LITERARY LANDSCAPE: A MEDIAWIKI FOR LITERARY READING AND WRITING

Leo F. H. Ma¹ and L. M. Mak²

¹ The Chinese University of Hong Kong, ²National Cheung Kung University

Abstract

For almost three decades, literary walk has been used by various education and public institutions in Hong Kong as an effective way to promote reading and writing to secondary school students. Funded by the Standing Committee on Language Education and Research of the Hong Kong Special Administrative Region Government in 2013, the Hong Kong Literature Research Centre (HKLRC) of the Chinese University of Hong Kong and the Chinese University of Hong Kong Library (CUHK Library) jointly kicked off a two-year proposal entitled "Fun with Learning Chinese Language through Literary Walk" aimed at promoting literary reading and writing skills to junior secondary school students in Hong Kong. In this paper, the authors discuss a key deliverable of this project, the Hong Kong Literary Landscape MediaWiki, jointly developed by the HKLRC and the CUHK Library, which provides literary walk materials on the wiki platform including video clips, critically selected literary works, literary maps, creative writings of the student participants, and so on. Apart from the project participants, the Hong Kong Literary Landscape

MediaWiki is also a useful tool for other secondary school teachers, students, and a wider group of audience in the Hong Kong community.

Keywords

Hong Kong Literary Landscape MediaWiki, Literary Walk, Reading and writing, The Chinese University of Hong Kong, Digital humanities.

Introduction

Despite the fact that literary walk has been adopted as a way to promote literature around the world, there is, however, no shared definition of what a literary walk should be (Dulwich Picture Gallery, 2020; Iowa City UNESCO City of Literature, 2020; Tokyo Metropolitan Government, 2020). In the context of Hong Kong, a literary walk usually consists of a docent and a group of participants. The docent designs a route for the walk by identifying some major landscapes and events of a specific area mentioned in the literature. While they walk through the area, the docent introduces these landscapes and events to the participants in order to demonstrate the cultural and historical context reflected in the literature. On the face of it, a literary walk looks very much like a historical walk, but the major difference is the text used for the walk. A literary walk usually makes use of poems, prose, and fiction to devise the route while a historical walk relies very much on historical documents and archives.

In the early 1990s, Lu Weiluan, a renowned scholar and writer in Hong Kong, put forward the idea of learning Hong Kong literature through literary walk. She believes that it is very important for students to have on-site learning experiences in order to better understand and appreciate literary works. In the past three decades, literary walk has been used by various education and public institutions in Hong Kong as an effective way to promote reading and writing to secondary school students. Funded by the Standing Committee on Language Education and Research (SCOLAR) of the Hong Kong Special Administrative Region Government (HK SAR Government), the Hong Kong Literature Research Centre (HKLRC) of the Chinese University of Hong Kong, and the Chinese University of Hong Kong Library (CUHK Library) kicked off a two-year proposal entitled "Fun with Learning Chinese Language through Literary Walk Project (Fun Project)." Apart from introducing the Fun Project, the authors also discuss a key deliverable of this project, namely *Hong Kong Literary Landscape MediaWiki*. (CUHK Hong Kong Literature Research Center and CUHK Library, n.d.) In this paper, the advantages of using MediaWiki as an effective open platform for creating content collaboratively are discussed, and the challenges of using an online platform to promote literary reading and writing are addressed.

Fun with Learning Chinese Language through Literary Walk: A Brief Outline

In January 2013, the SCOLAR of the HK SAR Government invited applications for the "Chinese Language Promotion 2013–2014" to promote creative and meaningful activity to improve Chinese writing skills of primary and secondary students. The HKLRC and CUHK Library jointly submitted a two-year proposal entitled "Fun with Learning Chinese Language through Literary Walk Project," which aims at promoting literary reading and writing skills to junior secondary school (equivalent to junior high school in North America) students in Hong Kong. The proposal was submitted to SCOLAR in March 2013 and was subsequently accepted in July 2013. The work team of the Fun Project consisted of four members: principal investigator, coinvestigator, project coordinator, and project assistant. The principal investigator and coinvestigator oversaw the direction, execution, and evaluation of the project while the project coordinator and project assistant were responsible for the project delivery including liaising with external parties, conducting publicity, coordinating literary walks, editing student writings, and setting up the *Hong Kong Literary Landscape MediaWiki*.

The Fun Project was designed in such a way that a literary walk was conducted in each district of Hong Kong. Administratively, Hong Kong is divided into eighteen districts in three major geographic areas: Central and Western, Eastern, Southern, and Wan Chai districts in Hong Kong Island; Kowloon City, Kwun Tong, Sham Shui Po, Wong Tai Sin, and Yau Tsim Mong districts in Kowloon and New Kowloon; and Islands, Kwai Tsing, North, Sai Kung, Sha Tin, Tai Po,

Tsuen Wan, Tuen Mun, and Yuen Long districts in New Territories. The Fun Project organized altogether eighteen literary walks in two years. To kick-off the project, an official invitation letter was sent to all principals and Chinese subject heads of the secondary school in Hong Kong to recruit student participants. In the past decade, the organizers have been actively promoting Hong Kong literature and have built up close connection with literary figures in Hong Kong. The project team identified emerging professional writers who published frequently on literary journals and websites to join the Fun Project. These emerging writers were not only young in age but also young in heart. For a designated district, a "young writer" was invited to serve as the docent.

After enrolling in the literary walk of a specific district, the student participants received a pack of reading materials critically selected by the docent. Apart from literary quality, these reading materials also cover the cultural and historical aspects of the respective district. The student participants were required to study the articles before attending the literary walk. On the event day, the docent delivered a workshop to the student participants by introducing the selected articles in more details so that they could grasp the main features of the articles. This arrangement facilitated a close interaction with the docent before the start of the literary walk. After the event, the student participants were required to submit a piece of creative writing in the form of poem, prose, or fiction on their experience and reflection of the literary walk.

Being a key deliverable of the Fun Project, the *Hong Kong Literary Landscape MediaWiki* serves as a repository of the output generated from the literary walks in eighteen districts, including critically selected articles, literary maps, video clips, creative writings of the student participants, and so on. The docents shared their views with the student participants about their creative writings using the discussion platform of the MediaWiki. In addition to the project participants, the *Hong Kong Literary Landscape MediaWiki* is also a useful open source to other secondary school teachers and students. Teachers can benefit from the *Hong Kong Literary Landscape MediaWiki* by making use of the online resources available on the wiki platform to design their own literary walks for their students. The *Hong Kong Literary Landscape*

MediaWiki is also beneficial to students because it provides an interesting and interactive way of learning Chinese language online.

Chinese Language Curriculum for Secondary School: Literary Walk and Chinese Language Learning

In 2001, as part of the education reform in Hong Kong, the Education Bureau of the HK SAR Government released a policy document on Chinese language learning titled *Chinese Language Curriculum Guide (Junior Secondary and Senior Secondary)*. As stated in this policy document, Chinese language learning comprises nine learning areas, namely reading, writing, listening, speaking, literature, Chinese culture, morality and affection, thinking, and independent language learning. Among these nine learning areas, reading, writing, listening, and speaking are considered as the fundamental learning areas that can also facilitate learning in the other five areas (Education Bureau, 2001). In other words, it is vitally important for students to build up their knowledge and hone their skills in reading, writing, listening, and speaking in order to succeed in Chinese language learning. Once they are competent in these four fundamental areas, their learning in the other five areas can be enhanced.

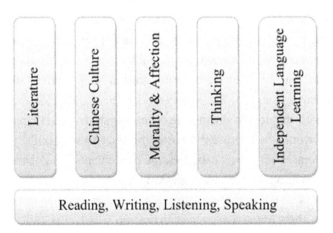

Figure 1 Nine learning areas of Chinese language. (Education Bureau, 2001).

According to the *Chinese Language Curriculum Guide*, the objectives of the four fundamental areas of Chinese language learning are the following:

Reading: To enhance reading skills such as comprehension, analysis, experience and appreciation, etc.; to master reading strategies; and to enjoy reading and do it diligently and seriously; increase the quantity and range of reading.

Writing: To enhance writing skills such as conception, expression and creative writing, etc.; to master writing strategies; and to enjoy writing and do it diligently and seriously.

Listening: To enhance listening skills such as comprehension and evaluation; to master listening strategies; and to enjoy listening and do it seriously; expand the range of listening.

Speaking: To enhance speaking skills such as conception, expression and response; to master speaking strategies; and to enjoy expressing and do it bravely, giving graceful response. (Education Bureau, 2001)

Reading, writing, listening, and speaking are essential learning skills in not only Chinese language but also other languages as well. It is very important for junior secondary school students to master these skills in their early stage of language learning. To this end, the Fun Project was aimed at enhancing the skills in these four areas of Chinese language learning of the student participants. In the workshop delivered by the docent, the participants could grasp a better understanding of the content and style of the literary works. Through face-to-face interaction with the docent during the event, the student participants had the opportunity to improve their listening and speaking skills. Through these interactive learning activities, the participants can enhance their reading, writing, listening, and speaking capabilities.

There is no doubt that literature is an excellent source for language learning. The *Chinese Language Curriculum Guide* also indicates that students can appreciate the beauty of language and acquire the sense of truth through literature learning. This is exactly the reason why literature is considered as one of the nine learning areas of Chinese language. In the *Chinese Language Curriculum Guide*, the learning objectives of Literature are the following:

- To experience the pleasure of literature reading and appreciate the beauty of it;
- To develop aesthetic insight, attitudes and skills;
- To enhance language learning interest and proficiency through the delightful reading experience;
- To share the unique but common thinking and affections in works to strengthen interpersonal communication and mutual understanding, and inspire life experience. (Education Bureau, 2001)

The Fun Project was designed to spark interest in language learning through literature among the student participants by reading and appreciating literary works in a relaxing and enjoyable setting.

Hong Kong Literary Landscape MediaWiki

Wikipedia was launched by Jimmy Wales and Larry Sanger in 2001. After developing its content by the Wiki community in the past two decades, Wikipedia is now the largest online encyclopedia in the world. Given the popularity of Wikipedia, a series of enhanced products among the wide variety of functions provided by Wikipedia, the content management, collaborative workspace, reference source, training guide, and so on, of Wikipedia are particularly relevant to library applications.

In the Fun Project, MediaWiki was adopted as the platform for the project deliverables for two reasons. First, MediaWiki supports very useful features such as easy navigation, editing, formatting, referencing, look and feel change, file uploading, user management, and so on. MediaWiki not only provides openly accessible data storage and retrieval service but also handles structured data including text, image, and multimedia files of the source data. It also supports

Chinese character that is critically important for the Fun Project. Second, MediaWiki is a collaboration and documentation platform that helps to collect and organize knowledge and make it available to people (Liginlal et al., 2010). It provides the collaborative editing function to facilitate the interaction between the docents and student participants of the Fun Project. Even though MediaWiki adopts open-source platform, it provides a secure environment for the Fun Project. With these resources available on MediaWiki, the project team could explore the best ways to support the project participants and to engage individuals from the wider communities (Poulter & Sheppard, 2020).

Besides selecting the best platform for this project, we also had to decide whether we should use a vendor-hosted solution versus a local-hosted solution. In terms of technical knowledge of the platform administrator, a vendor-hosted solution is less demanding and thus the platform can be setup in a comparative short period of time. Also, the platform provider takes care of the platform upgrade and data backup, which can be costly for a project with a limited budget. However, local-hosted solution guarantees the long-term preservation of the data and service by making use of the technical and human resources of the hosting institution. It also facilitates the customization of the interface and searching function. The downside of a local-hosted solution is that it requires additional resources for supporting the technical requirement. Given that the Fun Project was a two-year project and there was no budget provision for technical support, it was a sensible decision to adopt the vendor-hosted solution in order to roll out the platform as soon as possible in view of its tight schedule. Also, MediaWiki development is backed by Wikimedia Foundation with strong financial support. It is very unlikely in the foreseeable future that there will be any development and maintenance problem with the codebase of Mediawiki.

Hong Kong Literary Landscape MediaWiki: Key Features

The aim of *Hong Kong Literary Landscape MediaWiki* is to preserve and make accessible materials on literary walk in all districts in Hong

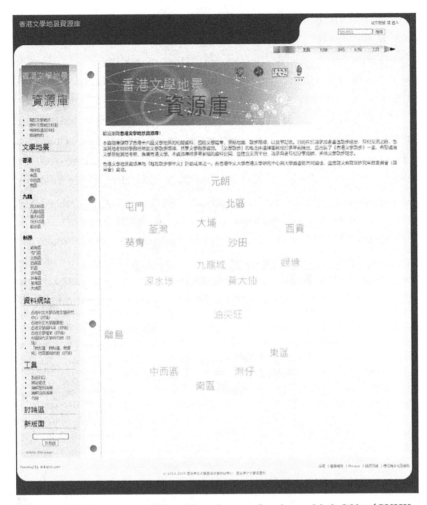

Figure 2 The home page of Hong Kong Literary Landscape MediaWiki. (CUHK Hong Kong Literature Research Center and CUHK Library, n.d.)

Kong. It is anticipated that, in the long term, *Hong Kong Literary Landscape MediaWiki* will be a repository of the archival materials on literary walk. The *Hong Kong Literary Landscape MediaWiki* is accessible by not only the project participants but also the wider public. This feature supports the mission of knowledge sharing with a larger group of audience of this project. The structure of the *Hong Kong Literary Landscape MediaWiki* was designed according to eighteen administrative

districts in Hong Kong, which contains materials related to the literary walks in each district. On the main page of *Hong Kong Literary
Landscape Media Wiki* (http://hkliteraryscenes.wikidot.com/), there is
a word map of these eighteen districts. By clicking the name of the district on the word map, it will bring you to the district subpage.

Each district subpage provides a list of critically selected articles
related to its district. If the copyright of an article has been cleared, it
also provides hyperlink to its full text. Apart from literary articles, the
district subpage also contains the project outputs, namely literary maps,
literary routes, project handouts, video clips, and the creative writings of
the student participants. The literary route highlights the literary landscape and relevant articles along its route. School teachers can make use
of these materials and handouts for their students to hone their skills
in reading and writing. They can also utilize project materials to devise
their own literary walk to enrich the learning environment outside of
the classroom.

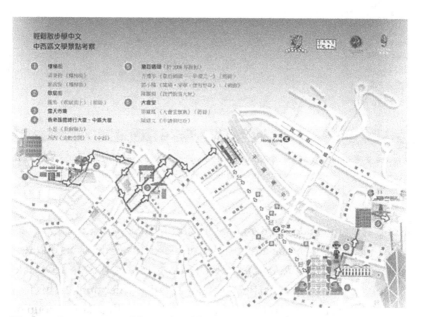

Figure 3 Literary map of Central and Western District. (CUHK Hong Kong Literature Research Center and CUHK Library, n.d.)

Hong Kong Literary Landscape MediaWiki:
A Collaborative Learning Platform

As a web 2.0 application, Wikis provide online collaborative function. The Wiki user is not only an information receiver but an information creator as well. Wiki applications, like Wikipedia, adopted a very simple markup based on UseModWiki because of its simplicity and security. As an open-source program, UseModWiki is a user-friendly computer language that can be learnt and used very easily. The *Hong Kong Literary Landscape MediaWiki* adopted the MediaWiki application to build up a literary reading and writing platform. By making use of the discussion platform, both the docents and the student participants are able to exchange their views and comments about reading and writing. This kind of interaction can facilitate a collaborative learning environment. After submitting their creative writings about the literary walks of their districts, the project coordinator created a separate subpage for each piece of writing submitted by the student participants. The project coordinator then invited the docents to comment on the creative writings in the discussion box after uploading these works. All student participants could respond to the comments made by the docent as well. They could add not only text but also photos and hyperlinks in the discussion box. This interactive process was an essential part of collaborative learning activities in the Fun Project.

Conclusion

The *Hong Kong Literary Landscape MediaWiki* is the first of its kind in preserving and providing access to literary walk materials in Hong Kong. Looking ahead, there are three major challenges in terms of sustainable growth and development of this Wiki project. First, there should be a sustainable funding support from public agencies. Given the success of the Fun Project, the organizers successfully solicited the funding support from the SCOLAR for three similar projects on literary walks for junior secondary students, namely Read/Write My City Project (2015–2017), Narrating Him/Her in My City (2017–2019), and

Fun Writing Literary Footprints Project (2019–2021). The deliverables of these projects have also been made available on the *Hong Kong Literary Landscape MediaWiki*. But what will happen after 2021 if there is no sustainable funding model for this Wiki project? Second, there is always a limit that we can successfully clear the copyright issue of the selected literary works that are used for literary walks. There is no doubt that the more full-text artifacts that can be made available on the *Hong Kong Literary Landscape MediaWiki* the better. Third, usually no more than twenty-five student participants were registered in a literary walk. How can the number of student participants be increased without comprising the quality of Chinese language learning? We consider these three major challenges vital to the success of the *Hong Kong Literary Landscape MediaWiki* as a repository of the materials on literary walks in Hong Kong. In the long term, it is anticipated that *Hong Kong Literary Landscape MediaWiki* can be used as a digital humanities resource to map the literary landscapes and activities in Hong Kong using spatial analysis and visualization technologies such as Internet-based GIS. The author believes that *Hong Kong Literary Landscape MediaWiki* will help to uncover a range of findings from historical, cultural, and societal perspectives that have not been addressed before.

References

CUHK Hong Kong Literature Research Center and CUHK Library. (n.d.). Hong Kong Literary Landscape. http://hkliteraryscenes.wikidot.com/.

Dulwich Picture Gallery. (2020, November 27). Bloomsbury literary walk. www.dulwichpicturegallery.org.uk/whats-on/tours-walks/2017/march/bloomsbury-literary-walk/.

Education Bureau. (2001). Chinese language curriculum guide (junior secondary and senior Secondary). Hong Kong: Hong SAR Government (in Chinese).

Iowa City UNESCO City of Literature. (2020, November 27). Lit walk. www.iowacityofliterature.org/lit-walk/.

Liginlal, D., Khansa, L., & Landry, J. P. (2010). Collaboration, innovation, and value creation: The case of Wikimedia's emergence as the center for collaborative content. In *Cases on technology innovation: Entrepreneurial successes and pitfalls*. Hershey: IGI Global (pp. 193–208). doi:10.4018/978-1-61520-609-4.ch010.

Poulter, M., & Sheppard, N. (2020). Wikimedia and universities: Contributing to the global commons in the Age of Disinformation. *Insights*, *33*(1), 14. doi: http://doi.org/10.1629/uksg.509.

Tokyo Metropolitan Government. (2020, November 27). Tokyo walking map. www.fukushihoken.metro.tokyo.lg.jp/walkmap/en/map/detail/sumida11.html.

Wikipedia. (2020, September 11). Wikipedia: Five pillars. https://en.wikipedia.org/wiki/Wikipedia:Five_pillars.

Wikipedia.(2020, September 28). Wikipedia: About. https://en.wikipedia.org/wiki/Wikipedia:About.

CHAPTER 17

STRUCTURING BIBLIOGRAPHIC REFERENCES: TAKING THE JOURNAL *ANAIS DO MUSEU PAULISTA* TO WIKIDATA

Éder Porto Ferreira Alves, [1] *Paul R. Burley,* [2]
and João Alexandre Peschanski [3]

[1] Grupo de Usuários Wiki Movimento Brasil, [2] Northwestern
University, [3] Faculdade Cásper Líbero

Abstract

This chapter provides a step-by-step process for large-scale contributions of articles from scholarly publications to Wikidata, a collaborative data store project of the Wikimedia Foundation. Tools and processes in Wikidata, Zotero, and Google Sheets in particular are described; they relate both to the Wikidata platform and standard spreadsheet programs. The case of the Brazilian journal Anais do Museu Paulista is used to illustrate the process that can then be replicated with other publications and in other contexts.

Author Note

Research by João Alexandre Peschanski is supported by the FAPESP grant project 2013/07699–0 and the Faculdade Cásper Líbero Interdisciplinary Research Center. We have no conflicts of interest to disclose.

DOI: https://doi.org/10.3998/mpub.11778416.ch17.en

Correspondence concerning this article should be addressed to João Alexandre Peschanski, Av. Paulista, 900, Bela Vista, São Paulo, SP, 01310–100 Brazil. Email: japeschanski@casperlibero.edu.br

Keywords

Wikidata, Scholarly literature, Bibliographic references.

Introduction

Wikimedia-supported knowledge projects have seen robust acceptance in the Global South, notably in Brazil. Wikimedia projects are attractive in Global South communities for decentering the use of the English language and the low cost of use and access. In contrast, institutional repository and data platforms are prohibitively expensive, either in cost or maintenance, for Global South galleries, libraries, archives, and museums (GLAMs). These tools additionally require technology out of the reach of Global South institutions. Resources for "community-owned infrastructure, and robust metadata to facilitate open scholarship practices" (ARL Task Force on Wikimedia and Linked Open Data, 2019) have grown in both size and depth in Brazil and other Global South communities. In contrast, the high cost of computer hardware, software, and Internet connectivity in Global South GLAMs, as well as a lack of technology specialists, is a constraint unlikely to change at present or in the near future. Internet connectivity in Brazil is limited to 74 percent in museums and 66 percent in libraries (Centro Regional de Estudos para o Desenvolvimento da Sociedade da Informação, 2018). Some of these infrastructure and technological obstacles are addressed by demonstrating the use of Wikidata to index items of scholarly articles in the Brazilian context.

Sources on Wikimedia Projects

Referencing reliable sources is an essential component of a Wikipedia article (Orlowitz, 2018), yet the quality of referencing has varied across Wikipedia instances in different languages (Lewoniewski et al., 2020). Some progress has been made in citation inclusion, but in general the addition of references to a Wikipedia article remains an excessively technical endeavor. An instance of a reference is limited to its article and cannot be shared among articles; more importantly, it is difficult to move a reference between different-language Wikipedias, even with the support of translation tools.

Wikidata is a free, collaborative knowledge base (Vrandečić & Krötzsch, 2014), and it can be used to overcome existing inefficiencies in the Wikipedia referencing model. The creation of items for scholarly articles and other periodical literature for a Wikimedia project is a useful contribution in its own right. A single, simple recent improvement to the article citation creation process in Wikipedia is the ability to create a reference based on a Wikidata identifier (QID), which can then be reused independently across different-language Wikipedias. A more advanced utility, not yet fully developed, would be a system in which article citations generated from Wikidata items are automatically updated or improved when the corresponding Wikidata item is enhanced.

Figure 1 highlights the imbalance of items for scholarly articles from North America and Europe in Wikidata in comparison to those elsewhere. This chapter specifically aims to motivate editors from the Global

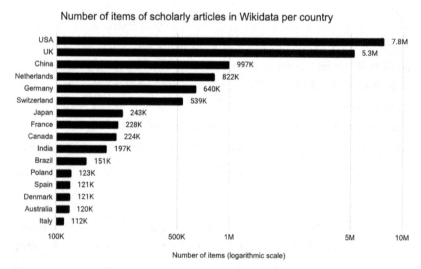

Figure 1 Number of items for scholarly articles in Wikidata by country of publication. Retrieved on September 26, 2020. Data available at https://doi.org/10.5281/zenodo.4051056.

South and underrepresented communities to engage in the large-scale contribution of items for scholarly articles and related academic literature to Wikidata. For these editors, tools and processes that are commonly used in resource-richer communities are often not helpful, as they depend on data that are already well-structured and easy to automatically feed to Wikidata. Commercial journal platforms and common metadata structures are well established in the Global North; in contrast, the situation in Brazil and elsewhere is ad-hoc. The process we present in this chapter is more easily replicable in Global South contexts.

Context

The edit-a-thon emerged among Wikimedia knowledge communities to increase content and depth of a subject area of common importance to its members or provide instruction on Wikimedia tools or practices. As the portmanteau of "edit" and "marathon" suggests, they are "in-person or virtual events where Wikimedia community members write or enhance Wikipedia articles, upload or edit metadata for images in Wikimedia Commons, add or enhance structured data in Wikidata, or other Wikimedia-related knowledge project activities" (ARL Task Force on Wikimedia and Linked Open Data, 2019). Edit-a-thons at Stanford University, Indiana University-Purdue, University of Indianapolis, and Laurentian University are described in the literature (Allison-Cassin & Scott, 2018; Keller et al., 2011; Lemus-Rojas & Pintscher, 2018). Descriptions of edit-a-thons outside the Global North in scholarly literature, however, are lacking.

The activities of Grupo de Usuários Wiki Movimento Brasil (English: Wiki Movement Brazil User Group), a national-level Wikimedia umbrella organization in Brazil, range from group editing projects to instruction on advanced tools. The user group has organized two distinct activity modalities: edit-a-thons, known as *maratonas de edição* or *editatonas* in Brazilian Portuguese, and Wikidata Labs. In contrast to the edit-a-thon, the Wikidata Lab emerged in 2017 as periodic events to share resources and capacities for the integration of Wikidata into other Wikimedia projects, especially Wikipedia. This series of events was awarded the 2019 WikidataCon Award, in the Category Outreach. Wikidata Labs evolved into connecting Wikimedians to GLAMs and set up a space for working directly on their collections.

The monthly events of the group, sustained activities, and tight community of practitioners of Wiki Movimento Brasil led to a large-scale project focused on content related to the Ipiranga Museum, commonly known as the Museu Paulista. The Museu Paulista opened in the late nineteenth century in a monumental building by the Italian architect Tommaso Gaudenzio Bezzi. The structure commemorated the independence of Brazil and its early collections emphasized the natural history of the country. The long directorship of the historian Afonso d'Escragnolle Taunay reoriented its collections to emphasize the independence movements and establishment of the federal republic of Brazil, the history of the state of São Paulo, and historical and cultural objects of the early twentieth century. The museum was integrated into the University of São Paulo in 1963. Bezzi's museum structure is now a federally protected monument in its own right. Activities of the museum include the maintenance and exhibition of its physical collection and support of research related to its activities. The museum closed in 2013 due to financial problems and is expected to reopen in 2022.

Wiki Movimento Brasil and Museu Paulista partnered on April 4, 2020, to organize Wikidata Lab XXI: Structuring Bibliographic References. The first part of the workshop was a webinar on how to automate the creation of Wikidata items of scholarly articles. The second part of the workshop was a collective effort among attendees to index articles from the primary journal of the museum, *Anais do Museu Paulista* (English: "Annals of the Paulista Museum"), into Wikidata. Twenty-six editors participated in the project, and their work resulted in creating 876 items: 511 for journal articles and 365 for authors. Ultimately, approximately 31,000 statements were added to Wikidata.

The *Anais* is a scholarly journal published by the Museu Paulista since 1922. It serves not only to disseminate scholarship on the museum itself, but it is also one of the primary history and museology journals in Brazil. The *Anais* dates to the early period of Taunay's directorship of the museum and reflects his focus on the formation of the Brazilian nation. Taunay's influence is mirrored in the journal's early subtitle, "Organ of the History of Brazil Section, and Especially of São Paulo, of the Paulista Museum" (Bittencourt, 2012). It draws heavily on contributions from academics associated with the museum and the University of São Paulo. Journal articles are, with few exceptions, by Brazilian scholars in Brazilian Portuguese. The editorial emphasis on the arts and history of Brazil continues to the present in the publication, which has a stated editorial objective to "discuss . . . themes related to material culture as a mediator of social practices, as well as innovative approaches to historical and museological processes." A new series of the journal was launched in 1993 (see figure 2).

ANAIS do MUSEU PAULISTA
História e Cultura Material

Nova Série   Número 1   1993
UNIVERSIDADE   DE   SÃO   PAULO

Figure 2 Cover of the first issue of the New Series of *Anais do Museu Paulista*, 1993.

Importing Scholarly Articles into Wikidata via Zotero: Step-by-Step Process

The eight steps below provide a detailed description of a process to ingest scholarly articles to Wikidata using Zotero, a bibliographic citation management software. The process is the same used to ingest a body of articles of the *Anais do Museu Paulista* into Wikidata.

Step 1: Download Zotero

In this step, we use Zotero, an open-source software to manage bibliographic data. Zotero Desktop is the desktop version of the tool and Zotero Connector is an extension for browsers to save online references to Zotero. The combination of the two tools aims to make bibliographic references fully integrated, interoperable, and synchronized. These tools are available to download at www.zotero.org/download/. Tutorials for how to work with Zotero are available at www.zotero.org/support/.

Step 2: Import a Set of Articles into Zotero

Begin by creating a list of identifiers and use the "Add Item by Identifier" button on Zotero Desktop to import them all at once (see top of figure 3). As of 2020, ISBNs, DOIs, PMIDs, and arXIv IDs are the only supported identifiers. Alternatively, add identifiers manually using the Zotero Connector extension in the browser by clicking on the "Save to Zotero" button at the top right corner of the article web page (see bottom of figure 3).

The challenge in this step is to decide on which alternative is less time-consuming or skill dependent: to produce a list of identifiers in a text file or spreadsheet or to add them one by one. If an article does not have any of the four identifiers, rely on Zotero Connector to add the article to the library.

Step 3: Create an Account on Wikimedia Projects

Users are not required to create an account or login in order to edit Wikipedia, Wikidata, or Wikimedia Commons. However, an account and

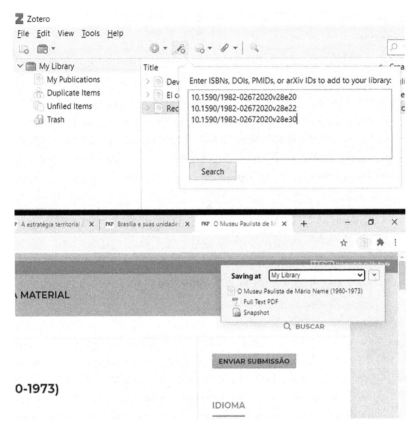

Figure 3 From top to bottom: screenshots of Zotero Desktop and Zotero Connector, showing usage of the "Add Item(s) by Identifier" and "Save to Zotero" buttons, respectively. Retrieved on September, 4, 2020.

username are required, for any functionality beyond basic edits. Additionally, Wikidata user access levels only allow experienced users to batch import datasets (Wikidata contributors, 2020). To access this functionality:

- Create an account by following the instructions at www.wikidata. org/wiki/Special:CreateAccount, and
- Make fifty valid edits or more and wait at least four days. This will establish you as an autoconfirmed user, and it will also allow you to use more advanced tools on Wikidata.

Step 4: Download, Install, and Set Up the QuickStatements Translator

Zotero and Wikidata are integrated with the use of a translator, a script that converts metadata stored in one format to another. The translator, which is called *Wikidata QuickStatements.js* and is part of a Zotero extension called *zotkat*, will generate a set of text commands to be imported into QuickStatements, an online tool program that can read and execute commands to create or edit a Wikidata item (Wikidata contributors, 2021). For this step:

- Download Wikidata QuickStatements.js file at https://github.com/UB-Mannheim/zotkat, and
- Paste the Wikidata QuickStatements.js file into the "translators" folder (see figure 4) of your Zotero installation.

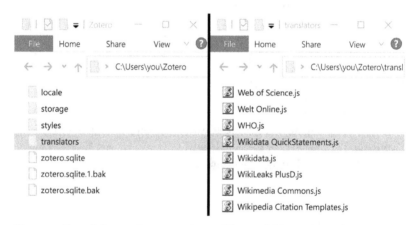

Figure 4 From left to right, screenshots of Zotero folder and translators folder. Retrieved September 9, 2020.

After this, restart Zotero and open "Program Preferences" under the Edit menu. To complete this step, highlight the "Export" tab, and select "Wikidata QuickStatements" under the "Default Output Format" dropped down menu, as indicated in figure 5.

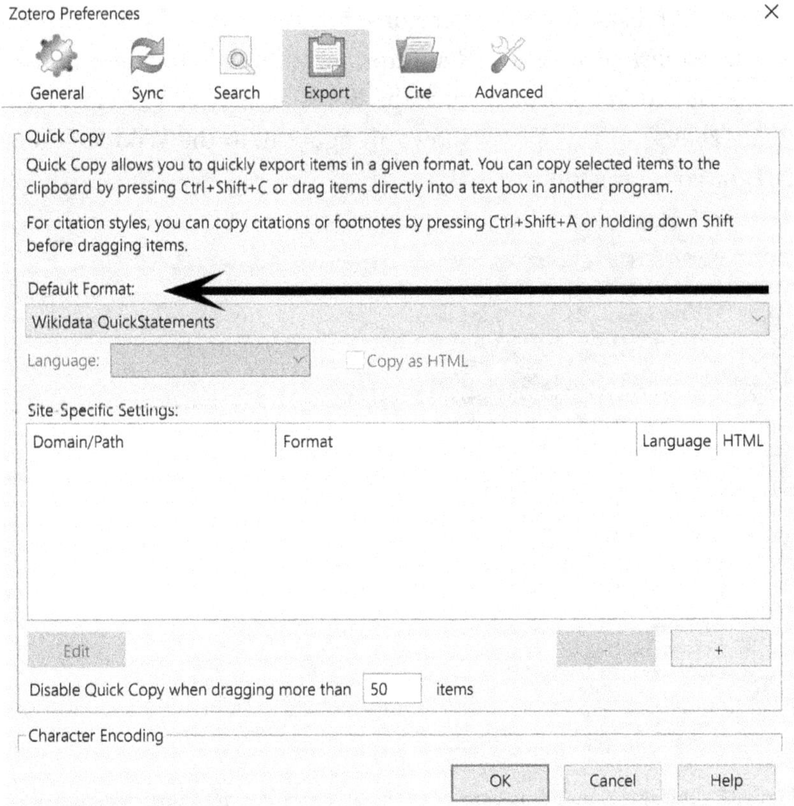

Zotero Preferences   ✕

| General | Sync | Search | Export | Cite | Advanced |

┌─ Quick Copy ──┐

Quick Copy allows you to quickly export items in a given format. You can copy selected items to the clipboard by pressing Ctrl+Shift+C or drag items directly into a text box in another program.

For citation styles, you can copy citations or footnotes by pressing Ctrl+Shift+A or holding down Shift before dragging items.

Default Format: ⬅━━━━━━━━━━━━━━━━━━━━━━━━━━━━━━━━━━━━━━

Wikidata QuickStatements   ∨

Language: [∨]   ☐ Copy as HTML

Site-Specific Settings:

Domain/Path	Format	Language	HTML

[Edit]   [   ] [+]

Disable Quick Copy when dragging more than [50] items

┌─ Character Encoding ───┐

[OK]   [Cancel]   [Help]

Figure 5 Screenshots of Zotero Preferences window, showing the Wikidata QuickStatements format chosen under "Default Format." Retrieved September 9, 2020.

Step 5: Check for Duplicates in Wikidata

It is important to not create duplicate items in Wikidata, so you will first need to check for your journal's articles in Wikidata before uploading new items. There are several strategies to check for duplicates. One strategy is to query Wikidata for items for scholarly articles from the journal on which you are working using Wikidata Query Service, a user-friendly interface to build and run data queries on Wikidata, providing an overview of the statements of a set of items. An example of a query of scholarly articles from *Anais do Museu Paulista* can be found at https://w.wiki/bYF. To run a similar query for another journal, switch the Brazilian journal Wikidata QID (Q50426299) in row 11, as shown in figure 6, to the Wikidata item QID of your target journals.

Figure 6 Query commands to generate a list of identifiers of the articles from *Anais do Museu Paulista*. Retrieved September 11, 2020.

Once you have performed a query, the data can be downloaded in several formats and compared to the list in Zotero. To do this:

- Download the query result in. csv format and open it into a spreadsheet software,
- Import your list of identifiers into another sheet of the same spreadsheet,
- Write a MATCH function to compare and match the identifiers from your list with the identifiers from the query result; for an example of a match function on Google Sheets, see https://support.google.com/docs/answer/3093378, and
- Exclude the articles with a match from your Zotero library.

Step 6: Upload to Wikidata via QuickStatements

To upload references to Wikidata, use the QuickStatements tool, mentioned before and available at https://quickstatements.toolforge.org/ along with Zotero. Begin in Zotero by:

- Selecting all the references you have imported and want to upload to Wikidata, and
- Clicking on "Edit" then "Copy as Wikidata QuickStatements" to copy the commands to the clipboard.

Then in the QuickStatements tool:

- Click on "Log in" at the right top corner to log in to your account,
- Click on "New batch" and paste the commands into the text field, and
- Click on "Import V1 commands." Look over the first articles to be uploaded, per Wikidata community guidelines, before clicking on "Run."

It might take some time for QuickStatements to upload the references to Wikidata, depending on the number of commands and the Quick-Statements server itself. Help on how to use QuickStatements is available at www.wikidata.org/wiki/Help:QuickStatements. Beware of the following possible mistakes and pitfalls: if the website of origin of your reference is not well structured, Zotero might import the items with duplicated information; Zotkat translator is not fully developed yet and some fields are not translated into QuickStatements commands, for example, the license; some properties present in Zotero do not yet exist in Wikidata and therefore are not imported.

Step 7: Check Completeness of Item Properties Using Wikidata Query Service

To check the completeness of data imported into Wikidata as part of a project, build a dashboard for Wikidata properties. An example of a dashboard for the *Anais do Museu Paulista* was generated using the

Wikidata Query Service at https://tinyurl.com/articles-by-journal-qid. In order to replicate the dashboard for a different journal using the query from the *Anais do Museu Paulista*, change the journal QID at row 39 of the query.

The zotkat tool does not import the "journal of publication" statement to Wikidata. The items created, therefore, do not initially have this declaration on Wikidata. In order to monitor them, build a query using their associated unique identifiers. An example query for a subset of *Anais do Museu Paulista* articles is available at https://tinyurl.com/articles-by-identifiers. To replicate the process for a different set of articles, substitute their identifiers at row 42 of the query.

Step 8: Add the "Journal of Publication" Statement using PetScan
To add the "journal of publication" statement to the items created, use PetScan (https://petscan.wmflabs.org), a tool that lists items based on a query code and can add statements to them in Wikidata. To do this:

- Add the identifiers of the articles created at line 42 of the query at https://tinyurl.com/articles-by-identifiers,
- Copy the query code and paste it into the SPARQL field at the "Other Sources" tab in PetScan (see the top half of figure 7),
- Click "Do it!" and wait until the results show up,
- At the beginning of the results list (see the bottom half of figure 7), include the journal of publication statement that needs large-scale editing at the top right corner. An example for including the journal of publication for scholarly articles of Anais do Museu Paulista is P1433 (property for "published in") and Q50426299 (item for "Anais do Museu Paulista"), and
- Click "Start QS" to open a Quick Statements window with the commands and follow the instructions as indicated before in step 6.

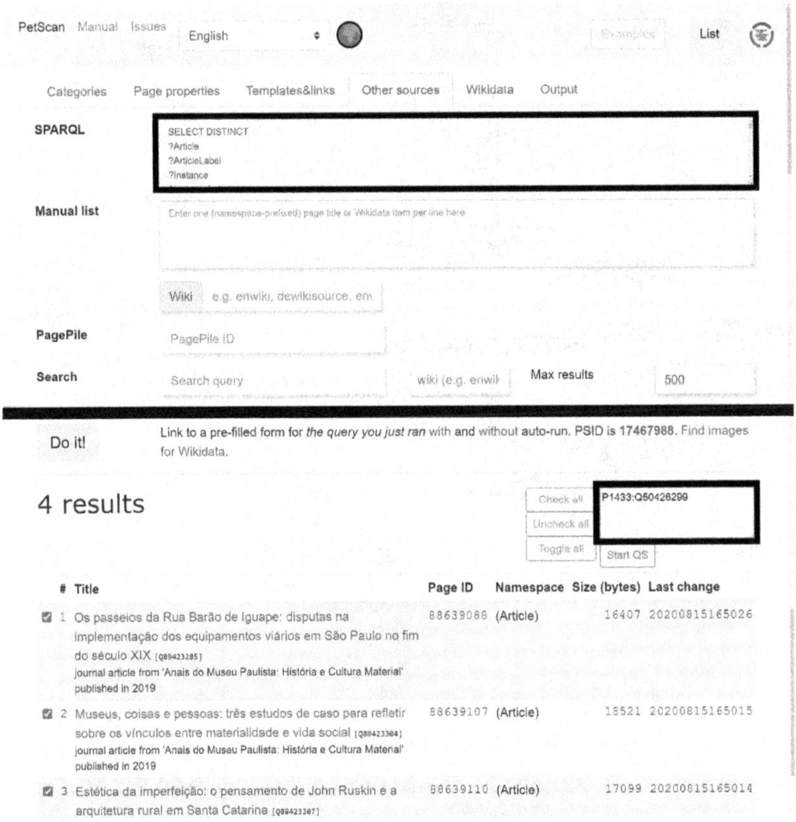

Figure 7 From top to bottom, screenshots of the Pet Scan tool, highlighting the SPARQL and Command list fields, and the results list. Retrieved from https://tinyurl.com/petscan-anaismp26092020.

Data Visualization

Bibliographic visualization is an important outcome of an initiative to create items on scholarly articles in Wikidata (see figure 8). Scholia is a web service to create scholarly profiles and their associated visualizations based on bibliographic information in Wikidata (https://scholia.toolforge.org/) (Nielsen et al., 2017). Profiles may be built for individuals, organizations, works, locations, events, awards, and research topics. In the case of academic journals, it displays lists of publications and research topics as well as information on authors and citations. Displays are built

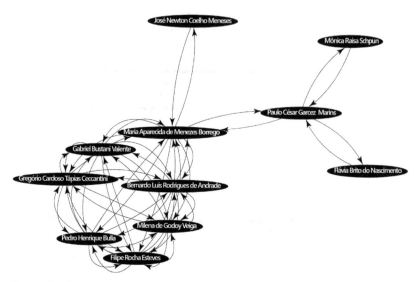

Figure 8 The coauthor graph—here, a fragment from Anais do Museu Paulista—is an output of the Scholia tool for publications. Available at https://w.wiki/XEw.

with the Wikidata Query Service; accordingly, information is updated in Scholia as items in Wikidata are added and enhanced. Scholia provides examples and a menu on the top to browse possible profiles. The profile of *Anais do Museu Paulista* may be found at https://scholia.toolforge.org/venue/Q50426299. Other bibliographic elements may be explored by changing the QID ("Q50426299") at the end of the previous URL.

Conclusion

The process laid out in this chapter demonstrates a strategy for how to democratize the contribution of scholarly literature to Wikidata and to facilitate the diversity of cultural and regional origin of the literature that is contributed to the project. We relied on Zotero and a set of Wikidata tools to provide a large-scale body of article indexing from the *Anais do Museu Paulista*, a scholarly journal of the Museu do Ipiranga. Our case study and related guidelines seek to motivate and illustrate the inclusion of bibliographic literature from the Global South without an advanced skill set, an information-heavy technology, or a well-structured dataset. The combination of tools and processes presented above forms a catalyst to promote knowledge equity in Wikidata, and in a wider context, bibliographic discovery and access.

References

Allison-Cassin, S., & Scott, D. (2018). Wikidata: A platform for your library's linked open data. *The Code4lib Journal, 40.* https://journal.code4lib.org/articles/13424.

Association of Research Libraries Task Force on Wikimedia and Linked Open Data. (2019). ARL white paper on Wikidata: Opportunities and recommendations (p. 59) [White paper]. *Association of Research Libraries.* www.arl.org/wp-content/uploads/2019/04/2019.04.18-ARL-white-paper-on-Wikidata.pdf.

Bittencourt, V. L. N. (2012). Revista do Museu Paulista e(m) capas: Identidade e representação institucional em texto e imagem [Revista do Museu Paulista in its covers: Identity and institutional representation through text and images]. *Anais do Museu Paulista, 20*(2), 149–54. http://dx.doi.org/10.1590/S0101-47142012000200006.

Centro Regional de Estudos para o Desenvolvimento da Sociedade da Informação. (2018). TIC Cultura: Pesquisa sobre o Uso das Tecnologias de Informação e Comunicação nos Equipamentos Culturais Brasileiros [TIC Cultura: Research on the use of information and communication technologies in Brazilian Cultural Institutions] (p. 4) [Report] *Centro Regional de Estudos para o Desenvolvimento da Sociedade da Informação.* www.cetic.br/media/analises/lancamento-pesquisa-tic-cultura-2018.pdf.

Keller, M. A., Persons, J., Glaser, H., & Calter, M. (2011). Report of the Stanford Linked Data Workshop, 27 June-1 July 2011. *Council on Library and Information Resources.* https://www.clir.org/pubs/reports/pub152/stanford-linked-data-workshop/

Lemus-Rojas, M., & Pintscher, L. (2018). Wikidata and libraries: Facilitating open knowledge. In Proffitt, M. (Ed.), *Leveraging Wikipedia: Connecting communities of knowledge* (pp. 143–58). ALA Editions.

Lewoniewski, W., Węcel, K., & Abramowicz, W. (2020). Modeling popularity and reliability of sources in multilingual Wikipedia. *Information, 11*(5), 263.

Meneses, U. T. B. de. (Ed). (1993). Anais do Museu Paulista: História e Cultura Material, (1993). *1*(1). https://www.revistas.usp.br/anaismp/issue/view/380

Nielsen, F. Å., Mietchen, D., & Willighagen, E. (2017, May 28). Scholia and scientometrics with Wikidata. *Joint Proceedings of the 1st International Workshop on Scientometrics and 1st International Workshop on Enabling Decentralised Scholarly Communication*. *1st International Workshop on Scientometrics and 1st International Workshop on Enabling Decentralised Scholarly Communication*, Portorož, Slovenia. https://doi.org/10.5281/ZENODO.1036595.

Orlowitz, J. (2018). The Wikipedia Library: The largest encyclopedia needs a digital library and we are building it. In Proffitt, M. (Ed.), *Leveraging Wikipedia: Connecting communities of knowledge* (pp. 1–25). ALA Editions.

Vrandečić, D., & Krötzsch, M. (2014). Wikidata: A free collaborative knowledgebase. *Communications of the ACM, 57*(10), 78–85. https://doi.org/10.1145/2629489.

Wikidata contributors. (2020, April 27). Wikidata:User access levels. In *Wikidata*. Retrieved January 20, 2021, from www.wikidata.org/w/index.php?title=Wikidata:User_access_levels&oldid=1167897989.

Wikidata contributors. (2021, January 13). Help:QuickStatements. In *Wikidata*. Retrieved January 20, 2021, from www.wikidata.org/w/index.php?title=Help:QuickStatements&oldid=1340541986.

CHAPTER 18

WIKISOURCE AS A TOOL FOR OCR
TRANSCRIPTION CORRECTION: THE
NATIONAL LIBRARY OF SCOTLAND'S
RESPONSE TO COVID-19

Gavin Willshaw[1]

[1] The University of Edinburgh

Abstract

This chapter focuses on the National Library of Scotland's Wikisource transcription correction project, an organization-wide effort during lockdown that generated 1,000 fully accurate transcriptions of 3,000 Scottish chapbooks, which the Library had uploaded to Wikisource, Wikimedia's online library of digitized, out of copyright works. The project, which contributed to the Library being awarded Partnership of the Year 2020 at the Wikimedia UK AGM, is thought to be the largest ever staff engagement with Wikimedia, and has had significant benefits to the Library and staff well beyond the original aims of the project. Initially set up to improve the quality of optical character recognition (OCR) transcriptions in order to make the chapbooks more discoverable and searchable, the project gave staff a purpose and sense of belonging during lockdown, provided an opportunity to work with a varied and fascinating collection, and enabled them to develop new skills in editing Wikisource, drafting guidance documentation, and managing projects. Further to this, the initiative greatly increased library staff engagement

DOI: https://doi.org/10.3998/mpub.11778416.ch18.en

with Wikimedia, led to the formation of a Wikimedia Community of Interest, and resulted in the embedding of Wikimedia activity in staff work.

Keywords

Wikisource, Crowdsourcing, Scottish chapbooks, National Library of Scotland, Staff engagement, Digital skills.

Introduction

Like many cultural heritage organizations, the National Library of Scotland faces a significant challenge when digitizing texts: how to efficiently generate accurate transcriptions that meet users' needs, not just for search and retrieval but also for computational analysis using text and data mining (Europeana Pro, 2019). The Library runs typed and printed text through OCR software to generate transcriptions automatically and makes these available online alongside digital images on its Digital Gallery (National Library of Scotland, 2020a). Unfortunately, these often contain spelling mistakes and errors as the software struggles to deal with issues such as faint text, hyphenation, and archaic letters including the long-s (ſ) (Alex, 2012). Such issues require human intervention to correct but the Library lacks the staff resource to undertake this work. One area that the Library has been interested in exploring is whether corrections could be crowdsourced using Wikisource, Wikimedia's online library of out of copyright, digitized books. When a book is added to Wikisource, a community of thousands of editors work together to improve transcriptions using the platform's in-built error correction module and then publish the book on Wikisource ("Wikisource," 2020). Recent developments in functionality mean that the completed books can be exported not only in PDF or ePUB format but also as TXT files ("Wikisource:WSexport," 2020). The Library wanted to explore whether out of copyright, digitized books from its collections could be uploaded to Wikisource, where transcriptions would be improved in collaboration with the Wikisource community and then reimported back into the Library's image repository to improve the quality of search on the Digital Gallery.

An opportunity to explore this workflow suddenly arose in March 2020, when the Library closed its doors as the United Kingdom entered lockdown in response to the COVID-19 crisis. The Library's ten-person digitization team, whose work almost exclusively required them to be on-site using cameras and scanners to digitize books and other items from the Library's collections, needed work that would have impact and advance projects, would be large enough to keep them occupied throughout lockdown, and would require minimal access to the Library's network or physical building space. This unique situation allowed the Library to test Wikisource at scale; within twenty-hour hours of lockdown the entire team was editing transcriptions for the Library's recently digitized Scottish chapbook collection (Hagan, 2016) on the platform.

Chapbooks are small printed booklets that were sold for a penny or less on the streets, at fairs, and at markets. Typified by the use of woodblock illustrations and covering a range of subjects such as murders, disasters, love stories, and biographies of famous people, they were staple reading material for much of the population in a time before modern communication systems were invented (Hagan, 2019). This depth of content makes them a particularly useful primary source for social historians of the period, while their engaging content matter and size—3,000 separate books ranging from eight to twenty-four pages in length—meant it was an ideal collection for exploring Wikisource as a tool for OCR correction. Within a few days of lockdown, it became apparent that there were several other members of Library staff who also had time to work on the Wikisource project. Like the digitization team, staff in roles that were public facing or required access to the Library building were also limited in what they could do while working from home. By the end of March there were over fifty members of staff taking part in the work; this number increased to seventy, which was over 20 percent of the entire Library staff (National Library of Scotland, 2020b), at the project's peak.

It was exciting to have this unexpected, possibly once in a lifetime, opportunity to focus staff resources on a Wikimedia project, but rolling it out to several dozen staff in just a few weeks created many challenges. Arguably the greatest of these was that the Library, and the country as a whole, was going through a huge change and staff had to adjust mentally and physically to their new reality. Most were using their own devices rather than Library laptops or PCs, so many were reliant on machines that were slow, out of date, or were shared with other members of their households. Furthermore, the level of Wikimedia knowledge and understanding across the Library was quite low. The layout of Wikimedia sites, the concept of Talk pages and etiquette of communication, and the use of basic HTML tags when editing source code were new to a lot of people, especially nondigital natives and those who didn't use digital technologies in their work.

In order to overcome these issues, the project team developed clear step-by-step instructions and guidance that covered all aspects of the workflow including how to set up a Wikimedia account and how to communicate with other users ("Wikisource:WikiProject NLS," 2020). A project support group was set up on Microsoft Teams where staff could discuss the issues they faced; additionally, all documentation was stored on Office 365, so staff could read and access documents without requiring VPN access to the Library's internal network. Rather than being assigned specific books to work on, staff were pointed to a Microsoft Excel spreadsheet that listed the books and the different workflow stages they were at; this allowed staff to select suitable items and to work on the project at a pace and time that suited them.

As mentioned above, the project team had very little time to plan this work in advance; one area that was initially overlooked in the rush to get the project started was codifying standards for the work being done. Wikisource has a Manual of Style ("Wikisource:Style guide," 2020), which outlines guidelines and recommendations to ensure consistency and standardization on the platform. These recommendations mainly focus on trying to achieve an accurate representation of the original item in the transcription. For example using the {{center}} tag to bring a heading into the center of the page, or the {{text-indent}} tag for indented paragraphs, while also ensuring that the spelling in the transcription matches that of the original image. While this works well for straightforward texts, for more complex items it can be extremely time-consuming to ensure that the transcription accurately matches the original item. For example, an incorrectly spelled word in a book should use the {{SIC}} tag to show both the incorrect spelling used in the original for historical accuracy, as well as the presumed correct spelling to aid with keyword search. It became apparent early in the project that to fully meet all of Wikisource's guidelines, the proofreader would have to spend a lot of time on each book. Bearing in mind that the Library's chief motivation for engaging with Wikisource was to generate and extract high-quality transcriptions, working in complete compliance with the existing standards would slow the process so much as to make it infeasible. Instead, the project team worked with key members of the Wikisource community to develop new standards that would allow a better balance between transcription quality and throughput. The agreed approach involved a focus on correct spelling and layout, while using some of the more common tags to ensure transcriptions aligned closely to the original text.

Discussion around standards helped the team develop the project workflow, splitting the work into five discrete tasks, which are outlined below ("Wikiproject NLS Workflow," 2020).

1. Upload multipage PDFs of digitized chapbooks and their associated metadata to Wikimedia Commons using the Pattypan bulk upload tool.
2. Create Index pages on Wikisource, link these to the files on Wikimedia Commons, and add another link and information to the project Excel spreadsheet.
3. Generate initial automated transcription using Wikisource's Google OCR engine then proofread to correct errors.
4. Validate the proofread transcription, publish to Wikisource (transclude), and link to author pages and Wikidata.
5. Export transcriptions as multipage PDFs, convert to single-page TXT files, remove header and footer information and tags, and reupload into the Library's Digital Gallery.

In developing the steps outlined above, the project showed it is possible to set up an end-to-end workflow to successfully improve transcription errors using Wikisource and reupload those transcriptions back into the Library's repository, which improves the search function of its digital collection. The project can be deemed a success: it has been estimated that at its peak there were more National Library of Scotland staff working on the platform than all other Wikisource editors combined; the project is also thought, anecdotally, to have been the largest ever staff contribution to a Wikimedia project. As of November 27, 2020, 1,064 of the 3,000 Scottish chapbooks in the collection had been fully transcluded, with an additional 535 books fully proofread ("Wikiproject NLS Progress").

However, despite all the effort in overcoming the challenges outlined above, the actual number of books fully transcribed has been quite low, and far lower than had been anticipated when the project started in March 2020. By the time the Library reopened in late July 2020, approximately 16,000 Scottish chapbook pages had been fully transcribed. Considering that approximately seventy staff had contributed to the project over a twenty-week period, the actual number of pages transcribed per person was only around ten per week. Based on this progress, it seems fair to conclude that if an organization's sole reason for engaging with Wikisource is to improve the quality of transcriptions from their digitized books, rather than using Wikisource they would probably be better building their own OCR correction module or buying one of the various commercial transcription packages or services that exist. The different stages of the Wikisource workflow take a lot of time: each Scottish chapbook was worked on by at least five different people as it progressed from upload to transcription export to the Library's gallery. Added to this, there are several manual elements to the process that are time-consuming, such as generating indexes on Wikisource by copying each individual URL from Wikimedia Commons, and frustrating, such as changing the OCR software from the default Tesseract engine to the far superior Google engine for every page. What is more, by adding books to Wikisource, there is an associated responsibility to manage the book once it is on the platform, to interact with and be guided by the existing community and to adhere as far as possible to their standards.

For the National Library of Scotland, however, the real benefit has been in areas far beyond correcting the quality of transcriptions, areas that had not even been considered at the start of the project.

The first of these was that Library staff experienced a huge amount of satisfaction and enjoyment from taking part in the project, with colleagues regularly tweeting about the interesting books they were working on and expressing their pride at being involved in the project in internal Library and Union lockdown surveys. For many, taking part in the project provided them with something tangible to work on, something to achieve and contribute to when their work environment had changed so dramatically. It gave people who didn't work with the collections on a day-to-day basis a much better sense of engagement with the Library and the materials it holds for the nation, and also helped them feel more connected with colleagues they hadn't seen since before the national lockdown.

Added to this, the Wikisource project has also given people opportunities to develop their digital literacy and skills by introducing them to Wikimedia projects and teaching them how to navigate the sites, contribute to open-knowledge initiatives, and learn how to use basic HTML and mark up for the first time. For the digitization team, who ran the project, the work had a secondary effect by giving them opportunities and responsibilities in a completely new area. Staff whose normal role was to digitize books—an important but often repetitive task—were given responsibility for different parts of the new workflow. One person, for example, became responsible for developing the internal guidance and training new staff as they joined the project, while another was responsible for liaison work with the Wikisource community on standards and workflow. A third member of the team took on the responsibility for file upload, which allowed them to learn to use the Pattypan tool to bulk upload files to Wikimedia Commons. These new responsibilities gave staff in the digitization team more confidence in their ability and raised their awareness of the wider digitization workflow and the impact digitized collections can have.

Furthermore, the project has helped to increase staff awareness of and engagement with Wikimedia projects more widely. All staff who

have taken part now have Wikimedia accounts, have been trained in the
basics of editing Wikimedia sites, and have received a bespoke Wikisource overview from Sara Thomas, Wikimedia UK Scotland Programme Coordinator, and Ewan McAndrew, Wikimedian-in-Residence
at the University of Edinburgh. Several Library staff also attended the
Wikipedia and archives webinar by Kelly Foster in April 2020 and the
Wikidata and cultural heritage collections session run by the Science
Museum in June 2020. All of this means that the Library now has a
better educated staff about the value of engagement with Wikimedia
projects and there is now a strong base to develop future Wikimedia-
related work. Members of staff who are now back to work at the Library
are still working on this project during quiet periods, meaning Wikimedia work is embedded in staff roles for the first time. Following the
success of this project, a Wikimedia Community of Interest was set
up at the Library, which has already had a significant internal impact.
There has been more staff engagement with the 1Lib1Ref campaign
and Wiki Loves Monuments, for which the Library uploaded over 100
images in the 2020 campaign (Wikimedia Foundation, 2020), an intern
was employed to write articles about the Library and its collections, a
member of staff attended the Wikidata Summer Institute, and plans
are in place to run a Bannatyne Manuscript Wikipedia edit-a-thon at
the end of the year in collaboration with the University of Saskatche-
wan. This project has been a catalyst for far greater Wikimedia activity
at the Library and collaboration with the Wikimedia community over
the coming years.

And finally, adding digitized books to Wikisource appears to have
improved access to and use of the Library's digitized collections.
Although no large-scale analysis has been undertaken, a sample of five
randomly chosen Scottish chapbooks on Wikisource was viewed an
average of five times per book, which, if expanded to cover the 1,000
chapbooks already published on Wikisource, would suggest around
5,000 page views per month for the entire collection, a figure that adds
to views on the Library's Digital Gallery site, and may well be higher
because of Wikisource's superior search engine optimization (SEO).
Indeed, another quick, internal test of five different random books

showed that the Wikisource version of a book appeared higher than the same item on the Library's Digital Gallery, with the Library's record sometimes not even appearing on the first page of Google results. The National Library of Scotland's experiments with Wikisource have shown that the platform is not necessarily the best medium to use if an organization is solely interested in improving the quality of its transcriptions through OCR, as it is a slow process, requires significant manual input, dialog and engagement with the Wikimedia community and agreement on standards. For the National Library of Scotland, however, the benefits of running this project have far outweighed these issues, and the improved transcriptions the Library has received have been more of a side benefit rather than the main reason for engaging with Wikisource. The project has brought a lot of positives to the Library, including raising the awareness off Wikimedia platforms among staff, kick-starting an internal Community of Interest, and building relations with the wider Wikimedia community, all of which should make activity in this area a more sustainable element of the Library's work in the future. This initiative has developed staff skills and empowered them to grow in new areas during a difficult and traumatic time in their working lives, it has helped to bring an important digitized collection to a wider public audience, and it has created a workflow that will allow work to ramp up again in the event of future crises and lockdowns. Aside from anything else, the Library's Wikisource transcription project has given a glimpse of what can be achieved when considerable staff resources are committed to an open-knowledge project.

References

Alex, B., Grover, C., Klein, E., & Tobin, R. (2012). Digitised historical text: Does it have to be mediOCRe? In *Proceedings of KONVENS 2012* (pp. 401–9). www.oegai.at/konvens2012/proceedings/59_alex12w/.

Europeana Pro. (2019, July 31). Issue 13: OCR. https://pro.europeana.eu/page/issue-13-ocr.

Hagan, A. (2016, March 4). Scottish chapbooks now online! *National Library of Scotland Blog.* https://blog.nls.uk/scottish-chapbooks-now-online/.

Hagan, A. (2019, August 27). Chapbooks: The poor person's reading material. *Europeana Blog.* https://blog.europeana.eu/2019/08/chapbooks-the-poor-persons-reading-material/.

National Library of Scotland. (2020a, September 24). Digital Gallery. https://digital.nls.uk/gallery/.

National Library of Scotland. (2020b, September 24). Meet our staff. www.nls.uk/about-us/working-at-the-library/meet-our-staff.

Wikimedia Foundation. (2020, September 24). Wiki Loves Monuments 2020. https://outreachdashboard.wmflabs.org/courses/National_Library_of_Scotland/Wiki_Loves_Monuments_2020.

WikiProject NLS. (2020, September 18). In Wikisource. https://en.wikisource.org/wiki/Wikisource:WikiProject_NLS.

WikiProject NLS Progress. (2020, September 18). In Wikisource. https://en.wikisource.org/wiki/Wikisource:WikiProject_NLS#Progress.

WikiProject NLS Workflow. (2020, September 18). In Wikisource. https://en.wikisource.org/wiki/Wikisource:WikiProject_NLS#Workflow.

Wikisource. (2020, September 15). In Wikipedia. https://en.wikipedia.org/wiki/Wikisource.

Wikisource:Style guide. (2020, August 4). In Wikisource. https://en.wikisource.org/wiki/Wikisource:Style_guide.

Wikisource:WSexport. (2020, July 16). In Wikisource. https://wikisource.org/wiki/Wikisource:WSexport.

CHAPTER 19

LEARNING FROM EACH OTHER: RECIPROCITY IN DESCRIPTION BETWEEN WIKIPEDIANS AND LIBRARIANS

Angela Yon[1] and Eric Willey[1]

[1] Illinois State University

Abstract

Librarians, archivists, and museum professionals are increasingly realizing the value of using and contributing information to Wikipedia through projects such as edit-a-thons and the 1Lib1Ref project. As the amount of knowledge in Wikipedia and Wikidata grows, the benefits to libraries in partnering with Wikimedia projects to enhance their own bibliographic records and catalog search results also increase. Conversely, librarians have created an immense number of bibliographic and authority records that Wikipedia and Wikidata editors can use both as resources in and of themselves and as examples of various approaches to metadata and knowledge creation. Despite some challenges there are numerous benefits for working to integrate library data with Wikipedia more closely.

This chapter will serve to highlight differences between Wikipedia resources and library catalog records, and how librarians and Wikipedians can learn from each other to improve description and discoverability in both Wikipedia and library catalogs for their respective users. It will also illustrate differences between

DOI: https://doi.org/10.3998/mpub.11778416.ch19.en

these two systems in order to reduce confusion and errors when data are merged uncritically. The discussion draws on experience gained from a previous Illinois State University Research Grant-funded project that used the Wikipedia List of African-American writers to enhance library catalog records.

Keywords

Authority control, Library of Congress Demographic Group Terms (LCDGT), Wikipedia lists, Metadata, Data integration, Cataloging, Wikidata.

Introduction

Librarians, archivists, and museum professionals are increasingly realizing the value of using and contributing information to Wikimedia projects, and as the amount of knowledge in Wikipedia and Wikidata grows, the benefits to libraries in partnering with Wikimedia projects to enhance their own bibliographic records and catalog search results increase. Librarians, archivists, and museum professionals have also created an immense number of bibliographic and authority records that Wikipedia and Wikidata editors can consult as information resources and examples of how to organize knowledge. Differences between Wikipedia resources and library catalog records provide opportunities for librarians and Wikipedians to learn from each other and improve description and discoverability in both resources for their respective users. The following discussion describes experiences gained from a previous Illinois State University Research Grant-funded project that explored using the Wikipedia List of African-American writers (Wikipedia contributors, 2020a) to enhance MAchine-Readable Cataloging (MARC) records with demographic group terms for authors.

Trends for the library catalog currently integrate the discoverability of local resources with features of the larger web environment. This mixture often draws from existing metadata in library catalog records. Examples include allowing users to refine searches using facets, using Functional Requirements for Bibliographic Records (FRBR) by showing a work in its representation of versions and editions, using linked data approaches for common entities, and integrating community-created systems like Wikipedia (Dempsey, 2012). As the largest library cooperative, OCLC has undertaken several collaborative partnerships between Wikipedia and libraries, such as the Wikipedia Visiting Scholar program and Project Passage (OCLC Research, 2020). OCLC has also urged catalogers to "integrate researchers' external IDs within library applications and services as appropriate" to facilitate the creation of high-quality linked data between resources (Smith-Yoshimura et al., 2014).

In recent years libraries have undertaken attempts to integrate the library's catalog data into the larger web environment for discoverability purposes. An additional goal for libraries is to share and benefit from knowledge created by larger community-based open systems, platforms, and hubs such as Google Search, Wikipedia, Amazon, LibraryThing, and Google Books, by bringing them into the library catalog setting (Dempsey, 2012). The open-source library catalog, VuFind, offers optional features that allow users to view rich linked data content, such as author biographies via Wikipedia (VuFind 4.1 Milner Library, 2020). Similarly, to improve the quality of services for both libraries and Wikipedia, Joorabchi and Mahdi (2018) designed a software system for automatic mapping of FAST subject headings that are used to index library materials to their corresponding articles in Wikipedia. Charting connections between the library catalog and other open systems, such as Wikipedia, creates a need for the implementation of linked data elements. The merging of data from different systems and its many descriptive forms under one discovery layer calls for linked data approaches so that the resources may be discoverable based on common entities and identifiers (Dempsey, 2012).

Both libraries and Wikipedia generate projects that allow users to refine searches with facets, lists, and categories. In 2013, the Library of Congress began exploring the creation of the Library of Congress Demographic Group Terms (LCDGT)-controlled vocabulary (Library of Congress, Policy and Standards Division, 2020). Through inclusion of new MARC fields in bibliographic records, the terms would allow catalogers to describe intended audiences and the creators of works. Library of Congress Subject Headings (LCSH) and their subdivisions already included information describing audiences and creators of resources (including demographic groups), but the format of the strings was not always clear to users in search results. With the use of LCDGT, there could be more precision in search results by faceted displays using these terms in the catalog, and clarity in the descriptions of the resources for users. Similarly, Wikipedia contains many lists of individuals in various demographic groups, often associated with a profession. Many of the Wikipedia lists correspond with the nine categories of the LCDGT vocabulary, one of which is ethnicity/ culture, which may indicate an agreement on what categories are useful between the two systems.

From 2017 to 2019, the authors led a project to examine the degree of agreement between the Wikipedia List of African-American writers (Wikipedia contributors, 2020a) and Library of Congress criteria for determining if a creator would be considered appropriate for description using the LCDGT term African Americans. For the project, African American history subject expert Trumaine Mitchell found that there was a high level of agreement between individuals on the Wikipedia list and those whose resources might be described as being authored by an African American by the LCDGT criteria (Willey and Yon, 2019). From that project, additional lessons were learned about differences in the structure of information between Wikipedia (especially Wikipedia lists) and traditional (MARC) library cataloging.

At the time, the principal investigators were researching the degree of agreement between Library of Congress criteria and decisions by Wikipedia editors as to which writers could be considered members of the demographic group African American. The possibility of using Wikidata or Wikipedia lists updated by bots such as Listeria to populate catalog search results was not considered during this research in favor of determining if the LCDGT criteria led to the same conclusions as those reached by Wikipedia editors. If there had been disagreement, that would have been a warning flag against integrating the two platforms; however, thankfully there was not. As this article reflects lessons learned during this project, there is limited discussion of Wikidata, although it represents a wealth of possibilities for additional research.

Similarities and Differences between
Wikipedia Lists and MARC Cataloging

The initial barriers for participating in the Program for Cooperative Cataloging (PCC) versus Wikipedia differ considerably. The PCC requires institutional participants to undergo training through the PCC Secretariat before creating or editing Name Authority Records (NARs). However, creating Wikipedia lists only requires familiarity with word processing software, so most people will be able to use the visual editor to create and make edits to Wikipedia lists and pages with minimal or no additional training, although several tutorials and guides are provided for users. In the analysis of Wikipedia lists, the subject expert was quickly able to learn how to add the Authority Template and the Library of Congress Control Number (LCCN) to Wikipedia pages where it was lacking and did so with accuracy and efficiency; however, no attempt was made to train them on the creation of NARs or the editing of existing NARs because of the greater amount of time required to learn Resource Description and Access (RDA) standards, International Standard Bibliographic Description (ISBD) punctuation, and other cataloging skills.

The process for making changes to PCC cataloging policy and Wikipedia policy also differs significantly. Partway through the creation of NARs in the project, PCC announced a moratorium on the use of the MARC 024 Other Standard Identifier field (Frank, 2018). In November 2020, PCC ended the moratorium and provided guidelines on the use of the MARC 024 field to link NARs to Wikidata identifiers, two years after the project. This allows NARs to link directly to Wikidata items, which are also used by the Authority Control Template in Wikipedia articles to provide links to NARs and other identifiers such as the International Standard Name Identifier (ISNI) and Virtual International Authority File (VIAF) (Wikipedia contributors, 2020b). No impactful changes to Wikipedia policy were encountered during the project, but it is understood that proposals can be made and implemented relatively swiftly if approved by the community. This is not intended as a critique of the PCC deliberative process but may be seen as an indicator that implementing changes in older established library standards such as MARC, which has undergone several changes and updates since it was developed in the 1960s, may require more deliberation and testing than changes to a relatively new system such as Wikipedia (developed in 2001). It may also be an indication that this is a larger conceptual step for cataloging systems than it is for Wikipedia.

A similarity between the two systems is that both Library of Congress and Wikipedia require citation of evidence to show why a person is described using an ethnic or racial group in some instances but not in others. In Wikipedia, the List of African-American writers includes a note to consult the Who is African American section (which has undergone several renamings since a section by that exact name was last present in 2012) of the African Americans article (Wikipedia contributors, 2020c) and the individual pages should include citations to reliable resources justifying any claims of race or ethnicity. This can, however, lead to cases such as Stanley Bennett Clay (Wikipedia contributors, 2020d) where they are included in the List of African-American writers (Wikipedia contributors, 2020a), but their page does not describe them as Black, African American, or any equivalent term, and they are not listed in the category: African-American writers page (Wikipedia contributors, 2020e). PCC policy also requires that NARs include a MARC 670 Source Data Found field for demographic information included in the record at the time of creation; however, catalogers can edit bibliographic records and include demographic information in the MARC 386 Creator/Contributor Characteristics field without the requirement to include citations showing how they reached that decision, as shown in figure 1. Therefore, both institutions can be said to have requirements that users cite information supporting any addition of ethnic group information to certain records, and practices that specifically associate individuals with an ethnic group, but do not require citations to convey that information.

Additionally, there are differences in the structure of the LCDGT and Wikipedia lists. The LCDGT are generally broken down to a single facet, because they are intended to be used in individually repeatable

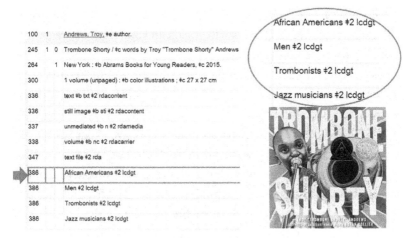

Figure 1 This image depicts Trombone Shorty by Troy Andrews, a bibliographic record, OCLC number 880349715 (OCLC Connexion, 2020).

MARC fields. Typically, two separate traits would be described using two different terms, one for ethnicity or culture and a second for nationality. The term "African Americans" is in the ethnic/cultural category but also describes a nationality. Therefore, the term "Americans" will also be included in a record. There is also no LCDGT for the occupation writer or author because creation of a bibliographic record is based on literary warrant. The overwhelming majority of entries in the Name Authority File (NAF) and bibliographic records are by writers, making that criteria nearly useless for sorting. Wikipedia lists cover many topics, but lists of people often seem to combine the criteria of nationality and profession (Puerto Rican comedians, for example). In order for library catalogs to incorporate Wikipedia lists into search results, these different approaches will need to be reconciled. Depending on how difficult this is, libraries may instead choose to incorporate information from Wikidata items or lists generated and automatically updated by tools such as Listeria (Manske, 2015). It may be easier for Wikipedia to generate lists from library records, as they can combine the individual facets to form a list with as many characteristics as desired. This may also indicate a difference in design philosophy with librarians expecting users to utilize facets to narrow search results in a library catalog, and Wikipedia users creating lists and categories with the expectation that users will engage in something more akin to browsing through search results.

Users of both systems face difficulty in creating complete and comprehensive lists of members of specific demographic groups. It was discovered that two authors with works in the local library catalog were not on the List of African-American writers but have Wikipedia pages. Benjamin Griffith Brawley was a prominent African American author and educator, and several of his books were standard college texts in the early twentieth century. Phillip Hayes Dean, an African American playwright, also has a Wikipedia page but was not on the List of African-American writers. Both have bibliographic records in the local library catalog with LCSH terms that included African American authors. This suggests that library catalogs may be useful in either populating or at least providing initial leads on populating demographic group lists, although they will only reflect members of that group for whom the library has holdings. Wikipedia also includes both Wikipedia lists and Wikipedia categories (and there are Wikidata items as well), and users may not always update all of these leading to lists and categories describing the same group but which include different items.

The Wikipedia List of African-American writers also included authors whose library bibliographic records did not record their status as African Americans, of course. One such author provided an interesting example in how Wikipedia lists can be useful in discovering works not directly cataloged by librarians. Clarissa Minnie Thompson Allen was included on the List of African-American writers but did not have an NAR or catalog record for their novel, *Treading the Winepress*. Investigation revealed that Allen's novel was serialized in *The Boston Advocate*, a newspaper, and not published as a stand-alone work. The portion that could be located has since been printed as an open-access book by the Illinois State University publications unit (Allen, 2019), but as catalogers rarely create records for individual parts of newspapers, Allen's work was never cataloged on its own record, and no NAR for Allen was created until long after the publication of her work. Historically marginalized creators often turned to publishing their works in formats other than monographs. Wikipedia lists can be useful in locating creators and works that may not have individual bibliographic records in the library catalog.

Mapping data to fields in a bibliographic record from similar categories in each system is an obvious example of how libraries and Wikipedia can provide each other with additional information to draw from; however, Joseph (2019) suggests a fresh approach of how Wikipedia can contribute to the library catalog. One of the challenges library catalogs face is the loss of historical revisions to bibliographic records. This change came consequently from the physical card catalog transition to the digital library catalog. "Analyses that were possible with physical catalog cards can no longer be performed, and tools that process digital records leave no traces of the information they add, remove, or update" (Joseph, 2019). In 2015, OCLC stopped printing catalog cards. Revisions and the historical context of classification are omitted in the online catalog, removing a source that librarians could reference for past analysis. Wikipedia, on the other hand, allows users to track changes in its digital environment through its discussion pages and revision pages. Joseph (2019) believes the library catalog can benefit from a similar practice, allowing analysis of changes and a larger field of subject domain experts to contribute to metadata decisions through discussion.

Library employees have easier access to databases, reference works, and special collections or archival materials than some Wikipedia members, which prove especially valuable in satisfying notability requirements for articles. While the Internet removes many barriers to access, older print materials are still largely held in libraries. Similarly, special collections materials are often only available through intermediaries or by on-site visits. Libraries also feel incentivized to provide citations from their special and local collections to bring greater visibility to those materials. In the analysis of Wikipedia lists, the subject expert began their search in Google Books but also utilized interviews found in library databases to conduct their research.

The volunteer nature of Wikipedia also makes it an excellent source of editors with rich and varied subject knowledge. Domain experts from around the world can apply their extensive knowledge to articles and lists, at their own discretion and convenience. Catalogers are also subject experts but will likely be expected to work on materials purchased by other librarians. Wikipedians' volunteer status allows them relative freedom in choosing topics to contribute. While librarians generally must justify metadata created during their work time to stakeholders, Wikipedians can investigate topics and create lists on subjects of their choice. For the analysis of Wikipedia lists, reference librarians stated that patrons sometimes requested works by African American creators, which gave the project more credibility when composing the grant request. It is also unlikely that the project would have proceeded beyond the theoretical phase without grant funds to hire a subject expert in African American history.

Wikidata and Future Work

There is consensus among institutions that the future of this reciprocal relationship with data will be very advantageous and valuable as the catalog moves to new forms of discovery in libraries (Bartholmei et al., 2016). In 2019, the Association of Research Libraries released a white paper by a task force of library professionals and expert Wikidata users with recommendations for librarians to use Wikidata to advance discovery of their collections, faculty, and institutions. Many cataloging systems do not produce linked data and cannot make data available as open linked data. Research libraries may lower this barrier with participation in the Wikidata community and infrastructure (Association of Research Libraries, 2019).

While the project under discussion used a list from Wikipedia, Wikidata offers a low-barrier, high-result method for creating and using linked data in libraries. It makes data not only visible but also reusable as linked data. In a 2016 International Federation of Library Associations and Institutions (IFLA) discussion paper, Stephan Bartholomei and others noted "the potential of Wikidata to draw linked open data and linked open data authorities together across the world's languages and many different ontologies and taxonomies has enormous potential to support researchers around the world" (Bartholmei et al., 2016).

The Library of Congress (LC), recognizing the potential of Wikidata as being a hub of identifiers, included links in their authority records out to Wikidata in spring 2019. They bulk loaded 400,000 more LC identifiers into Wikidata to add to the 650,000 IDs in Wikidata. This brought their total to about a million of their identifiers in the system. The majority of these identifiers are to their NAFs and 35,000 link to the Library of Congress subject heading file. Likewise, these links to Wikidata also appear on over one million Library of Congress Linked Data Service authority pages and in the data (Ferriter, 2019).

The PCC also acknowledges how Wikidata can be an important collaborative partner and system to help in the development of identity management and identifier creation for libraries and institutions. In September 2020, the PCC launched a Wikidata pilot project "to further advance the movement toward identity management" (PCC, 2020). Over seventy academic and cultural institutions across the globe will be part of the pilot to increase the movement toward identity management, and membership in PCC is not required to participate in the project.

Conclusion

Even though the project had a narrow scope (focusing on one Wikipedia list and MARC cataloging), the authors were able to learn many significant lessons about Wikipedia practices, cataloging, and how they interact. The practices and goals of catalogers and Wikipedians are often aligned, and even differences between the two group's practices can be seen as complementary rather than opposed. The Wikipedia-focused project also provided an excellent entry for the authors into associated services such as Wikidata and has led to further projects using that platform. With major institutions such as PCC backing Wikidata-related projects and Wikipedians-in-residence becoming increasingly accepted, additional opportunities for collaboration between Wikipedia and academic libraries are emerging. Critically, the reciprocity of knowledge and expertise between librarians and Wikimedians can significantly improve services and contribute greatly to the overall information landscape.

References

Allen, C. (2019). Treading the Winepress; or, a Mountain of Misfortune. *Undiscovered Americas*. https://web.archive.org/web/20200927134819/ https://ir.library.illinoisstate.edu/ua/2/.

Association of Research Libraries (ARL) Task Force on Wikimedia and Linked Open Data. (2019). "ARL white paper on Wikidata: Opportunities and recommendations." *Association of Research Libraries*. April 18, 2019. https://web.archive.org/web/20201110232835/www.arl.org/wp-content/ uploads/2019/04/2019.04.18-ARL-white-paper-on-Wikidata.pdf.

Bartholmei, S., Franks, R., Heilman, J., Joseph, M., McDonald, V., Raunik, A., Ridge, M., & Robertson, M. (2016). Opportunities for academic and research libraries and Wikipedia. https://web.archive.org/web/20200522082117/ www.ifla.org/files/assets/hq/topics/info-society/iflawikipediaopportuni tiesforacademicandresearchlibraries.pdf.

Dempsey, L. (2012, December 10). Thirteen ways of looking at libraries, discovery, and the catalog: Scale, workflow, attention. *EDUCAUSE*. https:// web.archive.org/web/20201106232835/https://er.educause.edu/arti cles/2012/12/thirteen-ways-of-looking-at-libraries-discovery-and-the-ca talog-scale-workflow-attention.

Ferriter, M. (2019, May 22). Integrating Wikidata at the Library of Congress. *The Signal*. https://web.archive.org/web/20201121143752/https://blogs.loc. gov/thesignal/2019/05/integrating-wikidata-at-the-library-of-congress/.

Frank, P. (2018). "024 (Other Standard Identifier) data in NACO records: Temporary moratorium." *PCCLIST@LISTSERV.LOC.GOV*, September 13, 2018. https://web.archive.org/web/20201202161342/https://listserv.loc. gov/cgi-bin/wa?A2=ind1809&L=PCCLIST&P=38986.

Joorabchi, A., & Mahdi, A. E. (2018), "Improving the visibility of library resources via mapping library subject headings to Wikipedia articles." *Library Hi Tech*, 36(1), 57–74. https://doi.org/10.1108/LHT-04-2017-0066.

Joseph, K. (2019). "Wikipedia knows the value of what the library catalog forgets." *Cataloging & Classification Quarterly*, 57(2–3), 166–83. https://doi. org/10.1080/01639374.2019.1597005.

Library of Congress, Policy and Standards Division (2020). "Demographic Group Terms Manual." https://web.archive.org/web/20201029185954/ www.loc.gov/aba/publications/FreeLCDGT/freelcdgt.html.

Manske, M. (2015, May 6). Überlistet. *The Whelming*. https://web.archive.org/ web/20201024200154/http://magnusmanske.de/wordpress/?p=301.

OCLC Connexion. (2020). *Trombone Shorty by Troy Andrews*. OCLC number 880349715. *OCLC*. https://web.archive.org/web/20201202154550/www. worldcat.org/title/trombone-shorty/oclc/880349715.

OCLC Research (2020). *Libraries Leverage Wikimedia. OCLC.* https://web. archive.org/web/20200927165544/www.oclc.org/research/areas/commu nity-catalysts/libraries-wikimedia.html

PCC Identity Management Home. (2020). Wikidata Pilot. *PCC.* https:// web.archive.org/web/20201030220924/https://wiki.lyrasis.org/display/ pccidmgt/Wikidata+Pilot

Smith-Yoshimura, K., Altman, M., Conlon, M., Cristán, A. L., Dawson, L., Dun- ham, J., Hickey, T., Hook, D., Horstmann, W., MacEwan, A., Schreur, P., Smart, L., Wacker, M., & Woutersen, S. (2014) Registering researchers in author- ity files. *OCLC Research.* https://web.archive.org/web/20200709205119/ www.oclc.org/content/dam/research/publications/library/2014/ oclcresearch-registering-researchers-2014.pdf.

VuFind 4.1 Milner Library. (2020). Author search for Langston Hughes. https://web.archive.org/web/20200929150211/https://i-share.carli.illinois. edu/vf-isu/Author/Home?author=Hughes,+Langston,+1902-1967.

Wikipedia contributors. (2020a). List of African-American writers. *Wikipe- dia, The Free Encyclopedia.* https://en.wikipedia.org/w/index.php?title= List_of_African-American_writers&oldid=855683364.

Wikipedia contributors. (2020b). Wikipedia:Authority control. *Wikipedia, The Free Encyclopedia.* https://en.wikipedia.org/w/index.php?title=Wikipedia: Authority_control&oldid=990543395

Wikipedia contributors. (2020c). Who is African-American. *Wikipedia, The Free Encyclopedia.* https://en.wikipedia.org/w/index.php?title=African_ Americans&oldid=496452616.

Wikipedia contributors. (2020d). Stanley Bennett Clay. *Wikipedia, The Free Encyclopedia.* https://en.wikipedia.org/w/index.php?title=Stanley_ Bennett_Clay&oldid=977742050.

Wikipedia contributors. (2020e). Category:African-American writers. *Wiki- pedia, The Free Encyclopedia.* https://en.wikipedia.org/w/index.php?title= Category:African-American_writers&oldid=969141150.

Willey, E., & Yon, A. (2019). Applying Library of Congress Demographic Group Characteristics for Creators. *Cataloging & Classification Quarterly,* 57(6), 349–68. https://doi.org/10.1080/01639374.2019.1654054.

Bookend: An OA Publishing Perspective, 2019–2021

Roberto A. Arteaga

From the initial conversations about what this publication could look like to the struggle of identifying a publisher, this project, like many, went through a series of ups and downs. But as drafts submissions arrived and peer reviewers returned their comments, this publication has been the one constant for my fellow editors and me. For some of us, this was the most complex scholarly project that we had undertaken, and for some of us, this was an extension of work previously done. But for all of us, this would be our first foray into Open Access (OA). To say that this task was an easy one would be a misrepresentation, given what we have all been going through the past couple of years. We are immensely grateful to our contributors, peer reviewers, publisher, and others who contributed along the way. Without them, this publication wouldn't be the same.

From the beginning, this project was envisioned as an OA publication. Motivated by previous work with Wikipedia, Laurie had identified the need for a more encompassing publication that more accurately captured the work that academic librarians are doing in

DOI: https://doi.org/10.3998/mpub.11778416.bookend.en   301 regards to Wikipedia and its sibling projects. During the early stages of this project, there were only a few publications that had attempted to do this (Ayers et al., 2008; Proffitt, 2018). This fact became the impetus for Laurie's interest in developing an OA publication that drew not just from the work of library workers in North America but also attempted to make it available at a more affordable price.

With this goal in mind, we began planning for this publication. From the beginning, we had a sense that identifying contributors might not be a difficult process given the increasing visibility of Wikimedia-related projects that librarians were writing, presenting, and talking about. We anticipated that issues might arise as we attempted to identify authors from outside of North America, and similarly as we tried to seek funding for this project. As it turned out, the challenges came from elsewhere, and in this case, it was an issue that affected us all. Needless to say, the COVID-19 pandemic was not something that we could have planned for, but we still managed to finish this project due to the privileged positions that we editors hold. Yet, this project is much different than we expected, and how could it not be? The pandemic has affected all spheres of life and diluted any boundaries between our homes and workplaces. Because of these circumstances, we wanted to dedicate some space to talk about this project, its successes and failures, the risks and challenges that we faced, and the forces that kept it going and almost stopped it. Last, we wanted to dedicate space to highlight and uphold the work of our contributors, both those who made it to the final publication and those who did not. Their efforts have not gone unseen and their work should not be left unheard.

Planning and Preparation

Funding and Selecting a Publisher

While seeking a more "traditional" publisher like ACRL or Library Juice Press, who are two well-respected, library-centric publishers, would have been an option, our timeline and how much time we could dedicate to the project were unfortunately limited. So, we chose the self-publishing route and began to identify a publisher that would be able to publish the final project within a reasonable timeline (ideally around summer 2021), could provide the right amount of services, would allow us to publish an openly licensed publication, offered an affordably priced physical version, and had reasonable publication fees.

Our initial search led us to Lever Press; however, that bid was not successful. After some research, we decided to seek a bid from Ubiquity Press, an OA press in the United Kingdom. Though we were not entirely familiar with them, the services they offered, particularly their post-publication offerings, drew us in with the promise of continued access and the ability to keep track of scholarly impact. This was important to us since our goal was to publish all of the chapters under a CC BY license. I will speak more about the licenses in the next section, but in short, we wanted our contributors to still maintain some ownership over their work. After a successful bid, we received a quote from Ubiquity that satisfied many of our requirements. However, we decided to seek another publisher since the initial quote[1] would have made seeking funding a more intensive process.

Soon after our Ubiquity bid, we identified another potential publisher: Maize Books, an imprint of Michigan Publishing. Thanks to our University of Michigan sponsors, we were able to secure a bid for this project at a price point that would not put too much pressure on us. Given the reputation of both the University of Michigan and Michigan Publishing and following the advice of some of our supervisors, we signed a contract with Maize Books to develop an OA publication that will be distributed both physically and digitally. After receiving an initial quote,[2] we refocused our efforts to finish the call for proposals and seek grant funding. Ultimately, this project was funded by the following grants:

- Creative Commons Global Network Community Activities Fund
- Wikimedia Foundation Rapid Grant
- Oregon State University Robert Lundeen Faculty Development Award

Creative Commons License

Wanting to follow Wikimedia's initiative and mission to "empower and engage people around the world to collect and develop educational content under a free license or in the public domain" (Wikimedia, 2018), the intention was always to have one Creative Commons (CC) license for all the chapters. In the early stages, we discussed the possibility of allowing contributors to pick their license, but after some deliberation, we decided to publish the whole volume under a CC BY license and be transparent about that from the beginning. We chose this license because it would allow for the largest dissemination and would allow for our contributors to still retain some ownership over their work. We also considered the possibility of publishing the whole volume under a CC 0, no rights reserved license, but ultimately we decided against this option since this may have impacted the number of contributors willing to publish their work under a public domain license and because this license might have made it difficult for our contributors to track the impact of their work, use their published work as part of any promotion processes, or even make it difficult to justify the value of the work they are doing.

"In the Time of COVID"

Perhaps due to the optimism expressed toward the beginning of the pandemic, we believed that simply extending the proposal deadline would let us get through the worst of things. Little did we know that our reality was about to be overturned and that we would be writing, peer reviewing, and publishing our work during a pandemic. To this day, it is sometimes difficult to fathom how this book managed to take shape. While you may only be hearing our perspective as editors, I hope that you instead consider and thank our contributing authors and peer reviewers for their labor, both academic and emotional. After all, they stuck with us until the end and made it all possible.

This publication is just a microcosm of what academia and teaching have become during the pandemic, and the fact that we were working with authors from different countries did not make this process any easier for anyone. There were times when we did not hear from one of our contributors and couldn't help but think that the unthinkable had happened. There were times when all we could do was try to act professional and continue to work as if everything was fine; after all, we had signed a contract, we had gotten grants, and the work had to be done. Throughout this whole process, we experienced all of the forces of academia magnified. First by the pandemic, and then by the negative influences of neoliberalism, the cult of busyness, and resilience narratives.

One place where this influence was felt was the peer review process. In general, there is some expectation of anonymity as part of this process, as the anonymity contributes to a sense of safety where the work being reviewed is only being critiqued on the basis of the work and not on the basis of the person. Unfortunately, because some of our grants required that we disclose who some of our contributors would be, it meant that we had to change our peer review process to a single-blind review. Though we did not experience many issues between contributors and reviewers, there is a slight sense that some of the "rigor" that the double-blind process would have afforded was lost. In a way, this is not something that we, as editors, were much concerned about, but knowing that some of our contributors will be using their contributions as part of a tenure and promotion process, there was some pressure on us to provide that additional level of support. Yet, because some of that veil had been removed, we had the chance to introduce a certain level of care to our peer review process. For example, instead of just asking for suggestions and revisions from our peer reviewers, we encouraged reviewers to comment on where the chapter they reviewed was excelling. For our parts as editors, our main focus was to build relationships—not just between ourselves and the documents we received but between ourselves and the people working on those documents. Yet this wasn't always an easy task, given the state of the world and the limited space for vulnerability that the peer review process allows.[3]

Advice and Recommendations

Needless to say, we were not the only academic endeavor that managed to be completed during the pandemic, regardless of our desire to shift to more pressing concerns. The fact remains, however, that we are able to do this work due to the great privilege that our jobs afford us, and to say otherwise would be a disservice to the efforts of essential workers that kept our workplaces, communities, and economies going. Without them, this publication would not be here.

From the beginning, this publication was designed to be open, and the many proposals that we received demonstrate the commitment that others bring to this cause. All in all, one of the biggest takeaways from this project is the realization that there is an increasing interest in open publications, given the response to our CFP. Thus, we hope that this volume is able to increase the number of people who care about improving access to knowledge and information, about reducing barriers to access, and about the many communities of practices around the world. If you are reading this, above all, I hope that you reexamine the reach of your work, both the everyday kind and the scholarly, and reconsider how you disseminate and share this work.

Beyond providing some transparency to a process that is often hidden away and seldom addressed, we would like to close this "bookend" by offering a few recommendations for those interested in pursuing similar endeavors:

- Remember that OA, like everything else, is not free. It may result in openly accessible publications, but there is still a cost attached to them. Going in with an expectation that you will have to raise the funds to fund a project will be essential to its success.
- Costs will vary depending on the publisher, but you should expect to raise at least $3,000 for any self-published project. In order to raise funds for your project, start at your institution, then look to organizations that align to the purpose of your publication.
- Recognize that the COVID-19 pandemic will result in further cuts and changes in funding across many institutions. In the near

future, funding opportunities might be limited and those that remain will have more strict guidelines and outcomes.

- If the goal is to develop a peer-reviewed publication, identifying a pool of qualified reviewers should be part of the initial planning process. Establishing clear rules and procedures will also help facilitate this process.

Notes

1 Ubiquity's book-processing charge (BPC) quote was about £7,500 for a twenty-chapter volume. The BPC quote included services like copyediting, index creation, cover design, and typesetting, among others.

2 Maize's initial estimate totaled $4,500 for a twenty-chapter volume. This estimate included services like copyediting, cover design, and typesetting, among others.

3 For more on the peer review process as a place for love and care, read Brito et al. (2014).

References

Ayers, P., Matthews, C., & Yates, B. (2008). *How Wikipedia works: And how you can be a part of it.* No Starch Press.

Brito, M., Fink, A., Friend, C., Heidebrink-Bruno, A., Moe, R., Shaffer, K., Robin, V., & Wharton, R. (2014, November 22). Love in the time of peer review. *Hybrid Pedagogy.* https://hybridpedagogy.org/love-time-peer-review/.

Proffitt, M. (2018). *Leveraging Wikipedia: Connecting communities of knowledge.* American Library Association.

Wikimedia Foundation Mission. (2018). Wikimedia Foundation. https://wikimediafoundation.org/about/mission/.

Contributors

Vicenç Allué Blanch, Autonomous University of Barcelona and Amical Wikimedia, Librarian. Librarian with a career in the field of university libraries. He holds a degree on Librarianship by University of Barcelona and master's degree in Documentation and History of Science by the Universitat Autònoma of Barcelona. From 1985 onward, he is the Head of Veterinary Library of this University. He is a member of the Catalan Association of Veterinary History, where he has developed projects of Open Access digitization through institutional repositories and Europeana. Allué Blanch is a Catalan Wikipedian since 2013 and has led and promoted activities related to open education, including the milestone of an official agreement between the University and Amical Wikimedia.

Roberto A. Arteaga is an academic librarian in the Pacific Northwest of the United States. His research interests include critical information literacy, instructional design, and e-learning. Off work, he listens to a lot of heavy metal and tries to find time to play video games, watch anime, and read. He can be found on Twitter at @irobarte.

Zhuzumkan Askhatbekova is a reference specialist who develops informational and instructional materials on library services and resources at American University of Central Asia. She holds an MLIS degree from University of Missouri, Columbia.

Jyldyz Bekbalaeva is a library director at American University of Central Asia. She holds an MLIS degree from University of Illinois and PhD in Linguistics from Kyrgyz National University.

Laurie M. Bridges is an Instruction and Outreach Librarian at Oregon State University at the rank of Associate Professor. She has co-coordinated several Wikipedia edit-a-thons, developed and cotaught an undergraduate course titled Wikipedia and Information Equity (which she taught for the third time in the spring of 2021), and has a forthcoming article about the motivations and activities of librarians in Spain who engage with Wikimedia projects (First Monday, 2021).

Maggie Bukowski is a Library Technician II for the UNLV University Libraries. She works to create student employee training programs and experiences that both support the goals of the UNLV University Libraries and foster student growth and development. She earned her Master of Arts in American History and BA in History from the University of Nevada, Las Vegas.

Paul R. Burley is a metadata librarian at the Northwestern University Libraries in Evanston, Illinois. He holds a Master's in Information Science from the University of Michigan and primarily catalogs materials in African and Asian languages. His interests include authority control and emerging bibliographic-linked data practices. He spends much of his free time on the Creative Commons-licensed photography of cultural heritage sites in both the United States and Brazil. His username across Wikimedia projects is Prburley.

Marta Bustillo, a College Liaison Librarian at UCD Library, has worked in a variety of roles in academic libraries for over twenty years.

Jesse Carliner is a Communications and Users Services Librarian at the University of Toronto Libraries. He is part of a team of service managers for user services in Robarts Library and provides reference and research support and library instruction. He is also responsible for external communications for the libraries, including social media and media relations. He manages the Wikipedian-in-Residence and Open Technology Specialist positions. He received his MI from the University of Toronto.

Kelsey Cowles, MLIS, is a Research and Instruction Librarian at the University of Pittsburgh Health Sciences Library System. Her work focuses on integrating the library into University initiatives relating to interprofessional education and community engagement. She previously served as Academic Coordinator for the Middle Atlantic Region of NNLM.

Francesc Xavier Dengra i Grau, KU Leuven and Amical Wikimedia, Biotechnologist, graduated in Biotechnology from the Universitat Autònoma de Barcelona and a master's degree in Environmental Sciences from the University of Copenhagen and the University of Natural Resources and Life Sciences, Vienna. He did research at the International Atomic Energy Agency and is currently pursuing a PhD in radioactive remediation at KU Leuven and the Belgian Nuclear Research Center. Editor of Catalan Wikipedia since he was fourteen years old, he has acted as Board Treasurer of Amical Wikimedia (2016–2020) and has led several educational projects in different universities of Catalonia, advised the National Library of Andorra, and trained the public libraries of his hometown, Cornellà de Llobregat.

Kristina M. De Voe is the English and Communication Librarian at Temple University and a 2020–2021 SPARC Open Education Leadership Program Fellow. Additionally, she is a Campus Partner for Affordable Learning PA (Pennsylvania's statewide OER initiative), advancing greater access and equity in education. She holds an MLIS from Kent State University and an MA in English Studies from the Ohio State University. Her other professional and research interests include critical information literacy, open pedagogy, and scholarly communications.

Odin Essers, MA, is the main curator of Maastricht University's Special Collections and the driving force behind several Wikimedia-related activities and projects. He regularly contributes to seminars and blogs to highlight the library's engagement with Wikipedia and Wikidata. ORCID ID https://orcid.org/0000-0003-1328-0622.

Carme Fenoll i Clarabuch, Universitat Politècnica de Catalunya, Librarian. She is a librarian with a long career in the field of public libraries and cultural management. She holds a degree in Librarianship and Documentation from the University of Barcelona and master's degree in Arts and Cultural Management from the Open University of Catalonia. From 2012 to 2017 she was Head of the Public Library Service of the Catalan Ministry of Culture, where she promoted the #Bibliowikis project. She has continued to be linked to Wikipedia as a volunteer. Since 2018 she has been working as Head of the Rector's Bureau of the Universitat Politècnica de Catalunya and she continues to be linked to the world of libraries, reading, and education.

Brittany Paloma Fiedler coordinates information literacy instruction for the university's first-year composition program and provides instruction, research support, and outreach for K-12, undergraduate, and graduate students. Her research interests include how traditionally underserved students engage with academic libraries, the experiences of librarians of color, and librarian-led professional development. Brittany earned a Bachelor of Science in Education and a Master of Arts in English Literature from the University of Nevada, Las Vegas and a Master of Science in Library and Information Science from the University of Illinois at Urbana-Champaign. She was a 2015–2016 ALA Spectrum Scholar and 2018 ALA Emerging Leader.

Francesc Fort i Silvestre, Amical Wikimedia, Economist. Licentiate in Economics from the University of Valencia. An editor of Wikipedia since 2008, he has been an active member in the movement. In 2016 he became the first Wikimedian-in-Residence in the Land of Valencia, in a joint project with the Valencian Museum of Ethnology. In 2019 he became the Liaison for Spanish Language Communities in the Wikimedia Movement 2030 Strategy Process.

Crystal Fulton, a UCD Academic Fellow, has researched and taught in the areas of information and digital literacies, information and communication behavior and public services, and social media for over twenty years.

Francesc García Grimau, Universitat de Barcelona, Assistant Professor.

Graduated with an Information and Documentation degree from the University of Barcelona and is currently studying for a Strategic Management of Information and Knowledge in Organizations Master's Degree at the Open University of Catalonia. He works as a Library Consultant at OCLC Spain, and also works as an assistant professor of the Department of Library Science, Documentation, and Audiovisual Communication of the University of Barcelona. He organized the Information and Communication Edit-a-thon of the Faculty of Information and Audiovisual Media at the University of Barcelona from 2015 to 2017 and has volunteered in Catalan Wikipedia for the #1Lib1Ref campaigns.

Ann Glusker, PhD, is Sociology, Demography, & Quantitative Research Librarian at University of California, Berkeley, where she helps plan in-person Wikipedia edit-a-thons. Previously she was Research and Data Coordinator for the NNLM Pacific Northwest Region. She has worked as a public health epidemiologist and medical librarian and is deeply committed to engaging all people with the use and understanding of data.

Aimee Gogan, MLIS, is Technical Information Specialist at the National Library of Medicine (NLM) Office of Engagement and Training. In her position, her primary roles are serving as the editor of the NLM Technical Bulletin and supporting programs that connect the public to NLM products and services.

Silvia E. Gutiérrez De la Torre has a MA in Digital Humanities by the University of Würzburg and King's College London. She is the Digital Humanities Librarian at the Daniel Cosío Villegas Library, cofounder of RLadies Mexico City (a local chapter of an international initiative to promote gender diversity in the RStats community), and a Wikipedian since 2011, which (she believes) is like being a closet librarian.

Henrietta Hazen is the coordinator of the Skills and Academic Support Team of Maastricht University Library. As such, she is responsible for information literacy activities (for students) by the library for and in collaboration with the faculties. ORCID ID https://orcid.org/0000-0002-1019-879X.

Chelsea Heinbach works to create meaningful learning experiences for undergraduate students new to the University of Nevada, Las Vegas through Urban Affairs and Engineering First-Year-seminar courses, the English Composition program, and cocurricular events. Chelsea is a cofounder of the Librarian Parlor (#libparlor), a community for librarians interested in conducting research. Her research interests include affective nature of research, dismantling deficit approaches to students, and the intersection between civic engagement and information literacy education. Chelsea holds a Bachelor of Arts in Literature from the University of Miami and a Master of Library and Information Sciences from the University of Denver.

Millie N. Horsfall is a Librarian and a Lecturer in the Department of Library and Information Science, University of Port Harcourt, Rivers State, Nigeria. She holds Bachelor's degree from University of Port Harcourt and Master's degree in Library and Information Science from Imo State University, Owerri, as well as a PhD degree from the University of Nigeria, Nsukka, (UNN), a certified Librarian of Nigeria (CLN) by Librarians Registration Council of Nigeria (LRCN), and a member of Nigerian Library Association (NLA) and Nigeria Association of Library and Information Science Educators (NALISE). She can be contacted via email: millie.horsfall@uniport.edu.ng.

Ji Yun Alex Jung serves as Open Technology Specialist at the University of Toronto Libraries, where he was previously Wikipedian-in-residence. He formerly co-organized Civic Tech Toronto and continues to contribute to a number of open-ended, decentralized projects both digitally and nondigitally. He spends a lot of time designing for easy collaboration and participation and only builds things that others can build on. He can be reached on his Wikipedia user page: User:Utl_jung.

Alicia Lillich, MLS, is the Emerging Technologies Specialist at the National Institutes of Health Library. She previously served as the Technology Coordinator for the NNLM MidContinental Region.

Jessica L. Lott is an Assistant Professor of Anthropology and the Associate Director of the Center for Applied Anthropology at Northern Kentucky University. She is a cultural anthropologist who studies gender and power, reproductive health, and kinship and personhood. In her teaching, she uses anthropology to help students engage with human diversity and the world around them. She strives to help her students feel ownership over their research and writing as part of her courses.

Leo F. H. Ma is Head of Upper Campus Libraries at the Chinese University of Hong Kong. Apart from managing branch libraries, he has spearheaded several digital humanities initiatives including Hong Kong Literature Database, Hong Kong Literary Landscape MediaWiki, and Modern Chinese Literature Research Portal. Currently, he is a Standing Committee Member of IFLA Academic & Research Libraries Section, Fellow of the Hong Kong Library Association, Advisory Member of LIS programs of the University of Hong Kong. He has published, as editor and author, more than twenty monographs, presented over sixty conference papers, and received more than thirty LIS and literary awards.

L. M. Mak was the former team member of the Hong Kong Literature Database (CUHK) and participated in the design and maintenance of Hong Kong Literary Landscape MediaWiki. He is now pursuing his PhD focusing on the changing cultural relations between Taiwan and Hong Kong in the late cold war period. His research interest ranges from literature, film studies to cultural studies.

Eduardo Martinez-Flores graduated in May 2020 from the University of Nevada, Las Vegas with a Bachelor of Arts in Criminal Justice. While enrolled as a student, he worked for the UNLV University Libraries as a Mason Undergraduate Peer Research Coach for four years. In this role he cotaught library instruction sessions alongside librarians and participated in outreach efforts to connect with students. In August 2020, Eduardo was EMT certified and started his career as a professional EMT. This new professional role is the first step in many to accomplishing his long-term goals of becoming a firefighter and arson investigator.

Ewan McAndrew is Wikimedian-in-Residence at the University of Edinburgh since 2016, supporting the university's commitment to gender equality and sharing knowledge openly—winning UK Wikimedian of the Year and Herald Higher Education Award. Ewan has volunteered with the Glasgow School of Art on their WW1 Roll of Honour project and worked as an English and Media teacher both in the Far East (Japan, Singapore, and South Korea) and in Scotland. Latterly, he hosted the first "Celtic Knot" conference focused on supporting minority language Wikipedia communities, completed an Information Management degree, and created a Wikidata-driven "Map of Accused Witches in Scotland" website.

Michael David Miller is originally from Flint, Michigan, and graduated from the Université de Montréal in 2013 with a Master of Information

Science. He is an Associate Librarian at the McGill University Library where he holds the position of Liaison Librarian for French Literature, Economics, and LGBTQ+ Studies. In 2011, he completed his undergraduate work, a BA in French Studies and a BA in Advertising at the Michigan State University. MDM began exploring the intersections of Wikipedia and liaison librarianship at the 2017 edition of Wikimania in Montréal. Since then, he has focused his Wikipedia work on the representation of Québec's LGBTQ+ history and culture in the Francophone Wikipedia (WikipédiaFR).

Rosan Mitola is the Interim Head of Educational Initiatives for the UNLV University Libraries. She leads the library instruction program and provides leadership for the Libraries' educational role on campus. Rosan also designs cocurricular learning experiences for students and oversees the Mason Undergraduate Peer Research Coach Program. Her research interests include peer-assisted learning in academic libraries, student employment as a high-impact practice, and dismantling deficit thinking in information literacy instruction and cocurricular outreach. She earned a Master of Library and Information Science from San José State University and a BA in History from University of Nevada, Las Vegas.

Aisuluu Namasbek kyzy is Assistant Professor at the Sociology Department of American University of Central Asia. She holds MA in Gender Studies from Central European University, Budapest, Hungary.

Adaora C. Obuezie is a Librarian and Lecturer in the Department of Library and Information Science, Nnamdi Azikiwe University (NAU), Awka, Anambra State, Nigeria. She holds her Bachelor's and Master's degrees in Library and Information Science from Nnamdi Azikiwe University, Awka, Anambra State, as well as presently pursuing her PhD program in Library and Information Science from the same university (NAU). She is a Certified Librarian of Nigeria (CLN) by Librarians' Registration Council of Nigeria (LRCN) and a member of Nigerian Library Association (NLA) and Nigerian Association of Library and

Information Science Educators (NALISE). She can be contacted via email: ac.obuezie@unizik.edu.ng.

Erin O'Neil is a white settler living in amiskwaciy-wâskahikan (Edmonton) on Treaty 6 and Métis territory. She is in her second year as a master's student in Digital Humanities at the University of Alberta, specializing in Gender and Social Justice Studies. Her research interests center on how the phenomena of apathy and ignorance manifest in digital spaces. Erin is the 2020 Wikipedian-in-Residence for University of Alberta Library.

Rebecca O'Neill is the Project Coordinator for Wikimedia Community Ireland. Her work focuses on improving the representation of Ireland on Wikipedia and the Irish language Wikipedia, Vicipéid.

João Alexandre Peschanski is a Professor of Journalism at Faculdade Cásper Líbero, in São Paulo, Brazil. He holds a PhD in Sociology from the University of Wisconsin-Madison. His research activity is funded by the Research, Innovation and Dissemination Center for Neuromathematics (2013/07699–0) and the Faculdade Cásper Líbero Interdisciplinary Research Center. He is currently the chair of the Wikimedia Foundation affiliate in Brazil, the User Group Wiki Movimento Brasil, and is a board member of the User Group Wikipedia & Education. His username across Wikimedia projects is Joalpe.

Amparo Pons Cortell, L'ETNO—Museu Valencià d'Etnologia and Amical Wikimedia, Librarian. Graduated with a degree in History and in Librarianship and Documentation from the Universitat de València. She is in charge of the Library of L'ETNO—Museu Valencià d'Etnologia, from where she has coordinated GLAM projects for the museum since 2016. In 2019, as Chair of the Official College of Librarians and Documentalists of the Land of Valencia (COBDCV), she signed formal agreements with Amical Wikimedia and Wikimedia España that aim to collaborate in training and raising the awareness of Valencian chartered professionals toward

Wikimedia projects and activities. She is a partner and collaborator of Amical Wikimedia and Wikimedia Spain.

Éder Porto Ferreira Alves is a software developer based in São Paulo, Brazil. He holds an undergraduate degree in Applied Mathematics from the University of São Paulo. He is a technical assistant at the Research, Innovation and Dissemination Center for Neuromathematics (RIDC NeuroMat). On Wikimedia projects, his interests include the automatization, adaptation, and optimization of wiki processes and tools that facilitate the contributions of others in the wiki universe. His username across Wikimedia projects is Ederporto.

Raymond Pun is an Education and Outreach Manager at the Hoover Institution Library & Archives, Stanford University. Ray is a coeditor of several books including *The Sustainable Library's Cookbook* (2019) and *Asian American Librarians and Library Services* (2017). He holds a Doctorate in Education from California State University, Fresno, a Master of Library Science from Queens College, City University of New York, a Master of Arts in East Asian Studies, and a Bachelor of Arts in History from St. John's University.

Sarah Severson is a Digital Projects Librarian at the University of Alberta Library in amiskwaciy-wâskahikan (Edmonton) on Treaty 6 and Métis territory. She works with a team to support the Library's Publishing and Digital Production Services, which includes an open journal and educational resources publishing program and digitization. She is interested in how open knowledge paradigms are changing the online publishing landscape and alternative forms of publishing and has been working with different Wikimedia projects for years.

Adrienne Shaw is Associate Professor in Temple University's Department of Media Studies and Production. She is author of *Gaming at the Edge: Sexuality and Gender* and founder of the LGBTQ Game Archive (www.lgbtqgamearchive.com). She cocurated Rainbow Arcade, an exhibit of thirty years of LGBTQ video game history at the Schwules

Museum in Berlin Germany. In addition to the exhibit catalog, she has written for and coedited three anthologies. Presently, she is an associate editor for the Journal of Communication and series editor for NYU Press's Critical Cultural Communication series.

Margie Sheppard, MLS, is the Outreach and Technology Coordinator for the NNLM MidContinental Region, based at the University of Kansas Medical Center. She has an undergraduate degree in nursing and works with libraries and community organizations interested in improving the health and well-being of their communities by connecting them with NLM products and updating their technology needs.

Nicolette Siep, PhD, is information specialist of the Skills and Academic Support Team of Maastricht University Library. In liaison with academic faculties, she develops, coordinates, and delivers information literacy activities, including those involving Wikimedia, to bachelor and master students.

Kai Alexis Smith is an information activist, scholar, educator, and librarian. She is the Architecture and Planning Librarian at MIT. Kai has roughly ten years of experience working with these subject-specific communities and contributing to open knowledge. She serves on the Simple Annual Planning Grant Committee advocating for equity, diversity, and inclusion from the Wikipedia movement. Kai is a comoderator for the Architecture and Planning Section and Executive Board member of the Art Libraries Society of North America (ARLIS/NA). Kai is the founder of the Wikipedia project BIPOC in the Built.

Jennifer L. Sullivan is a Health Sciences Librarian at Upstate Medical University in Syracuse, New York. Her focus is on science literacy, information literacy, cultural competence, and the medical humanities. She finds immense joy in working with and building relationships with her students, and in guiding them toward greater competence and confidence in their levels of information fluency and research efficacy.

Shirin Tumenbaeva is Assistant Professor at the International and Comparative Politics Department of the American University of Central Asia. As a DAAD scholarship holder, she completed an MA in Political Science at the University of Mannheim.

Elaina Vitale, MLIS, is a Research and Education Librarian in the Biomedical Libraries at Dartmouth College, where she works with medical students, faculty, clinicians, nurses, and patients. Elaina was previously the Academic and Data Services Coordinator for the NNLM Middle Atlantic Region.

Liz Waltman, MLIS, is the Outreach, Education and Communications Coordinator for the NNLM Southeastern/Atlantic Region, based at the University of Maryland, Baltimore. She is responsible for the development of training opportunities and outreach initiatives for library and health professionals and coordinating all communications for the regional medical library.

Eric Willey is an associate professor and the Special Collections and Formats Cataloger at Illinois State University. He has previously worked as an intern at the Illinois Regional Archives Depository at Western Illinois University, as a project assistant with the McCormick-International Harvester Collection at the Wisconsin Historical Society, and as an associate curator at the Filson Historical Society in Louisville, Kentucky. He is currently a cofacilitator of the LD4-Wikidata Affinity Group. For further publications, see orcid.org/0000-0002-7514-0011.

Gavin Willshaw is the Digitization and Digital Engagement Manager at the University of Edinburgh Library, where he manages a team of photographers, audiovisual technicians, and videographers who digitize the University's heritage collections for teaching, learning, research, and engagement. He previously worked as the Mass Digitization Service Manager at the National Library of Scotland, where he oversaw the Wikisource transcription correction project that forms the focus of this chapter. Gavin is an experienced Wikimedian and has run several edit-a-thons, citation hunt sessions, and other Wikimedia-focused activities both at work and in his hometown of Portobello, Edinburgh.

Amanda J. Wilson, MSLS, is Chief of the National Library of Medicine Office of Engagement and Training (OET), in which she leads the capacity-building, training, and engagement programs connecting NLM products and services with the public.

Tess Wilson, MLIS, is the All of Us Community Engagement Coordinator for the NNLM Middle Atlantic Region. She is also an advocate with Library Freedom Project and a coauthor of the book *All Ages Welcome: Recruiting and Retaining Younger Generations for Library Boards, Friends Groups, and Foundations.*

Angela Yon, Assistant Professor, Cataloging and Metadata Librarian, Illinois State University. She received her MSLIS from the University of Illinois at Urbana-Champaign, with a concentration in data curation. She currently serves as the principal investigator on the Council on Library and Information Resources (CLIR) grant project "Step Right Up: Digitizing Over 100 Years of Circus Route Books." For further publications, see orcid.org/0000-0003-4125-2397.

Index

Note: Page numbers in *italic* and **bold** indicate figures and tables; Page numbers followed by "*n*" indicate chapter notes.

American Library Association, 71
American University of Central Asia
    (AUCA), 5, 7–9, 15
Amical-way, 159, 163, 166, 169
Amical Wikimedia, 158, 161–66, 168
Anais do Museu Paulista, 264–74, *265*
Andorran Copyright Law, 165
Appiah, Kwame, 96
Archives of Gender and Sexuality, 115
Art+Feminism, 22, 123, 139, 220, 222
Article for Creation (AFC), 225, 226
Association of College & Research
    Libraries (ACRL), 64, 302
    *Framework for Information Liter-
    acy in Higher Education*, 55,
    64, 68–72, 80
Association of Research Libraries, 296
Athena Scientific Women's Academic
    Network (SWAN), 204
AUCA. *See* American University of
    Central Asia (AUCA)
authentic learning, in cultural
    anthropology, 64–76
    advice and recommendations, 74–76
    assessment, 85
    assignment, 67–68, 80, 83–85
    disciplinary information literacy
    empowering learners, 74
    gender bias, 73–74
    information literacy, as social
    justice, 71–73
    *Framework for Information
    Literacy in Higher Education*,
    68–71
    Authority Is Constructed and
    Contextual, 69–70
    Scholarship as Conversation,
    70–71
    learning outcomes, 80, **81–83**
    literature review

editing Wikipedia, in higher
    education classrooms, 66
    librarians–faculty
    collaboration, 66–67
    semester lengths, 85–86
    Wikipedia editing assignment, 80
    Authority Is Constructed and
    Contextual, 69–70, 73

B

Backer, Alice, 98
BAnQ. *See Bibliothèque et Archives
    nationales du Québec*
    (BAnQ)
BDCV. *See Biblioteca Daniel Cosío
    Villegas* (BDCV)
Berson, Amber, 220–21
Bezzi, Tommaso Guadenzio, 264
bibliographic references, structuring,
    260–75
    context, 263–65
    data visualization, 273–74, *274*
    sources on Wikimedia projects,
    261–63, *262*
    Zotero, importing scholarly
    articles into Wikidata via,
    266–73, *267–70, 273*
Biblioteca Daniel Cosío Villegas
    (BDCV)
    WIR in, 177, 182–91
    collaboration, 184–86
    fireplaces, building, 186–91,
    188
    #1Bib1Ref, 183–84
    strengths, leveraging, 184–86,
    185
*Bibliothèque et Archives nationales
    du Québec* (BAnQ), 115
Bibliothèques de la Ville de Montréal,
    115

#Bibliowikis
  in Catalonia's public libraries,
    158–70
  volunteer-driven philosophy,
    162–67
  deployment, 163–65
  strengths, 165–67
  threats, 165–67
  uncertainties, 165–67
  weaknesses, 165–67
BIPOC (Black, Indigenous, and
  People of Color), 94,
  96, 101
BIPOC in the Built, 99
Bizdin Muras, 7
Blackening Wikipedia, 98
Black Lives Matter movement, 92
Black Lunch Table (BLT), 97, 98
Black scholars, encyclopedic
  knowledge of, 94–96
Black Wikipedians, 91–102
  future of, 99–101
  libraries and archives, 93–96
  responsibility of, 96–99
BLT. *See* Black Lunch Table (BLT)
Blyden, Edward W., 95
Bobiwash, Rodney, 219, 238
Bourg, Chris, 93, 94
Brawley, Benjamin Griffith, 294
Brightspace, 54
Brooklyn Public Library, 98
Buolamwini, Joy, 99

C
Carliner, Jesse, 218, 219, 227–28
Carroll, Emma, 204
Catalan language, 159–60
Catalan librarians, Wikipedia's
  benefits and opportunities
  for, 161–62

Catalan Wikipedia (Viquipèdia),
  158–62, *161*
Catalonia College of Music
  (ESMUC), 168
CC. *See* Creative Commons (CC)
  license
CDC. *See* curriculum development
  consultant (CDC)
CEAS. *See* Colegio de Etnólogos
  y Antropólogos Sociales
  A.C. (CEAS, College of
  Ethnologists and Social
  Anthropologists)
censorship, 14
chapbooks, 279
Chávez, Micaela, 182
Chinese Language Curriculum
  Guide (Junior Secondary and
  Senior Secondary), 251–53,
  251
Chinese University of Hong Kong
  Library (CUHK Library),
  247, 248
  "Fun with Learning Chinese
  Language through Literary
  Walk Project (Fun Project)",
  248–54
Chiu, Alfred Kaiming, 94
Cisneros, Jaime, 189
Citation Hunt, 76
#CiteNLM edit-a-thons, 144–56
  academic libraries, as partners,
  152–56
  collaboration, 153–54
  evaluation, 155–56
  host selection, 153
  implementation, 153–54
  campaign history and evolution
  background, 147
  2018 campaigns, 147–49

2019 campaigns, 149–50
2020 campaigns, 150–52
#CiteNLM Guide for Organizers,
150, 154
civic activism, 14–15
COBDCV. *See* Official College
of Librarians and
Documentalists of the Land
of Valencia (COBDCV)
Colegio de Etnólogos y
Antropólogos Sociales
A.C. (CEAS, College of
Ethnologists and Social
Anthropologists), 184
Colegio Nacional de Bibliotecarios
(National College of
Librarians), 186
COLMEX. *See* El Colegio de México
(COLMEX)
Concordia University Library
Wikimedian-in-Residence,
220–21
Connaught Laboratories, 235
copyright debt, 199
Coren, Ashleigh, 147
Creative Commons (CC) license, 9,
22, 23, 168, 189
critical information literacy,
18–32, 66
existing infrastructures, 21–23
iterative collaboration, 23–24
representation, 27–28
technology and culture through
Wikipedia, understanding,
24–27
critical pedagogy, 19
Crockford, Ally, 201
crowdsourcing, 144–56
cultural anthropology, authentic
learning in, 64–76

advice and recommendations,
74–76
assessment, 85
assignment, 67–68, 80, 83–85
disciplinary information literacy
empowering learners, 74
gender bias, 73–74
information literacy, as social
justice, 71–73
*Framework for Information
Literacy in Higher Education*,
68–71
Authority Is Constructed and
Contextual, 69–70
Scholarship as Conversation,
70–71
learning outcomes, 80, **81–83**
literature review
librarians–faculty
collaboration, 66–67
Wikipedia in higher education
classrooms, editing, 66
semester lengths, 85–86
Wikipedia editing assignment, 80
culture through Wikipedia,
understanding, 24–27
curriculum development consultant
(CDC), 126, 127

D
data visualization, 273–74, *274*
Data Visualization Internship, 204
Davidson, Cathy N.
New Education, The, 31
Dean, Phillip Hayes, 294
Design Justice Network, 101
Dewey Decimal Classification
System, 94
Dewey, Melville, 94
Díaz Roble, Tajëëw B., 190

CPSIA information can be obtained
at www.ICGtesting.com
Printed in the USA
LVHW021013161121
703429LV00011B/175